SUCKER PUNCH

THE HARD LEFT HOOK THAT DAZED ALI AND KILLED KING'S DREAM

By
JACK CASHILL

NELSON CURRENT
A Subsidiary of Thomas Nelson, Inc.

Published in Nashville, Tennessee, by Nelson Current, a division of a wholly-owned subsidiary (Nelson Communications, Inc.) of Thomas Nelson, Inc.

Nelson Current books may be purchased in bulk for educational, business, fundraising, or sales promotional use. For information, please e-mail SpecialMarkets@ThomasNelson.com.

Library of Congress cataloguing-in-publication data
on file with the Library of Congress.

ISBN 1-59555-033-X

Printed in the United States of America

05 06 07 08 09 QWK 5 4 3 2 1

To Joe Frazier and the late Joe Louis,

two gallant Americans who deserve
much better than the nation's cultural
and media elite has seen fit to offer.

TABLE OF CONTENTS

TABLE OF CONTENTS

Prologue

MARCH 1971

On March 8, 1971, my friends from grad school—Rick, Stanley, and Joan—and I drove from Purdue in my yellow VW bug to watch a large screen presentation of the first Ali-Frazier fight.

Given the imperatives of student poverty, we headed not south to Indianapolis, which was forty miles closer, but north to Gary, which was five dollars cheaper. The moment we walked into the theater, however, I understood what the others did not: five bucks or no, Gary was a mistake.

Other than the fifty or so guys sitting together in makeshift bleachers by the exit door, we were about the only white people in the joint. Of the four thousand or so in attendance, Joan was the only white woman—period. This was of some concern to me as she would soon be my wife. Many times, before and since, I have found myself in venues with comparable ratios, but never one in which the racial tension was so raw and palpable.

Given her pro-Ali perspective at the time, Joan remembers the small group of guys in the bleachers as "Mafiosi." I remember them more benignly as "hardhats." A popular phrase of the era, "hardhat" evoked an independent, illiberal, blue-collar patriotism. Unlike my friends, Joan included, I knew these guys. I had grown up with their spiritual kin in the no-nonsense, inner wards of Newark, New Jersey. They were my uncles and cousins and boyhood friends. They were pulling for Joe Frazier. So was I.

Seven years earlier, if you had told me I would one day root against Ali, I would have said, "Sure, and I'll cast my first presidential vote for Richard Nixon." I had admired Cassius Clay, as he was then known, almost as much as I had John Kennedy. As it happened, JFK had edged out Nixon for the presidency in a controversial split decision just two months after Ali won his Olympic gold.

I was the only Frazier fan I knew at Purdue. The night before the fight, when we gathered at our habitual watering hole, my grad school buddies vied with each other to express their passion for Ali. Among their many professions of fealty, one has stuck with me, if only for its crudeness.

"I would stand on this table and piss in my pants if Ali were to walk in that door," said Ron, a fellow not usually known for his excesses. Still, if Ron's emotion was extreme, his attachment was the norm. I suspected that on the more excitable campuses—Bloomington and Madison and Boulder and Berkeley—the Ali juju was surging even more feverishly.

I forget how much I bet on the fight. Joan was shocked when she found out and took comfort only in my winning. The pickings were easy. Knowing little of the sport's sweet science, my Purdue friends bet their hearts. They even gave away odds. I bet my instincts. I had been following the fights since my dad took me as a six-year-old to meet local hero Two Ton Tony Galento, the aptly named palooka who knocked down Joe Louis in the third round of their 1939 fight. The occasion was the neighborhood movie premiere of *On the Waterfront*, in which Two Ton had a bit part as a union goon—no stretch there.

In Gary that night, I could have used Two Ton Tony. On the way to the restroom before the fight, several large gentlemen blocked my way and inquired rather bluntly into my choice of boxers. "Who you for, mother f***er?" I didn't hesitate. "Ali," I said. They let me pass. As much I respected Joe Frazier, I wasn't about to die for him.

In Gary and beyond, no fight had so racially polarized America since Jack Johnson squared off against Jim Jeffries in Reno sixty years earlier. This, I thought, is what Ali had wrought. He had the crowd not so much pulling for him as against the imagined race traitor, Joe Frazier, and anyone, black or white, who dared cheer for him. Gary, that night, was a cauldron of hate, a harrowing, volatile place to be. Still, the fight proved to be worth the risk. It was both brutal and brilliant, as only great fights can be. Going into the fifteenth, it seemed to all of us too close to call.

"OK," I said to my friends between rounds, "we're out of here." They thought me daft and resisted. I explained patiently that if Ali lost a fight that the crowd expected him to win, there would be hell to pay, and we'd likely do the paying. "But we're for Ali," Stanley protested.

How had it come to this? I wondered. How could so many seemingly smart young Americans be so utterly delusional?

Some years later, equally smart young intellectuals would routinely sing Ali's praises not just as a boxer, but as a man of conscience, a peacemaker, a racial healer, a Mandela, a Gandhi. All but alone in his public dissent, Joe Frazier has insisted otherwise. "What has he done so great for this world?" he asks rhetorically of Ali. "Everything that he has done was against this country."

What Ali did, great or otherwise, was to channel the spirit of his age. "He is all that the sixties were," writes legendary sportswriter Jimmy Cannon of Ali. "It is as though he were created to represent them." In Gary that March night, he captured the ethos of that decade all too well. It wasn't pretty. I was there, and I know what I saw.

ACT ONE

THE CREATION OF THE MYTH, 1942–1975

THE YEAR THAT TRIED MEN'S SOULS

Muhammad Ali, born Cassius Marcellus Clay in Louisville, Kentucky, on January 17, 1942, grandson of a slave, began boxing at the age of twelve, and, by eighteen, had fought 108 amateur bouts.

In the very first sentence on Ali's life in her essay, "The Cruelest Sport," noted author Joyce Carol Oates shares with the reader one observation beyond the superficial: Ali was born the "grandson of a slave." Oates apparently sees this as the defining fact of Ali's existence.

More influential than Oates or anyone else in interpreting Ali to the world was sportscaster Howard Cosell. In his 1973 book, *Cosell*, he holds back until the second sentence of his seventy-page Ali bio before declaring, "He was a descendant of slaves."

We all have grown so used to this shame-on-us school of storytelling that we take it for granted. Today, those who shape our culture—writers, critics, publishers, broadcasters, movie and TV producers—routinely calculate the essence of individuals, especially racial minorities, not as the sum of their blessings but rather as the sum of their grievances.

In the traditional hero saga, the individual is expected to overcome hardship and injustice. In the grievance narrative, he nurses them like grudges. If they seem inadequate to evoke guilt or anger—the two desired responses from the audience—the narrator reserves the right to embellish or even invent additional offenses.

It was not until the 1960s, with the emergence of paralyzing concepts like "structural poverty" and "institutional racism," that this kind of narrative took root in American popular culture. The earlier postwar years were years of mounting hope. As late as 1961, for instance, Jack Newcombe dared to write a smart, upbeat biography of reigning heavyweight champ Floyd Patterson without ever mentioning Patterson's race or that of his opponents, let alone his descent from slaves.

The heroic possibilities of the grievance narrative did not fully emerge until the latter half of the decade, after the death of John Kennedy and the escalation of the war in Vietnam. As told by those who have mythologized the sixties, the youth of America rose up to throw off the shackles of racial paternalism, sexual repression, and imperial ambition. In this context, heroism was achieved not so much through individual accomplishment as through individual awareness of grievances and a collective reordering of the society. Ali came as close to fulfilling this idea of the hero as any public figure of that era. Indeed, as seen through the looking glass of this fabled decade, his life has taken on the quality of myth.

The flame of the sixties burned brightly into the early 1970s, and it continues to illuminate much of what we read and see today. As an example, in his otherwise fair-minded 2001 biopic, *Ali,* director Michael Mann shows the viewer a young Ali being shepherded to the back of a segregated bus, learning of the lynching death of Emmett Till, and being casually harassed by the cops during his morning workout—and all of this just under the opening credits.

Oates follows a similar script, rejecting any number of alternate ways to introduce the young Ali. She could have informed the reader that he was the much-loved offspring of two devoted parents, Odessa Grady Clay and Cassius Marcellus Clay Sr., which may explain his confidence. He had a skilled muralist for a father, a mathematician for an uncle, and a math teacher for an aunt, which may account for his creativity and instinctive smarts. As to his drive, that likely derived from his status as the first child in an ambitious African-American household.

Oates chooses instead to introduce Ali the way Malcolm X might have, not as an American, but as a victim of America, the grandson of a slave. This introduction would have made a little more sense if Ali actually *were* the grandson of a slave, but he is not. A boy born seventy-seven years after the passage of the Thirteenth Amendment was unlikely to have a grandparent who had been enslaved even as a child. Oates should have intuited as much or, if not, at least checked her facts. She did not need to. So widely accepted is the grievance narrative in the American media, especially on racial matters, that facts are challenged or even questioned only when they defy the gloomy orthodoxy.

Ali's grandparents were very much alive during his youth. The oldest of them, paternal grandfather Herman Clay, was born about 1878. His paternal grandmother, Edith Greathouse Clay, was born later still. Pride took a different turn in Herman Clay's day. He boasted of having famed American statesman Henry Clay, the "Great Compromiser," as his grandfather. His daughter, math teacher Mary Clay Turner, puts her seal of approval on the claim. "Henry Clay was Cassius's great-great-grandfather," she tells *Sports Illustrated* writer Jack Olsen, "and that's no family legend."

Ali himself bore the name of another white Clay, the abolitionist firebrand Cassius Marcellus. In his more spontaneous days, Ali reveled in the euphonic ring of his birth name. "Don't you think it's a beautiful name?" he would ask reporters. "Say it out loud: Cassius Marcellus Clay."

After Ali joined the Nation of Islam, he would deny any specific knowledge of white blood in the family. "If slaveholder Clay's blood came into our veins along with the name," he proclaimed, assuming the worst, hoping for it even, "it came by rape and defilement." By this time, Ali had made the grievance narrative his own. Although a chronic complainer, his father was outraged when Ali abandoned the "slave name" of Cassius Clay in 1964. Cassius Sr. despaired that his son and the Muslims were "trying to rub that name out" just as he was "trying to make it strong."

Ali's paternal aunt, Eva Clay Waddell, took a more generous view of her lineage as well. "No doubt some Clay and Greathouse ancestors were white," she told a reporter in 1980, "but that doesn't concern me one way or the other. It's nothing to hide. Those things happened back then."

On Ali's mother's side, the bloodlines are clearer. Odessa Clay was born a Grady. "My white blood came from the slave masters, from raping," Ali liked to claim, but his mother's grandfather was an adventurous lad from the old sod, Abe Grady of County Clare. Grady came to America after the Civil War and married Odessa's grandmother, Dinah. Their son would become Odessa's father. "He looked exactly like a white man," Odessa would remember. She herself could pass, at least in her son's eyes. "Mama, when you get on the bus, do people think you're a white lady or a colored lady?" Ali asked his mom when he was four.

Odessa's other grandfather, Tom Morehead, had a white father and a black mother. He had fought on the Union side in the Civil War. By all accounts, Tom Morehead was something special. "He wasn't afraid of nothing," Ali's aunt, Gillie Bell Morehead Plunkett, would recall. "He was some nice-looking man, too, the best-looking man I ever saw: tall and straight, light-skinned, had long black curly hair and dimples in each cheek. He carried himself with pride, didn't bow to no man." Other than the hair and dimples, writers would come to describe Ali very much the way Aunt Gillie described Tom Morehead.

Although Oates is silent on its significance, the time of Ali's birth is as extraordinary as his heritage. Winston Groom subtitles his recent best-seller, *1942, The Year That Tried Men's Souls*. He does not exaggerate. Six weeks before Ali was born, the Japanese bombed Pearl Harbor. During the week of his birth, the Japanese struck the main line of American resistance in the Philippines, a "Thrilla in Manila" of real consequence. The notorious Bataan death march would begin soon after.

In England, one city after another lay in smoldering ruins from the German blitz. The Germans, meanwhile, continued their advance through Russia, murdering Jews and other offending parties as they pushed East. In the month of Ali's birth, the first gas chamber went on line in Auschwitz. Three days after he was born, the Germans held the Der Wannsee Conference in Berlin to coordinate the "Final Solution." A day later, Rommel launched an offensive across Northern Africa.

In 1942, wherever one looked in the world, horror reigned—Europe, China, the Middle East, North Africa. Almost everywhere, that is. In assessing Ali's early life, Oates might have posed this sequence of questions: For every one hundred children who entered the world in January 1942, how many were born in a modern hospital? How many had two loving parents? How many drove away in their father's car? How many returned to a home with indoor plumbing, running water, and electricity? Indeed, how many could sleep at night without worry of a bomb crashing through their roof?

Of that one hundred, there could have been no more than two or three so blessed, Ali among them. For all the maddening indignities of the pre-civil rights South, Ali was born into a life more secure and comfortable than that of almost any child anywhere in the world. Neither Oates nor others of her literary caste would give Kentucky, or even America, credit for that. Instead, they encouraged Ali to reject his heritage and to repudiate its gifts—his faith, his country, even his name. His brother Rudolph—a.k.a. Rahaman Ali—would do the same.

For all of his gripes, and they were many and often racial in nature, Cassius Sr. retained a certain pride in his own accomplishments, as he should have. "I dressed them up as good as I could afford," he said of his two sons, "kept them in pretty good clothes. And they didn't come out of no ghetto. I raised them on the best street I could afford: 3302 Grand Avenue in the west end of Louisville."

The esteemed "ring doctor," Dr. Ferdie Pacheco, who has written arguably the most intimate and insightful of all books on Ali, describes Ali's early life "as distinctly middle-class." He continues: "They lived in a nice house . . . the children, Cassius and Rudy, dressed well and went to a good school. The problems of the ghetto were alien to them."

Pacheco raises still another question that Oates might have posed: Just how many children born in 1942 were the first born in a brood that would number no more than two? Ali was the golden child in the Clay family. No doubt the attention lavished on him by his parents and extended family would shape the man he became.

The story of Ali's adolescence reads like the script of an Andy Hardy movie. In a homey 1992 piece for *Sports Illustrated*, William Nack interviews any number of Ali's childhood friends. To a person, they tell of an eager, funny, charming, popular boy who deeply loved his mother, fainted with his first kiss at seventeen, and graduated from high school a teacher's pet and a virgin. Perhaps more than any other factor, the charmed circumstances of Ali's early life set him apart, certainly among heavyweight champions.

BORN IN 1895, Harry "Jack" Dempsey was the ninth of thirteen children. His ne'er-do-well Mormon father uprooted the family from West Virginia near century's end and took them westward by horse and wagon. When sober, his father scratched out a subsistence living in a series of Colorado towns, Manassa among them. Dempsey would later wear the sobriquet "Manassa Mauler" with pride. It gave him a more fixed sense of provenance than he had ever felt.

JOE LOUIS, BORN Joe Louis Barrow in 1914, was the seventh child of Munrow and Lily Reese Barrow, an Alabama sharecropping family. Although Munrow's mother was reportedly a full-blooded Cherokee, Louis was "mostly of black blood" and "proud of that." At the age of two, Louis's father was sent to the Searcy Hospital for the Negro Insane. A few years later, Lily met and married a widower named Pat Brooks. The combined family had sixteen children, the whole lot of whom the parents took to Detroit in search of a better life. Brooks, according to Louis, "was a good stepfather who worked hard and did the best he could."

ROCCO FRANCIS MARCHEGIANO, known to the world as Rocky Marciano, was born to Pierino and Pasqualena Marchegiano in the tough, working-class burg of Brockton, Massachusetts, in 1923. He was the second of seven children. Although an Italian immigrant, Pierino enlisted to fight in World War I and was gassed in the Argonne Forest. He never fully recovered but still managed to eke out a living in a Brockton shoe factory. "Even during the tough times," remembers Rocky's brother Sonny, "we didn't know we were poor."

THE POLICE IN Brooklyn's notorious Bedford-Sty had nicked young Floyd Patterson thirty or forty times for stealing and truancy by the time he was ten. Born in 1935, Patterson was the third of eleven children. His parents, desperately poor, moved from one dreary cold-water flat to another. He shared his bed with more brothers than Ali had. At ten, he was sent to Wiltwyck, a home for wayward boys in upstate New York. He would later dedicate his autobiography to Wiltwyck, "which started me in the right direction."

CHARLES "SONNY" LISTON might just as well have been born in the twelfth century for the silence that shrouds his early, undocumented life. Although he would fudge the date repeatedly in the future, best evidence marks his year of birth as 1928. Liston was the twenty-second child of a vicious sharecropper father and a browbeaten mother, the father's second wife, too put upon to protect Sonny from his father's abuse. Amidst this chorus of hard times stories, Liston's stands out. "Dickensian" doesn't do it justice. He grew up almost feral. Alone among all the boxers profiled, he could not even count on the love of his mother. Soon after Ali was born, Liston left Arkansas for St. Louis to seek out his mother, who had already fled her brutal husband. There, he launched a life of primal terror, most of it out of the ring. Liston was the first ogre young Ali would have to slay.

JOE FRAZIER WAS the second and most formidable. Although Ali and his enthusiasts would paint Frazier as the "great white hope," it is hard to imagine a more profoundly African experience in America than Frazier's. His family hailed from Gullah country, outside of Beaufort, South Carolina, the one part of the South most spiritually in touch with the African motherland. Born in 1944, two years after Ali, Joe was the twelfth of Dolly and Rubin Frazier's thirteen children. An overseer and moonshiner, the senior Frazier had his arm shot off in a fight over a woman. In this part of the world, no one was shocked. Young Frazier was helping his father almost full-time by the age of six or seven. "I never had a little boy's life," he would say. This background would count for nothing in the Ali myth.

THE THIRD AND youngest of Ali's epic foes was George Foreman. He was born in 1949, the fifth of seven children to Texan sharecroppers J. D. and Nancy Ree Nelson Foreman. Soon after his birth, the family moved to Houston. This was a particularly troubled time for the Foremans because J. D. was not George's biological father. Knowing this, J.D. rambled away from the family home even more than usual. "Hunger shaped my youth," says Foreman. Only the improbable combination of a loving mother and the newly created Job Corps spared the brutish young George a life of crime and punishment.

OF THE SERIOUS contenders in Ali's generation, only Ken Norton, a year younger than Ali, had as charmed an upbringing, and he admits it. "I definitely can hold claim to a wonderfully happy childhood," Norton remembers, "having never felt deprived in any way, shape, or form." As an African American, he was not unaware of the prejudice that lingered in his hometown of Jacksonville, Illinois, but he did not define himself by it.

THE IRONY, OF course, is that despite the relative ease of his early life, Muhammad Ali alone among these champions would wear the mantel of victim. This was doubly ironic since Ali was not instinctively inclined to self-pity. Rather, the script dictated grievance, and Ali gamely played the part.

To elevate Ali, to sustain the moral force of the chosen narrative, the guardians of the Ali myth have had to either subvert or suppress two key series of facts that were unfolding at the time of Ali's birth. The subversion involves Joe Louis. The suppression involves Elijah Muhammad, the self-appointed Messenger of Allah, the storied head of the Nation of Islam, and the single most influential individual in Ali's adult life.

"To some," writes Thomas Hauser, Ali was "the greatest hero to come out of the Vietnam War." That "some" seems to include Hauser, whose authorized oral history, *Muhammad Ali: His Life and Times*, is the Bible of the Ali library. For Ali to be "the greatest hero," his defenders have had to pull off two cultural coups. The first was to redefine "war hero" to mean draft resister. This would take time. The second and simpler strategy was to deny or demean Louis's contribution to the war effort.

Less than one week before Ali's birth, and only five weeks after the United States entered World War II, Joe Louis enlisted in the U.S. Army. He did not have to. The world heavyweight champion was twenty-seven years old at the time with a wife and a mother depending on him for support. He was unlikely to be called in the near future. However, the events of Pearl Harbor inspired him to act. "I was mad. I was furious, you name it," Louis would recall in his autobiography, a book published in 1978, long after such sentiments were fashionable. "Hell, this is my country. Don't come around sneaking up and attacking it."

Given his influence, Howard Cosell set the tone for undercutting the validity and honor of Louis's contribution. Although Cosell did his World War II duty in Brooklyn, he felt free to dismiss Louis's service as a "soft, cushiony, showcase job." Like others, he implied that Louis cut a deal at the beginning, but in fact Louis did no such thing. He enlisted without any knowledge of what he would be called on to do or where. He endured basic training like any other grunt. The Army then dispatched him to a cavalry division at Fort Riley in Kansas because of his improbable skill as a horseman.

Life had been kind to Joe Louis. In those glory years before the war, he had made millions of dollars, part of which he had invested in a Michigan horse ranch. There he and his wife, Marva, learned to become competitive "equestrians," a word admittedly new to Louis's vocabulary. "I love this country like I love my people," Louis would remember. "No place in this world could a onetime black cotton picker like me get to be a millionaire."

It was Louis's unapologetic patriotism even more than his war record that threatened the Ali myth. To justify Ali's defiance, the mythmakers would have to undermine Louis's very character. This would not be easy. Louis reigned unbeaten as heavyweight champ from 1937 to 1949. Only a decade separated Louis's retirement in 1951—after a misbegotten comeback—and Ali's professional debut. Only two decades separated Louis's honorable discharge from the Army and Ali's rejection of the draft. The memory of Louis's behavior was still fresh, especially among Ali's detractors.

In truth, no American of his generation did more for the cause of civil rights than Joe Louis, perhaps no American of the century. Told honestly, Louis's story speaks well not only of the man but also of the nation he helped to mold.

In February 1933, the month before FDR was inaugurated, eighteen-year-old Joe Louis Barrow held down a decent job at the River Rouge Ford complex west of Detroit. This very fact contradicts so much of what we think we know about that time and place. Yes, even in the very darkest month of the Great Depression, there were good jobs to be had. African Americans held many of them. The Henry Ford we are encouraged to think of as an anti-Semite was not a practicing racist. As it happens, his company would later employ Malcolm X.

Louis dropped the "Barrow" lest his mother know that he had begun to box. Like every able American male, black or white, he had a dream. "I knew I wasn't going to stay where I was," he remembers, "but I wasn't sure just where I was going." He did not turn to boxing out of desperation. He turned to it as the best way to follow his dream given his various gifts. Impressively, the Ford plant extended him a six-month leave with a guaranteed job on return so that he could pursue his ambitions.

Much has been made about the self-imposed restrictions under which Louis boxed: no taunting, no gloating, and especially no cavorting with white women. His black managers and trainers made it clear to him from the beginning: "Don't become another Jack Johnson." Johnson, the only black heavyweight champ before Louis, effectively surrendered his crown in 1913 when he fled the country to avoid conviction on a Mann Act rap. In 1915, broke and desperate, he lost the title officially when Kansan Jess Willard knocked him out in the twenty-sixth round of a still controversial fight in Cuba.

"White man hasn't forgotten that fool nigger with his white women," trainer Jack "Chappy" Blackburn reminded Louis, "acting like he owned the world." In the 1930s, most black Americans had little use for Johnson, Louis and Blackburn in particular. Blackburn had once worked with Johnson as a sparring partner and, as he tells it, inadvertently showed him up. Johnson retaliated by trying to destroy his career. When Louis came of age under Blackburn's tutelage, Johnson went out of his way to belittle Louis. "It didn't do him much good," Louis remembers. "He was working as a strong man in Robert Ripley's Flea Circus, and by my standards that ain't shit. And the black people who were rallying around me put him down for talking against me."

Reserved by nature, Louis would not have been inclined to taunt his opponents in any case. As to white women, and there were many, Louis made a point to be discreet. He was discreet with black women as well. As a married man during his glory days, it paid to be. Besides, women like Lana Turner and Lena Horne insisted on it.

In 1935, Louis fought an Italian giant and former world champion by the name of Primo Carnera. For the first time, Louis sensed how much symbolism could be invested in a boxing match. With Mussolini's Italy at war with Ethiopia, many American blacks let him know that he was fighting for the honor of Africa. "They put a heavy weight on my twenty-year-old shoulders," said Louis, no pun likely intended. He won and pocketed an extraordinary $60,000, about thirty years worth of work at the Ford plant.

The symbolic stakes would get much higher. In 1937, Louis beat Jim Braddock, the Cinderella Man, for the title. In 1938, he squared off against German Max Schmeling in front of seventy thousand people in Yankee Stadium. By this time, Hitler's intentions were clear to the world. Although he was an anti-Nazi with a Jewish trainer, Schmeling found himself cast as the poster child for the Master Race. Louis served as head chef for the melting pot. "Now here I was a black man," he recalled, "I had the burden of representing all America." Shortly before the fight, in fact, President Roosevelt had invited Louis to dinner at the White House and told him, "We're depending on those muscles for America." Louis dispatched Schmeling in the first round.

"America was proud of me," Louis recalled. "My people were proud of me, and since the fight, race relationships were lightening up—who the hell could ask for more." Even black poet Langston Hughes, known at the time for his sharp critiques of the American experience, approved of Louis's service: "Joe Louis is a man / For men to imitate / When his country needed him / He did not stall or fail."

This was a watershed moment in American sports. Historically, fans have tended to root for their ethnic or racial champions, a natural enough phenomenon. Louis, for instance, enjoyed a popularity in

America's black communities that has never been equaled. His influence on the next generation of black boxers was profound.

As Ali relates in his autobiography, "My father walked up and down Boston Street after my first victory, predicting, 'My son is going to be another Joe Louis.'" Joe Frazier has similar recollections, "Uncle Israel looked at me and, noting my stocky build, told the others: 'That boy there . . . that boy is gonna be another Joe Louis.'"

But on the occasion of the Schmeling fight, the great majority of white Americans cheered a black man over a white. What is less well understood is that white fans continued to support Louis against a long series of white opponents even after the Schmeling fight, especially after he joined the Army.

"Joe was the first black American of any discipline or endeavor," tennis star Arthur Ashe once noted, "to enjoy the overall good feel, sometimes bordering on idolatry, of all Americans regardless of color." Born in 1943, Ashe was just old enough to remember. Louis could not forget. "The cheers were for me and I loved every minute of it," he reflected after a fight late in his career. "It sounded like old times again."

America had come a long way in a short period of time. The day after winning the crown in 1919, Jack Dempsey had quietly promised that he would not fight a black man, and he was as good as his word. There was nothing quiet about champ John L. Sullivan's boast a generation before that. "I will not fight a Negro," he proclaimed. "I never have and I never shall." Through his skill and his character, Louis had prodded America forward.

Louis's service in World War II further endeared him to the nation. Although the Army quickly realized he would be of more use as a morale builder than as a cavalry sergeant, Louis paid his dues. He served 46 months; traveled over 70,000 miles in his "soft, cushiony" job, many of those in war zones; fought 96 exhibitions; and was seen by more than 5,000,000 soldiers, more than a few of them in hospitals.

Among those soldiers inspired by a Louis visit was staff sergeant

Angelo Mirena. "To have actually met him," recalls Mirena, "was one of the highlights of my English tour of duty." Mirena had an older brother who boxed and who was also named Joe. Like Louis, Joey Mirena fought under an assumed name lest his parents find out. When Joey's brother Chris got into fight management, he used his brother's new name. So did Angelo when he went to work for Chris. And that's how these South Philly sons of Italian immigrants—Joe, Chris, and Angelo—all came to be known by the Scottish name of Dundee. Only in America.

Louis did more than entertain the troops. He used his considerable weight to challenge segregation within the ranks, usually with success and often through the sheer force of his will. Boxing great Sugar Ray Robinson traveled with Louis on the American end of his exhibition tour and affirms the impact that he and particularly Louis made. On one occasion, in fact, Robinson had to intervene lest Louis clobber a white Southern MP who insisted on belittling him. When adjudicated, the Army ruled in Louis's favor. Louis even succeeded in opening the doors of the Fort Riley baseball team to a man who would do some serious door-opening after the war, Jackie Robinson.

In 1948, the year after Robinson desegregated major league baseball, Harry Truman desegregated the U.S. military. Louis had made it impossible not to. Such was the opinion of Truman Gibson. A black attorney admitted to the bar of the Supreme Court in 1939, Gibson had met Louis while serving as an aid to the secretary of war and had arranged Louis's exhibition tour. He would go on to head up the International Boxing Commission.

The virtues that the press, black and white, admired in Louis were the same ones they admired in any champion: intelligence, courage, self-restraint, modesty. To call them "white values," as some Ali enthusiasts are inclined to do, is to flatter white people unduly. When Rocky Marciano seized the crown the year after Louis retired, the press was pleased that he lived up to Louis's standards. "He is an intelligent guy and enjoys the homage all champions know," wrote Jimmy Cannon of Marciano. "But he doesn't take advantage of his position. Only Joe Louis in my time had this grace." "Like Joe Louis," Budd Schulberg observed, "[Marciano] has innate taste and graciousness."

Young Ali fans, however, had little real knowledge of Joe Louis or of the times that produced him. The Ali mythmakers have filled in the gaps. As they tell it, when they bother to tell Louis's story at all, Louis was not the proud and defiant champion of the people that Ali was, but rather an accommodator, someone who went along to get along, "a white man's black man," as Cosell would have it.

Ali upped the ante during his period of Vietnam resistance calling Louis an "Uncle Tom" and worse after Louis criticized him for refusing the draft. "Louis is the one without courage," said Ali at the time. "Louis, he doesn't know what the words mean. He's a sucker." When Louis is written of sympathetically today, as in the recent book, *Heroes Without a Country: America's Betrayal of Joe Louis and Jesse Owens,* it is typically as a victim, a role in which he never saw himself even during his dispiriting, post-ring, IRS-hounded career.

WHILE SUBVERTING LOUIS'S history, the guardians of the Ali myth have also chosen to suppress certain inconvenient facts that have shaped Ali's life and career. And none is more inconvenient than the disposition of Elijah Muhammad in the month of Ali's birth and Joe Louis's enlistment, January 1942.

Elijah Muhammad was born Elija Pool, later modified to Elijah Poole, in 1897. Like Joe Louis, he was the seventh child of a struggling but deeply Christian family in the Deep South. His father, in fact, was a preacher. Like Louis, he came to Detroit to seek his fortune, arriving in 1923 with his wife, Clara. Once there, he quickly found a job with a company whose name—critics might scoff—fit him perfectly, the American Nut Company.

Although the job paid more than twice what he had been making in the South, Muhammad hated it. He devoted his energy instead to Marcus

Garvey's United Negro Improvement Association, a hugely popular exercise in back-to-Africa black nationalism. Alas, soon after Muhammad arrived in Detroit, the Feds busted Garvey on a credible mail fraud charge. Garvey blamed his downfall on the middle-class "light-colored Negroes." He felt, with some justification, that they resented his popularity. In any case, as Garvey's fortunes swooned, so did Muhammad's. He took to drink and became a burden to his own family.

To help pull himself out of his funk, Muhammad turned to the Moorish Science Temple of America, an organization that the charismatic Noble Drew Ali had founded in Newark, New Jersey, in 1913. Drew Ali described his religion as "Islam" and his followers as "Muslims" and laid the groundwork for the Nation of Islam that would follow.

From the beginning, intramural violence would plague this organization and its spin-offs. Drew Ali was indicted for murder in 1928, and not without good reason. Given his fix, he welcomed the timely arrival of a man who could sustain his mission, the enigmatic David Ford, better known as Wallace Fard. After the police roughly intervened in still another internecine squabble, the enraged Fard swore that he would bring "America to its knees in the very near future." The 1929 stock market crash followed as if by divine inspiration, and Fard took delight in having called it down. Needless to say, this prophecy impressed his followers.

It certainly impressed Muhammad's wife, Clara. She persuaded her husband, who had started drinking again upon the demise of Drew Ali, to meet Fard. "I know you think I'm white," Fard told him at that first meeting. "But I'm not. I'm an Asiatic black man. I have come to America to save my long lost uncle."

Fard did look Caucasian and indeed was. Best evidence—his hatred of Hinduism being exhibit A—pegs him as a native of what is now Pakistan. Among Fard's stops on his way from Karachi to Detroit was San Quentin, where he had idled away a few years on a narcotics rap. The "uncle" he had come to save was the African American, and few among them needed saving like Elijah Muhammad. He transferred his loyalties to Fard in a Detroit minute.

Much has been made about the rather adventurous creation myths that Fard shared with Muhammad, the tales of a big-headed black scientist named Yakub who had grafted the white race from the black thousands of years ago in a gene-manipulation experiment. But it was not Fard's cosmology that attracted the FBI in the 1930s. It was the company he kept.

As early as 1933, the prescient Fard was predicting a war between the United States and Japan. He was soon elaborating that a hovering "Mother Plane" would launch smaller planes, which would drop poison bombs and eliminate white America. That plane was to have been designed and built in Japan.

In that same year, 1933, to avoid legal complications, Fard changed the name of his organization to the Nation of Islam, the name by which it is still known. He also created the Fruit of Islam, a paramilitary group not unlike the SA of Adolph Hitler, who had assumed power that same year in Germany. By this time too, Fard had granted his now loyal acolyte the name Elijah Muhammad and appointed him Supreme Minister.

Fard and Muhammad did more than talk about their "Asiatic brothers." They conspired with them. They got in particularly deep with Japanese agent Satohata Takahashi, who had burrowed into a variety of black nationalist organizations, and his protégé, Ashima Takis. In a 1933 rally transcribed by the FBI, Takis told his black audience, "You are the most oppressed people on earth. If you join the Japanese and other colored races, you will be in command of the whites." As Karl Evanzz notes in his courageous book on Elijah Muhammad, *The Messenger,* "This ideological confluence marked the beginning of the federal government's monitoring of Muslims in America."

After Fard disappeared one step ahead of the law, Muhammad assumed control of the Nation of Islam, claiming that Fard had appointed him as his successor. Throughout the decade, Muhammad peppered nearly every speech with boasts of Japanese superiority.

"The Japanese will slaughter the white man," Muhammad promised repeatedly. To prop up Muhammad's leadership and encourage a little treason, Takahashi promised each Nation of Islam follower a single-family detached home in Hawaii. All they had to do was to support Japan in a war against America. By decade's end, Fard's war prophecy was looking more and more inspired. The Feds certainly thought so. They listed Muhammad as a "threat to national security" and arrested Takahashi for immigration violations.

Were he still a drinker, Muhammad would have been popping champagne corks on December 7, 1941. That was the day, of course, that "Allah's Asiatic Army" bombed Pearl Harbor. In the weeks that followed, as Evanzz relates, "Muhammad and his followers reveled in newspaper accounts of Japan's exploits."

As it happened, Congress had extended the draft age to forty-four a year earlier. A generation later, it would lower the passing percentile on intelligent tests from 30 to 15. In each case, neither intentional, the change just barely netted a prominent member of the Nation of Islam. In each case, that member refused to register. Muhammad's refusal set the precedent for Ali's. Not knowing Muhammad's history, and not particularly caring, Vietnam-era resisters would see Ali's resistance as moral and principled, as they imagined their own to be. That is one of the many drawbacks of not knowing history.

To say the least, Elijah Muhammad lacked Muhammad Ali's resources to fight the draft. On September 20, 1942, federal agents found the Messenger hiding ingloriously under a bed in a Washington D.C. house. A week later, Ashima Takis pled guilty to forging a money order and turned state's evidence against the Nation of Islam. Three weeks later, a grand jury indicted Muhammad for conspiracy to commit sedition.

Among the evidence presented against Muhammad in his subsequent trial was a lecture he had delivered at the Chicago temple in August 1942.

"You shouldn't fear the devil when he tells you that you must go and fight in this war. You should refuse to fight," he told his followers. "The newspapers are lying when they say that the Japanese are losing. We are going to win."

As history records, "we"—the Japanese/Nazi/Nation of Islam axis—did not exactly win the war. Nor did Muhammad win his legal battles. After three years in a federal hoosegow, he was released to what he regarded as a larger prison, the "wilderness of North America," one year and one week after the Second World War came to its terrifying end.

FRIDAY NIGHT FIGHTS

On May 17, 1954, the United States Supreme Court declared that "separate educational facilities are inherently unequal." The decision effectively denied the legal basis for academic segregation in Kentucky and twenty other states and swept all legalized segregation closer to the dustbin of history. At the time, Muhammad Ali was twelve.

Like the succulent fruit dangled over the head of the starving Tantalus, such seemingly real racial progress was mere illusion. Or so the Ali myth insists. Indeed, in one of his less charitable moments, the radicalized Ali would call the architect of *Brown v. Board of Education*, the legendary Thurgood Marshall, "an ugly American."

To understand the Ali myth, it is essential to understand the presumed forces of darkness in the zero-sum morality play called the sixties. "White America" is the mythical place to which Joyce Carol Oates, Ali biographer Thomas Hauser, and other Ali faithful have consigned their less enlightened fellow Caucasians. As they tell it, "white America" inevitably misbehaves in matters racial. "How ingloriously white America responded to Ali," writes Oates in a typical bit of condescension.

Oates and people like her could position themselves as morally superior only if they had someone to feel superior to. This role was assigned to the hardhats in Gary and elsewhere across the fruited plain. I know something about them and the notorious "white America" they were said to inhabit. In reality, however, it was never overly white, and we mostly just thought of it as America. I tell my story only to shed light on theirs.

In 1954, I was six years old. My parents, my two older brothers, my baby sister, and I had just moved to my new block on the second floor of a coal-fired triplex, 7 Myrtle Avenue, Newark, New Jersey. Three black families inhabited an identical triplex at 9 Myrtle Avenue when we moved there. Two more black families inhabited the duplex at 11 Myrtle; two more the duplex at 13. There were several more black families on the Roseville Avenue side of the block, including a dentist. As a six-year-old, I helped my older brother deliver papers. Later, I would have my own paper routes, so I knew everyone who lived everywhere and had been in most of their houses.

My father was a Navy vet and cop, "Big Bill," a kind-hearted, six-foot, two-hundred-plus-pounder, who presided benignly over our nightly TV from an easy chair in a back corner of the living room. He imposed his will on our viewing only on Friday nights when he and every other father, white or black, in an archipelago of urban enclaves from Newark to New Orleans, turned the dial to NBC's *Gillette Cavalcade of Sports*, better known as the *Friday Night Fights*.

In mid-century America, only major league baseball held more sway over the public than professional boxing, and in our part of the world, it was a close call. Other than my baby sister, we all watched the fights religiously. I grew up thinking that every little kid could sing the Gillette theme song and name the heavyweight champs in order.

It was in the autumn of 1954 that Two Ton Tony Galento came to the Tivoli theater, just two blocks from our house, for the "Neighborhood Premiere" of *On the Waterfront*. The movie had long since premiered in New York and even in downtown Newark. We didn't care. We didn't care that it was Two Ton and not Marlon Brando. Everyone went.

Two Ton was the first celebrity I had ever seen. He had somehow managed to knock down Joe Louis, but even more impressively, he had fought a bear, a kangaroo, and, yes, an octopus. Apparently, he beat the bear and the kangaroo, lost to Louis, and fled the water tank in a panic when the octopus squirted him with its ink jets. Galento accomplished a lot for a guy who worked the light bag while smoking a cigar. I still remember how thrilled I felt upon seeing all two tons of him, how thrilled we all felt.

At the time, every enclave in the archipelago had its own hero. In New Jersey, North Bergen had Jimmy Braddock, who used to work the Hoboken docks where *On The Waterfront* was filmed. Essex County had Two Ton. Bayonne was nurturing a lad who would one day enshrine the city in boxing lore. That, of course, would be the "Bayonne Bleeder," Chuck Wepner. After watching Wepner knock down Ali in a 1975 mismatch and then hang on improbably until the fifteenth round, a young Sylvester Stallone went home and wrote the screenplay for *Rocky.* He set it in South Philly, another such enclave, and borrowed much of Rocky's lifestyle from Philadelphian Joe Frazier.

Camden, New Jersey, had "Jersey Joe" Walcott. Across the river in Philadelphia, in September 1952, Rocky Marciano ended what the black-owned *Amsterdam News* called a "Glorious Fistic Era" when he knocked out Walcott in the thirteenth round of their title match. Walcott was the third consecutive black fighter to hold the crown during a fifteen-year span, Ezzard Charles and Joe Louis having come before him.

In the 1950s, the men in their easy chairs were pleased to just watch the fights and cheer their local heroes. Many of them had done more fighting than they had ever cared to in the decade just past. Now, they contented themselves with the simple things in their lives, and America respected their contentment.

That was all about to change.

TOMORROW'S CHAMPION

For the hardcore Ali faithful, the real story of 1954 was not how the Supreme Court desegregated the schools but how "The Greatest" discovered boxing. The story begins with the bicycle, a new sixty-dollar Schwinn with red lights and chrome trim that his father had bought him for Christmas. To the reader, this bike might seem unexceptional, but one cannot imagine Floyd Patterson or Joe Frazier or Sonny Liston or Mike Tyson ever having received such a present. On this particular day, Ali and a friend rode their bikes to a major black business exhibition in the center of Louisville.

The boys parked their bikes and went in. When they came out, Ali discovered to his horror that his had been stolen. He was distraught, not only at the loss of his bike but also at the fear of his father's wrath. In tears, he sought out a policeman.

The people in the neighborhood sent him to a nearby boxing gym run by one Joseph Elsby Martin, a Louisville police officer, badge number 474. "I stood there, smelling the sweat and rubbing alcohol, and a feeling of awe came over me," remembers Ali. After having Ali fill out a report, Martin gave him an application for the boxing program and encouraged him to join. Ali returned home to the expected tongue-lashing, one that even he felt was deserved, and said nothing to his parents about the application.

The following Saturday, he was home watching TV, then still something of a novelty, and happened to catch a program called *Tomorrow's Champions*. There, working the corners with one of his boxers, was Joe Martin. The combination of boxing and potential TV exposure intoxicated the young Ali. At that moment, an extraordinary career was born.

As it happened, Muhammad Ali discovered boxing during the only four years in the last seventy when a white American ruled the heavyweight ranks. "One night I heard Rocky Marciano fighting on the radio," Muhammad Ali would tell *Sports Illustrated's* Jack Olsen many years later. "And it sounded so exciting. Here I was, a little Louisville boy riding around on a bicycle, no money, half hungry, hearing about this great man, Marciano."

To satisfy the terms of the Ali myth, Ali would often paint a grimmer-than-real portrait of his early life. But here his enthusiasm for Marciano seems genuine. One senses in the young Ali's excitement a boy who had yet to yield to the sway of race.

THERE WAS MUCH in Rocky Marciano's story that deserved Ali's awe and, as with Louis, much that challenges the basics of the Ali myth. Journalists of the time greatly admired Marciano's work ethic, his keen sense of family, his patriotism, and above all his humility. As Ferdie Pacheco observes, "Humility was a quality much appreciated in American heroes." In this particular virtue, Marciano stood out. The *San Francisco Examiner* called Marciano "probably the humblest of heavyweight champions." "By the end of his career, to the media and the masses," comments Sullivan, "Rocky Marciano was no longer an Italian hero. He was, instead, an American hero."

Born in 1923, the child of immigrants, Marciano dropped out of high school as a sophomore with little more than the wistful ambition of becoming a major league baseball player. He never got close. Still, Marciano refused to settle for the time-clock life that his father led. "He wanted to be successful," remembers his brother Sonny. "And I think that alone separated him."

In 1943, the Army called and Marciano listened. He served two years with the 150th Combat Engineers, much of that time overseas. In this regard, he was hardly exceptional. My own father, and the fathers of all my friends, did the same. This service impressed a whole generation of otherwise ordinary men with a distinctive sense of duty, and they expected the same of others.

In Marciano's most significant role, he helped ferry supplies to the invasion beaches of Normandy. He returned stateside in 1945 looking for some way to distinguish himself. He found it in the ring. Marciano fought his first legitimate fights in Army tournaments at Fort Lewis. A late starter, he turned twenty-two that year, the same age as Ali when he first won the world championship. It was not until 1947 that Marciano got serious about amateur boxing and not until 1948 that he fought his first real professional fight.

Few of the savvy old ring hands saw much of a future in Marciano. For a heavyweight he was small, light, thick-legged, and notoriously short-armed. On top of all that, his style was crude and awkward, even at his best. He did have two things going for him, however, a powerful right hand and an extraordinary will to succeed.

On October 26, 1951, the ascendant Marciano squared off with the one man he least wanted to face. It was not that he was afraid of Joe Louis, but rather, as a friend recalls, "Rocky worshipped the guy." Louis was his idol. In 1951, on the comeback trail, Louis was still the idol of many. Although overwhelmingly white, the crowd at Madison Square Garden that night was "a Joe Louis crowd." Adds Marciano biographer Russell Sullivan, "Louis had built up a reservoir of public affection during his long and glorious career."

In the eighth round, Marciano put a seriously beaten Louis out of his all too obvious misery with a pair of left hooks. Marciano then returned to his dressing room and cried. "Rocky didn't really have too many guys that he looked up to," his brother Peter would tell Sullivan. "But Joe Louis was one of them."

Even in a fight free of Louis sentiment, the white fans did not automatically embrace Marciano because he was white. "If anything," reports Sullivan, "more fans were pulling for Walcott, given the fact he was from nearby Camden, New Jersey." Sullivan notes that this pattern would hold through Marciano's four title defenses against black challengers: "If some people cheered for the white champion, others did for the black challenger."

Whites in general may not have flocked en masse to Marciano, but his fellow Italian-Americans most certainly did. "They rooted for him— passionately," Sullivan notes. Indeed, they cheered him with as much passion as blacks had Joe Louis or Jews had Max Baer. In terms of fan behavior, in fact, it makes more sense to think of blacks not as the opposite of whites, but rather as a distinct ethnic group like Jews or Italians.

All other factors being equal, it seems fully human to cheer on one's racial hero. More than just human, it seems altogether appropriate to cheer on an ethnic hero. As Marciano's career makes clear, factors other than race informed the passions of much of the white audience. Even today, however, few factors trump ethnicity.

For all the current talk of diversity, America was more culturally diverse in Marciano's day and less constrained by law or custom. My mother, who was born the same year as Marciano, was not allowed to play with Italians. Typically, Italian families had arrived in America a generation later than the Irish. The difference between the customs of that first generation of Italians or Jews or even Southern blacks and those of their fellow citizens was real and occasionally provocative.

In the great experiment that was America, any number of such groups lived together side by side with little civic authority to discipline their behavior. Given the imperfections of human nature, they coexisted uneasily. Such an experiment had never been tried before. There were no ground rules. In retrospect, one marvels at how relatively well these disparate groups got on.

At the beginning of the Marciano ascendancy, for instance, my mother's younger brother, my Uncle Bob, married an Italian girl, my Aunt Lucille, the daughter of immigrants, she with the wild black hair, peasant blouses, and loop earrings. The courtship could not have pleased my grandfather, but times were changing, and he knew it. Like Louis before him, Marciano helped make that change possible.

UNLIKE LOUIS OR Marciano, Ali would drive a wedge between races during the years when it mattered most. Although the blame—or credit—for Ali's racial posturing is usually laid at the Nation of Islam's door, the roots of it can be traced to Louisville.

At the Columbia gym, the young Ali found not just a passion but a second home and a surrogate father in Joe Martin. Martin passed up promotions on the police force lest one jeopardize the work he really loved, molding the kids in his charge, none of whom was more special to him than Ali. They would spend six years together. There are many reasons Ali sought refuge in the gym, but Martin advances an unspoken one: "The kid was scared to death of his father."

By all accounts, Cassius Clay Sr. was a volatile, insecure man, a dedicated parent when sober, a powder keg when not. One friend described him to Jack Olsen, who did the most in-depth reporting on Ali's early life, as "just a frustrated little guy who can't drink." Dr. Ferdie Pacheco describes the life of the senior Clay as "one of anguished depression."

"He grew up in an atmosphere of impending explosion," says Olsen of Ali, and there are police reports to prove it. Clay's wife, Odessa, called the cops on her husband several times, once for cutting the young Ali. These incidents only deepened the senior Clay's resentment toward the police, Joe Martin included.

From the time he was a little boy, Ali and his brother, Rahaman, heard from their father story upon story of racial injustice, some real, some exaggerated, some fully apocryphal or wildly conspiratorial. What he learned from his father, observes Pacheco, was "a deep distrust of the white man." Says Olsen of Clay, "He set up an environment that made the Black Muslims or some other hate-white movement perfect for the kid."

Ali's no-nonsense Aunt Mary implicated her brother in what she clearly saw as a wrong turn in Ali's adult life. "If Cassius tells you he's the way he is because he was kicked around by white people," she told Olsen, "he's just trying to give you an answer, that's all." From an early age, Ali was hearing one thing about the white man and experiencing another, a dichotomy that would shape his life.

For all his flaws, Clay loved his son deeply and eventually warmed up to his amateur career as Ali gained more exposure. But the father did not have a lock on his son's yet unformed spirit. His mother infused Ali with her own particular gift, an "inner sweetness of character" as Olsen describes it. "Odessa was a light-skinned beautiful woman who was soft-spoken, kind, gentle, and religious," observes Pacheco, a sentiment from which no one dissents. In the battle for Ali's soul, however, Odessa had few allies, at least not early in his career.

At the peak of his powers in 1975, the then thirty-three-year-old world champ reflected back on his Louisville days. The vehicle was an autobiography, *The Greatest: My Own Story*. Black scholar and Ali icon-oclast Gerald Early has deconstructed the book's unusual composition. According to Early, Richard Durham, the Marxist-oriented editor of *Muhammad Speaks*, is the coauthor of the book in name only. Durham's job was to tape any number of conversations with Ali or between Ali and others and then give them to an "editor" for writing. That editor was Toni Morrison. Ali's is surely the only boxing autobiography ghosted by a Nobel Prize winner. To further confuse the authorship issue, Herbert Muhammad, the son of Elijah and the manager of Ali, had to sign off on every page.

Not surprisingly, their collective retelling of Ali's Louisville experience rendered his story poorer, tougher, and blacker, and it does so at the
expense of Joe Martin. Unaware of the hurt such charges could deliver,
Ali, not for the last time, casually painted a white benefactor as something of a racist. "Most of Martin's boys were white," says Ali, "and most
of those he tried to seriously recruit were white." If this were true, one
has to question why Martin actively recruited Ali when Ali had no record
and showed no obvious potential.

Ali tells the reader, too, that only "in the all-black part of town," the
East End, did any serious training take place. As Ali remembers, when he
went to see the man behind that training, Fred Stoner, the word got back
to Martin who dressed Ali down and made him feel "degraded." As a
result, Ali had to stay with the unsophisticated Martin who merely guided
Ali through all 108 of his amateur fights and on to win six Kentucky
Golden Glove Championships, two National Golden Gloves tournaments, two National AAU titles, and eventually an Olympic gold medal.

"All of the publicity about my boxing origin and the early development of my boxing skill describes Joe Martin as the incubator," Ali recalls
with a stunning lack of grace and candor. "But my style, my stamina, my
system were molded in the basement of a church in the East End."

IN 1954, IT was not events in the East End of Louisville that would
shape Ali's life, but in the east end of the world, the far east, specifically
Indochina. In May of that year, 25,000 Communist troops attacked the
fewer than 3,000 French soldiers in the shrinking French stronghold of
Dien Bien Phu. Despite fierce resistance from the French, the
Communists breached their defenses and forced their surrender. At least
2,200 French died in the battle along with about 8,000 Vietnamese.

Only after French rule ended in the North did the Vietnamese begin
to understand what terror was really like. "The scale of violence was
extraordinary," reports the authoritative French work, *The Black Book of
Communism*. Through a combination of lethal "land reform" and

Stalinist intra-party purges, the victorious Democratic Republic of Vietnam (DRV) executed an estimated 50,000 of its own citizens and imprisoned as many as 100,000 more. Millions meanwhile fled to the South, including at least 600,000 Catholics.

In 1954, Muhammad Ali could not even begin to suspect that events in this far-off world would influence his boxing career, but they most certainly would.

RUMBLINGS

DAD AVENGES $3 ROBBERY
Three 11-year-old boys were arrested by the detective father
of a 9-year-old boy whom the trio stopped on the street
and robbed of $3 yesterday in front of 55 Myrtle Avenue.

So reads the lead of a small human-interest story on page 19 of the June 14th, 1957, edition of the *Newark Evening News*. Prey to the unknowable logic of motherhood, my mom chose to paste this quirky little account of my first official mugging in her scrapbook. I was in the fourth grade at the time.

As the *Evening News* told the tale, I was returning home from the grocery store where I "had gone on an errand"—a quaint notion—when the three boys stopped me. One boy held his hands over my eyes while the other boys rifled my pockets. The trio then fled. I reported the incident to my father, "Detective William Cashill of the Youth Aid Bureau," and then we "toured the neighborhood" until I pointed out the boys. The three confessed and were released to their parents' custody. End of story.

Not quite. The truth, as always, was a bit more complicated. The three "older" boys were black. I did not resist when the one kid put his hands over my eyes because I thought the hands belonged to a friend of mine from the block. "Earl," I joked, "is that you?" By the time I realized it wasn't, the boys were gone, and so was the money. Like Ali with his bicycle, I worried as much about my parents thinking me careless as about the crime itself.

I trudged home crestfallen to our house, a ramshackle old relic at 29 Myrtle that my father was rehabilitating around us. I told my tale of woe to my mother, who prided herself on being no one's fool. Her first instinct was to challenge it. Only when satisfied that I was on the level did she explode. That day marked the first time I ever heard her use the words "black" or "bastard."

Lest the reader think my mother a bigot, allow me to share one other story. Just a few months prior, my Cub Scout den mother invited us all to bring a new kid to the next meeting at her house. I brought my good friend Albert, a classmate since kindergarten. All seemed to go well enough until meeting's end. Just as I was leaving, the den mother took me aside and dressed me down for bringing a colored kid. I didn't tell Albert, but I did tell my mother. Enraged, she picked up the phone, called the den mother, and roasted her royally. That day marked the first time I ever heard my mother use the words "guinea" or "bitch." Politically incorrect she may have been, but my mother did have a rough sense of justice and was prepared to enforce it. Albert went on to become one of Cub Pack 115's most decorated scouts.

On the day of the mugging, we didn't tour the neighborhood, as reported, but went straight to the nearby Roseville Avenue School. I remember the principal as a heavyset white woman who assured us that none of her boys would ever do such a thing. She suggested we go look at the Eighth Street School a half mile away. My father quietly reminded her that the crime took place about one hundred feet from her school's playground, that the boys in question were colored, and that her school had myriad colored boys from which to choose. "Well, you can look," she sniffed.

As we left the office, my father said, "The trouble with Jews is that they believe the coloreds can do no wrong." It was the first and only time I heard my father offer an opinion about Jews.

My father and I went from class to class. Other than race and the back of one boy's nylon shirt, I had no way to ID the perps. As we entered the last unvisited classroom, a goofy-looking kid in the first row pulled a book up in front of his face and held it there shaking.

"Dad," I said hopefully, "I think this kid might be one of them." When my father asked him to come up front, he blurted out, "I didn't take that boy's three dollars." As cops will tell you, crime rarely attracts the best and brightest. The kid quickly ratted out his buddies. Better still, the word somehow spread that I fought the kids off valiantly when they attacked me. I did nothing to discourage those rumors. For a moment or two, I was something of a hero in the neighborhood, a half-pint Tony Galento.

IN JUNE OF 1957, thirteen-year-old Joe Frazier decided that he'd had enough of school. "The fact is I didn't learn quick, and I didn't learn easy," recalls Frazier. So he quit and went to work full time on a series of backbreaking jobs in and around Beaufort, South Carolina, jobs that helped make him the hard man he eventually became.

Compared to Beaufort, Ali's Louisville was an Eleanor Roosevelt garden party. "Let's just say," remembers Frazier of Beaufort, "that its attitudes had me wanting to leave there from the time I was a boy." When his father finally got his family a TV, Frazier began to sense "a world beyond Beaufort of comforts and joys." This new TV America and the old South would soon conspire to propel Frazier northward.

Frazier was living life hard and fast for a kid his age and priding himself on his badness. One night he found himself squaring off in the streets of downtown Beaufort against a white kid several years his senior. What the kid didn't know was that Frazier had already decided that he was destined to be a world champion, "the next Joe Louis." He had been perfecting his lethal left hook on a homemade backyard heavy bag. Once hit, the white kid went down as if he had been shot.

"Son, if you can't get along with white folks," his loving mother had told him after the fight, "then leave home because I don't want anything to happen to you." One day, without fanfare, Frazier packed his bags, headed down to the Greyhound station, and bought a one-way ticket for New York on "the dog."

"It was 1959," Frazier recalls. "I was fifteen years old and on my own."

IN 1959, THE seventeen-year-old Ali traveled to Chicago with Joe Martin for a Golden Gloves tournament. It was there, Ali claims, that he first encountered the Nation of Islam. What Elijah Muhammad and his followers were saying about black pride caught his attention. When he returned to Louisville, he attempted to do a term paper on the Nation, but the teacher dissuaded him. From the perspective of both blacks and whites, Ali admits, "The Nation of Islam was a pretty scary bunch."

IN THE SPRING of 1959, Floyd Patterson was the heavyweight champion of the world. At my house, we all liked the modest, self-effacing Patterson. Not only had he had won an Olympic gold medal, but he had also converted to Catholicism. Both played well on Myrtle Avenue. Patterson was set to square off against the Swede, Ingemar Johansson. One day, over at my friend Roger's house, we talked about the fight with Roger's father. The father shocked me when he told us he was rooting for Johansson.

"Why?" I asked naïvely.

"He's white," said the father.

"But Patterson's an American," I shot back.

Roger's father and I looked at each other as if we had come from different planets, his a Protestant and not particularly patriotic one. On

June 26, Johansson knocked out Patterson in the third round. I avoided Roger's house in the aftermath. I did not want to hear the old man gloat.

Some months later, Roger accompanied me as I walked my afternoon paper route. As we descended into the vestibule of a large apartment building, three older black kids grabbed us, and one stuck a gun into my back. It was likely an air rifle, but I was not in a position to question the owner about make and model.

"How much money you got?" said the one kid.

"A nickel," I answered truthfully. They roughed us up some for the hell of it but allowed me keep the nickel. I chose not to tell my father about the incident. Roger told his. Within a year, his family had beat it out of Newark and settled in a distant suburb, the closest one they could afford some fifty miles away. Roger was the first of my friends to go. Within five or six years, almost all of my friends would be gone.

IN THAT SAME spring of 1959, ten thousand miles away, the Vietnamese Communists of the North made a secret decision to try to spread the war in the South and to support it by sending troops and arms. They did this despite the great cost to the people of North Vietnam and the great tragedy to the people of the South. Noam Chomsky and others in the antiwar movement would insist, even after the truth was known, that the North began sending aid in 1964 only in response to the American buildup. They were wrong. The fix was in early on.

LOST GOLD

So what I remember most about the Summer of 1960 is not the
hero welcome, the celebrations, the Police Chief, the Mayor, the
Governor, or even the ten Louisville millionaires, but that night
when I stood on the Jefferson County Bridge and threw my
Olympic Gold Medal down to the bottom of the Ohio River.
Muhammad Ali, The Greatest, 1975

Before learning he wasn't supposed to feel this way, Ali considered the
events of September 1960 the most exhilarating of his young life.

How could he not have? He was eighteen years old at the time. After
overcoming his dread of flying, with much persuasion and hand-holding,
Ali headed off to Rome to represent the United States in the Summer
Olympics as a light heavyweight. He charmed his fellow Olympians with
his brash innocence. And he won the gold.

"I stood there so proudly for my country," an older and wiser Ali
remembers in his 2004 memoir, *The Soul of a Butterfly*. "I felt like I had
whupped the whole world for America."

After his Olympic victory, a Russian journalist tried to provoke a propaganda coup on the subject of racial injustice. Ali refused the bait. "Tell your readers we got qualified people working on that problem," he said, "and I'm not worried about the outcome."

Although he would disown this sentiment in years to come, Ali had answered the question in pitch perfect, mid-continent, Rotarian patois, and he did so truthfully. "Qualified people" were on the verge of resolving "the problem," at least to the degree that such a problem was capable of being resolved.

"To me," added Ali, "the USA is the best country in the world, including yours." In 1960, we all agreed. Ali made us see and celebrate our common bonds. Alone in his time, he had the potential to obliterate race and its obligations much the way Michael Jordan would do a generation later when the task was easier and the stakes much lower.

When Ali returned to Louisville in mid-September, he shared his first major poem with the happy throngs who greeted him at the airport. It was entitled, "How Cassius Took Rome."

> To make America the greatest is my goal
> So I beat the Russians, and I beat the Pole,
> And for the USA won the medal of Gold.
> Italians said, "You're Greater than the Cassius of Old."
> We like your name, we like your game,
> So make Rome your home if you will.
> I said I appreciate your kind hospitality.
> But the USA is my country still,
> 'Cause they're waiting to welcome me in Louisville.

I was twelve years old at the time, and this was the Ali who totally charmed me—cocky, proud, funny, and so resplendently, flamboyantly American.

Ali charmed Louisville too. Its citizens turned out to greet him, black and white both. They lined the streets of the city all the way downtown. The mayor told Ali that his gold medal was the key to the city. When Ali returned to his house, he discovered that Cassius Sr. had painted the front steps of the house red, white, and blue. There, Cassius Sr. regaled the crowd that followed Ali with the singing of "The Star Spangled Banner." As suspicious as he was of the white man, Ali's father had not abandoned his faith in America. Other than the Nation of Islam and a few old Bolsheviks, no one really had.

Not surprisingly, Ali received his share of management offers, including ones from Archie Moore, Rocky Marciano, and Cus D'Amato. As Ali remembers it, the men he hoped would manage him rejected him. Joe Louis turned him down because he thought Ali more of a braggart than a fighter. Ali's idol, Sugar Ray Robinson, had too much going on. "I'm still a fighter myself," Robinson remembers telling the young Ali. "I couldn't possibly be fighting myself and managing you at the same time." Either because of that perceived slight, or more likely because of Robinson's unyielding Christianity, Ali and his Muslim censors would all but edit Sugar Ray out of the story of Ali's life.

Ali carries the grudge into his largely benign 2004 memoir. In this retelling, Ali tries to meet Robinson in New York before heading off to Italy. He waits outside of his Harlem club until Robinson arrives. "He never really looked at me," Ali recalls. He just gave the eighteen-year-old a quick pat on the shoulder and said, "Later, boy, I'm busy right now."

In his own autobiography, *Sugar Ray,* written in 1970, Robinson casually tells of their first meeting outside the Harlem club. In this much more believable account, Robinson and Ali talk amiably for several minutes, and it is here that Robinson explains why he can't manage the young Ali. There was no insult given or taken, the proof of which, as shall be seen, is that Ali continued to turn to Robinson at critical moments in his life.

"IT SEEMED LIKE the only people who showed any interest in me," Ali recalls in *The Soul of a Butterfly,* "were white southerners." As Ali tells it, the first such southerners to express an interest in his management were his trainer Joe Martin and his backer, Kentucky aluminum magnate William Reynolds. This seems true enough. What defies all right reason is the alleged crudeness of their approach. In the 1975 retelling, Martin shoves a $75-a-week contract in front of Cassius Sr. and insists that he sign it immediately before talking to a lawyer. "The slave trade is over," Cassius Sr. thunders as he rejects the contract.

Martin then secures Ali an interim job at Reynolds's estate. Here, Reynolds's employees vie with each other to hurl racial insults at Ali and then make him eat on the front porch with the dogs. This hyperbolic account serves an essential function in the Ali myth. It is through this and other post-Rome revelations—"the hidden turning point" Ali calls it—that Cassius Clay begins to fashion his own origins story, the birth of Muhammad Ali. In the Nation of Islam tradition, this birth has to be painful, as first real exposure to the white devil always is.

What Ali and his handlers could not deny, however, was the timely intervention of William Faversham. A millionaire sportsman, Faversham recruited ten of his like-minded buddies and formed what has come to be known as the "Louisville Sponsoring Group." This hometown booster group offered Ali the best starting contract yet offered a fighter, one that Ali's authorized biographer, Thomas Hauser, admits was "fair and generous for its time."

The syndicate would take half of Ali's earnings for the first four years and 40 percent for the next two, but would assume all training, travel, and promotional costs. The six-year deal included a monthly stipend of $333 against earnings, an entirely thoughtful pension fund, and a $10,000 signing bonus, worth about $65,000 in today's dollars.

True to form, Ali would do his best to denigrate the motives of his sponsors. In his autobiography, for instance, he imagines his sponsors sitting ringside and waving at him "as though saying, there's our horse," one who had come to do battle with the "other white manager's horse." Still, there was no denying the exceptional terms of his contract.

THE MIDDLE CLASS home, the loving parents, the Olympic gold, the glorious hometown reception, the generous white sponsors, and the inevitable pink Cadillac do not make for a compelling grievance narrative. So for his 1975 autobiography and the movie that it spun off, *The Greatest,* Ali and his handlers had to concoct an event powerful enough to undo it all. For symbolic reasons, they focused on the Olympic gold.

The book offers the most extravagant account. In this version, Ali and his friend Ronnie stop at a diner to duck an impending rainstorm. Outside waits a gang of motorcycle outlaws, resplendent in Nazi regalia and Confederate flags. Inside, the manager tells Ali that gold medal or no gold medal, "We don't serve no niggers."

Ali rises to the occasion. "This is supposed to be the land of the free and the home of the brave," he tells the patron and his sheepish clientele. "You're disgracing it with your actions." Under Ronnie's prodding, Ali reviews the list of his sponsors, thinking of which one to call to intervene, but each, he realizes, is somehow tainted by his Confederate past.

For page after preposterous page, Ali describes in heart-pounding detail how the motorcycle gang chases him and Ronnie to a climactic showdown on the Jefferson County Bridge. Here, two of the gangbangers, "Frog" and "Kentucky Slim," pull out their chains and attack the innocent duo. After a violent, bloody encounter, the good guys prevail, and the evildoers slink away, begging for mercy.

The Olympic gold medal had purchased Ali no refuge from America's racist heritage. It could not even secure him a meal at a local diner. "Suddenly I knew what I wanted to do with this cheap piece of metal and raggedy ribbon," says Ali. He proceeds to the highest point of the bridge, and presumably the deepest point of the river, and throws it in. The *New York Times,* by the way, described the book as "honest" and "very convincing." The *Detroit Free Press* called it "the greatest, most honest contribution to sports literature perhaps ever."

The motorcycle chase proved too much even for Ring Lardner Jr., the unrepentant Stalinist who wrote the screenplay for the movie, *The*

Greatest. The defining moment in this major studio production comes instead when the young Ali innocently enters a restaurant where one of his millionaire sponsors is eating. Ali suggests he bring his black friend in as well, but the sponsor responds, "Don't make waves." The suddenly disillusioned Ali then proceeds to the bridge and throws the medal in. "It's phony, gold plated, and ain't worth a damn," he says of the medal, but as the movie audience is led to understand, he is really speaking about the American dream.

At best, only one of these two accounts is true. Almost assuredly, neither is. Ali was still wearing his Olympic trunks with "U.S.A." on the side when he started fighting professionally several weeks after the alleged incident. When Jack Olsen wrote his book in 1967, three years after Ali formally joined the Nation of Islam, the gold medal legend had yet to crystallize. "It was retired later," Olsen writes casually of the medal, "some of its silver underwear exposed where months of constant wear had rubbed off the gold." Hauser's comprehensive 1991 biography makes no mention of any incident involving the gold medal. Ali's sidekick Bundini Brown would tell *Sports Illustrated* writer Mark Kram, "Honkies sure bought into that one." Ali's best friend Howard Bingham admits that the story was "concocted."

The breakdown in accountability begins at the top. Random House editor-in-chief James Silberman tells Hauser that he often had to rely on the uncorroborated testimony of Ali or Herbert Muhammad, and so parts of the book may or may not be true. He consoles himself, however, with the nonsense that "if you check Winston Churchill's version of history, you'd find it somewhat at odds with other versions by historians." Historian Thomas Hietala meanwhile flirts with parody in his indulgence of the book's obvious fraud. "While inaccurate in detail," he writes of Ali's rumble with the motorcycle gang, "the story was metaphorically true."

When sportswriter Kram asked Ali about the medal years later, Ali just shrugged and said, "Who remembers?" In his revealing book, *Redemption Song: Muhammad Ali and the Spirit of the Sixties,* Mike

Marqusee surely remembers. "It was because of the gap between Olympic ideals and American realities," Marqusee writes on the book's second page, "that . . . Cassius Clay had flung his gold medal into the Ohio River." The Anglo-American Marqusee is a serious writer. Much of the reporting he does in the book is sober, solid, and sometimes highly critical of both Ali and the Nation of Islam.

Although the Nation of Islam is by almost any definition a rightwing organization, its angry deconstruction of the American ideal played into leftist and even Soviet hands. Ali, in fact, would become well-known throughout the Eastern bloc. The Soviet journal *Pravda* reported extensively on what it called "the campaign of persecution against Muhammad Ali by racists who wanted to curtail forever the career of the Black Hope."

Such propaganda was not something new. The Comintern, the international Soviet propaganda arm, had been quietly slipping toxins into the melting pot since the Sacco and Vanzetti trial fifty years prior. Although largely free of Soviet influence, the New Left was not above a little racial mischief of its own.

The Greatest, released in 1977, represented an unlikely fusion of interests. Hollywood Ten veteran Lardner adapted a book largely written by leftist author Toni Morrison on a film project overseen by the Nation of Islam. "Although most of the work is innocuous," notes one leftist Web site of Lardner's contribution, "the screenplay still has the courage to include Malcolm X's line, 'A white man is a blue-eyed devil,' and Ali's protest against the Vietnam war: 'No Vietcong ever called me nigger.'"

NOT ALL RACIAL coming-of-age stories paint so bleak a picture. Historically, in fact, they have tended to do just the opposite. Boxing great Archie Moore's story is typical and instructive. As Moore tells the story in his 1971 memoir, the aptly titled *Any Boy Can*, a serious car accident leaves him and his black manager desperate and in danger of dying alongside an Oklahoma road. A car pulls up. Two white interns, who "didn't care that [Moore] was a black man," get out and tend to the bleeding boxer. They insist he go with them to the hospital, and, in so doing, save his life.

"I felt that God had sent these people to save me," writes Moore. The incident proves to him that "there were good people and bad people among all races." As a tank town boxer in the 1930s, Moore had endured more and various racial slights than Ali and his Muslim handlers could even imagine. This roadside rescue proved to be an important lesson for Moore and the beginning of wisdom. The grievance narrative, by contrast, instructs its heroes to ignore good deeds and to revel in bad ones, even invent them if necessary.

Many of Ali's contemporaries wrote or cowrote autobiographies, among them Joe Louis, Sugar Ray Robinson, Floyd Patterson, Joe Frazier, Ken Norton, George Foreman, and Larry Holmes. Each of these is a tribute to the American dream. Each author describes the virtues necessary to succeed in America and the opportunity available to those who practice such virtue. Only Ali writes a grievance narrative.

In his 1975 autobiography, Ali distinguishes his story from Robinson's—and by extension all the other black boxers of his era—by alluding to his superior racial awareness. "[Robinson] stayed out what I call the real fighting ring, the one where freedom for black people in America takes place." Ali ruminates that had Robinson become his manager, he, too, would have stayed out of that ring. "I'm glad he had no time."

SONNY LISTON IS the one heavyweight champ who never wrote an autobiography. Almost no one would have bought it, and he would not have been able to read it himself. In that same September of 1960, the unlovable Liston beat California tough guy Eddie Machen to emerge as the number-one heavyweight contender of the world. The road to the top had been a long and lonely one, and it took Liston thirty-two ugly years to get there.

Liston had fled his Arkansas home at fifteen. "The only thing my old man ever gave me was a beating," he remembered. After a short stay with half-brother E. B. Ward who lived nearby—"He was all to hisself," recalls Ward—Liston headed for St. Louis to find his mother. What he mostly found was trouble. In late 1949, he first entered the logbook of official-dom as "unknown negro #1." He and two of his buddies had mugged an innocent St. Louis pedestrian.

"He was always a rough boy," his mother once told a reporter. "He liked the rough side of life." When caught after a string of such robberies, Liston listed his age as twenty-two. If accurate, that would have made him thirty-six at the time of the first Ali fight.

In June 1950, Liston headed off to the state penitentiary in Jefferson City, the one place in the world where he would feel at home. "I didn't mind prison," he would recall. The prison's Catholic chaplain was also its director of athletics, and he encouraged Liston to channel his natural aggression into the sport of boxing. With his astonishing 15" fists (meas-ure your own) and 84" reach, and a body that had known little but hard labor since age eight, Sonny Liston was one very frightening natural. "After four weeks of fighting," Father Edward Schlattmann tells Nick Tosches, the tough-minded author of *The Devil and Sonny Liston*, "nobody in the penitentiary would get in the ring with Sonny."

The sponsoring group that greeted Liston upon his release from Jefferson City had a lot more history in the fight game than Ali's and a good deal less heart. Its members had old-line boxing names like John J. Vitale, Blinky Palermo, and Frankie Carbo. They groomed Liston not just to box but to break legs on demand. The cops arrested him fourteen times between 1953 and 1958. Even when not on the job, Liston free-lanced in miscellaneous bad behavior. A 1956 assault on a cop netted Liston nine months in the City Workhouse.

"In those days bad niggers were not the darling middle-class iconic commodities and consumers of a white-ruled conglomerate culture," says Tosches. "In those days, bad niggers were bad news." In 1960, Liston had almost no one in his corner save for the mobsters that owned him.

IN SEPTEMBER 1960, Floyd Patterson was once again the heavyweight champion of the world. In June of that year, before thirty-two thousand fans at New York's Polo Grounds, a hard left hook from Patterson put Ingemar Johansson on the canvas for the first time in his career. Another left hook put him out. The kind-hearted Patterson was the first heavyweight ever to regain the championship. He would not be the last.

IN OCTOBER 1960, six weeks after returning from Rome, Ali fought a West Virginia cop named Tunney Hunsaker. It was his first professional fight. Six thousand excited partisans turned out at Louisville's Freedom Hall. Never in the course of his long career would Liston ever experience the kind of affection or enthusiasm Ali experienced on that very first night in Louisville.

A week after Ali's triumph, John Kennedy edged out Richard Nixon on points. My family and friends cheered JFK on the way they had Billy Conn and Jim Braddock before him. He was our tribal hero. What is more, he had pulled the whole neighborhood together, the Irish and Italians Catholics and the black Protestants.

Despite some troubling signs, we had no reason to believe that the neighborhood would not always stay together. Progress was in the air that gilded autumn of 1960. Racial barriers were falling. The income gap between blacks and whites was narrowing. Crime rates were still low and seemed more or less stable. And Patterson was champ once more.

INVENTED LIVES

In November 1960, right after Ali's first professional fight, his Louisville sponsors sent him to California to train with Archie Moore. Moore called his remote training camp the "Salt Mine," and the name fit. When Ali arrived, he discovered that training also included doing his own fair share of the chores.

"I wanted [Ali] to respect me as a man and as an instructor and fall in line with the learning process," Moore tells Hauser. "And that seemed to amuse and sometimes anger him." Unlike most of his boxing peers, Ali had never held a real job and never would. He chafed under the discipline. When given the opportunity to spar with Moore, thirty years his senior, Ali took out his resentment in the ring.

"I was jabbing him and moving, circling, whipping in uppercuts, stunning him with right crosses," recalls a contrite Ali years later. He went home for Christmas in 1960 and never came back. "To tell you the truth the boy needed a good spanking," Moore observes, "but I wasn't sure who could give it to him." Had Ali stayed with Moore, the Nation of Islam never would have found him.

When the Moore deal fell through, Bill Faversham and some of his

Louisville colleagues went to Miami to interview the veteran trainer Angelo Dundee. They were impressed. Eager to start training at Dundee's legendary 5th Street Gym, Ali left for Miami almost as soon as he got back to Louisville. He was still just eighteen years old. Unlike Moore, the laissez-faire Dundee gave Ali all the freedom he wanted both in the ring and out. He had little choice. At the time, he was managing or training at least a dozen fighters, most of them world-class. "He's Italian and he passes for White, but he's got a lot of nigger in him," said a young Ali of Dundee. "I get along with him. He never bosses me, tells me when to run, how much to box. I do what I want to do."

In the gym, Ali was a wonder. He loved to train and loved to box and needed very little guidance. Outside the gym, he was a total naïf and needed all the guidance he could get. Neither Dundee nor the Louisville sponsors could provide it. "The Louisville people should never have sent him to Miami," Odessa Clay lamented. "They let the Muslims steal my boy." "No, it was that idiot Rudy who did it," Cassius Sr. countered.

A year younger than Ali, Rudy/Rahaman lived his life fully and contentedly in his brother's shadow. Jack Olsen describes Rahaman as "a study in sibling obedience." The relationship, however, was more complex than it seems. Rahaman's contempt for whites ran much deeper than Ali's and likely infected Ali. "I hate whites," Rahaman would tell writer and former light-heavyweight champ, Jose Torres. "They are no good. I don't even smile at them. I hate them. I hate them."

Dr. Pacheco backs up the Senior Clay on the issue of Ali's drift to the Nation of Islam. As Pacheco recalls, Rudy used to spend his ample free time at Red's Barber Shop in Miami's Overtown section, long a hub of Muslim activity. There he fell under the spell of a man known as Cap'n Sam, a former numbers runner turned Muslim recruiter. Sam used Rudy to get to Ali. "[Sam] invited me to a meeting," Ali confirms in his Hauser interview, "and, after that, my life changed."

The story of this first introduction to the Nation of Islam would be told so many times in so many different ways that even the participants may not remember the exact sequence, especially since Ali flirted with the Nation while still in high school. In the most dramatic and improbable version, the one presented in the movie, *The Greatest*, a Muslim selling newspapers rescues an immature Ali from a rendezvous with a white prostitute and escorts him into a storefront mosque where Malcolm X is preaching.

Sensing the potential of a recruit with Clay's visibility, Elijah Muhammad sent his minister for the Deep South, Jeremiah Shabazz, to continue Ali's education. "We taught him first that God is a black man," Shabazz tells Hauser. "And as far as white people were concerned, we taught him that the white man is the devil." By this time, according to Shabazz, Ali had been sufficiently indoctrinated so he "didn't have problems with our claim that the white man was evil."

Muhammad Ali first met Malcolm X in Detroit in 1962. Ali and his brother had driven up from Miami—Ali still did not like to fly—to hear Elijah Muhammad speak. In Detroit, however, he found himself captivated by the charismatic Malcolm, and Malcolm by him. "Every Muslim was impressed by the bearing and the obvious genuineness of the handsome pair of prize-winning brothers," recalled Malcolm.

For Malcolm, the road to Detroit was a circuitous one, the road to Mecca more circuitous still. Malcolm traces the road's origins to 1931, when Malcolm Little was six. One night, his father, the Reverend Earl Little, stormed out of their Lansing, Michigan home after an argument with his mother. Malcolm later attributed the family tension to death threats from a reactionary Michigan group known as the Black Legion. The Reverend Little, a Baptist minister, had allegedly stirred the anger of Michigan's least tolerant whites by preaching the back-to-Africa message of Marcus Garvey and his United Negro Improvement Association (UNIA).

Reverend Little did not come home that evening. The police found his body on the streetcar tracks, his head crushed, his torso nearly severed. The insurance company ruled it a suicide. This was not a reality Malcolm could handle. In his autobiography, *The Autobiography of Malcolm X,* he tells coauthor Alex Haley, "Negroes in Lansing have always said that [my father] was attacked, and then laid across some tracks for a streetcar to run over him." Later in that same book, his speculation has calcified into hard fact. To embarrass a State Department official from Michigan while both were in Africa, Malcolm publicly claims, "My own father was murdered by whites in the state of Michigan."

In Spike Lee's movie, *Malcolm X,* the imagery becomes harder and more vivid still. The viewer sees some shadowy and reckless Black Legionnaires throwing the Reverend Little's battered body in front on an oncoming streetcar and yelling, "That'll teach you, nigger."

In an equally inflammatory opening scene in both the book and movie, set six years before Reverend Little's death, Ku Klux Klan night riders attack the Little's Omaha home. They do so again because of the Reverend's work on behalf of Marcus Garvey. Malcolm's mother would cite the attack as the reason for the family's move to Michigan.

As much as I envy Malcolm his grievance, I don't believe it. At times, I have felt the urge to tell my own family history along more heroic and ideologically useful lines, as Malcolm has, but I have resisted for any number of good reasons. I understand the urge, however, and sympathize with those who have yielded.

In the summer of 1960, my father drove us all in his 1950 Buick to visit Nana and Gramps, who had lived in St. Petersburg since before I was born. The trip proved an eye opener in many ways. I had never really seen the South before or experienced it. This was not Newark. Here, even as a twelve-year-old, I could sense the power that accrued to being white, the power to do evil or to do good or to do nothing at all.

On the way down, we pulled into a rest stop in Georgia and saw a black couple with a little girl my age, all dressed in their Sunday best. It was Monday. Our New Jersey license plates encouraged the father of that family to approach the father of ours. He explained that they had been stranded overnight for want of jumper cables. My always-handy father happily obliged. "This is wrong," my father muttered as we drove away, disturbed that no one else had helped.

As much as I learned about the South, I learned even more about my own family. After we had been in Florida for a few days, I asked my father a question he had likely been expecting, "How come you call your father 'Bernie?'" It was only then that I learned the heretofore untold story of my father's childhood.

When he was a boy, his father, William Jennings Bryan Cashill, had gone to work one day and did not return. At first, no one was too alarmed. In early Irish-America, alcoholics were known to disappear for a few days here and there. But this time, my grandfather never came back. He left behind a crippled wife and an eight-year-old son, my father, who took his departure hard. Not a single word was ever heard from him again. Some years later, the saintly Bernie, a retired Norwegian merchant seaman, carried Nana off to Florida and became our "Gramps."

The story floored me. I had no idea. For years thereafter, I would imagine great adventures for my missing grandfather and glorious homecomings. Kids need to fill the void. But as I would soon learn, there is a romance to a missing grandfather that there is not with a missing father.

During that same visit, I came across my father's high school yearbook. I was surprised to see him in uniform in the football team picture. When I asked why he never talked about playing on the team, he said that it was because he never actually did. He spent every Saturday doing chores for his crippled mom. "Big Bill" could practice but never play. His yearbook held another surprise. Under his class of 1936 picture—Newark Central, Junior Soprano's alma mater—it listed as his choice of college "Georgia Tech." In truth, my father had little more hope of going to Georgia Tech than Sonny Liston did.

From Florida on I sensed about my father an ineffable sadness that no one else seemed to. No doubt, hundreds of people read the following *Newark Evening News* headline two years later in a state of shock approaching outright disbelief. I was not one of them.

COP'S DEATH HELD SUICIDE
Newark Father of Four Found Shot in Head at His Home

The first time I read the article that follows this headline was in researching this book. I was aware of it back then, and of its general thrust, but I chose not to read it. Ignorance gives the survivors more freedom to construct their own death narratives, as Malcolm X almost surely did. The real cause of the Reverend Little's despair, like my father's own, likely sprang from the grinding reversals of everyday life.

In my father's case, an Italian challenger had beaten the Irish incumbent in a Newark mayor's race and sent many of the Irish cops to Siberia, my father among them. As a youth aid detective, my father could walk to work, wear a suit, and be home for dinner. Now, he was taking a bus in uniform downtown at midnight to do an idiot job. What galled my parents even more is that they had voted for the Italian.

At about the same time my father lost his detective job, Gramps died. Nana and her sister, Lil, were forced to move in with us. They were a bitter, fractious pair. My mother didn't like them even when they lived in Florida, let alone when they lived upstairs, in the process exiling my parents to a foldout couch in the living room. My brother and I appreciated the sisters for their porn stash, but that was not a point we could openly argue in their favor. Almost immediately after my father's death, my mother booted them. She was a survivor and one tough broad.

Malcolm's mother was neither. Two years after the death of his father, when Malcolm was eight, she was institutionalized for mental illness, and the family was scattered. With his world in disarray, Malcolm could use all the mythic reinforcement he could find. In the Nation of Islam, he found it—or at least he thought he had.

Unlike Christianity or even Islam, the Nation allowed for no afterlife. Malcolm had only anger to console him. It is likely that Elijah Muhammad and his lieutenants helped Malcolm craft the mythic dimensions of his life much as they would later do with Ali. In addition to his own involvement with Marcus Garvey and UNIA, there is one story, in particular, that might have inspired the Messenger. It took place in Detroit in 1936, his base city. Quite by chance, the victim's family name was the same as his, Poole. It involved the aforementioned Black Legion, a very real and scary crew of poor whites hostile to all "aliens, Negroes, Jews and cults and creeds believing in racial equality or owing allegiance to any foreign potentates."

On a May night in 1936, this black-hooded band kidnapped Charles Poole, an organizer for the Works Progress Administration, drove him to a remote corner of southwest Detroit, and gunned him down along the side of the road. His killers had accused him of beating his wife.

There may have been pockets of America where groups like the Black Legion operated with impunity in the 1930s. Michigan was not one of them. Authorities promptly arrested twelve suspects, convicted eleven of them for first degree murder, and sent them all off to prison for life. There is, however, an interesting twist to this case. Poole was white. If this fact robs the death saga of the Reverend Little of its uniquely racial character, it might comfort those who read race into every act of American justice.

Such a reading today is all but required. "At the age of six," the Web site Marxist.org says of Malcolm X, "his father was assassinated by the Ku Klux Klan." From the Marxist perspective, there is not a whiff of doubt about the way he died. And since the Ku Klux Klan is more symbolically rich than the Black Legion, all credit is given to the Klan.

Unfortunately, the Marxist take on Malcolm's history—and racial history in general—has fused with that of black nationalism to become the mainstream of American intellectual thought. "He was a troubled spirit who was forced to cope with the trauma of the murder of his father for being a 'uppity nigger,'" claims the *Black Collegian* as a way of explaining Malcolm's undeniable rage. *The Encyclopedia Britannica* is no more prudent: "Malcolm saw his house burned down at the hands of the white supremacist Ku Klux Klan. Two years later his father was murdered."

None of this holds water. In the *Autobiography*, Malcolm learns of the

Ku Klux Klan attack on the Little's Omaha home only from his mother, who was conveniently alone with her children when it was supposed to have happened. Soon to be institutionalized, she was not the most reliable of sources. Nor does his father's decision to flee Omaha make sense to the adult Malcolm. "I am not sure why he made this decision [to move]," writes Malcolm of his father, "for he was not a frightened Negro, as most were, and many still are today."

The Marcus Garvey angle does not bear scrutiny either. In the days leading up to his death in 1931, the Reverend Little would not have been militating on behalf of Garvey if for no other reason than Garvey's UNIA was long since defunct. Garvey had been deported to Jamaica three years before Little's death and imprisoned on a mail fraud charge three years before that. Besides, most white hate groups had wished Garvey's back-to-Africa movement all the success in the world. "Like Elijah Muhammad in 1961," Marqusee notes, "[Garvey] even made overtures to white supremacists. Including the Klan."

IF THERE WAS ever a black man that even the Nation of Islam considered evil, it would have to have been Sonny Liston. Liston biographer Nick Tosches once asked veteran black boxing executive Truman Gibson if Liston had a sense of right and wrong. Gibson hesitated and then answered thoughtfully, "None." The NAACP openly pulled for Floyd Patterson to beat Liston, claiming, "He represents us better than Liston ever could or would." Even JFK got in the act, telling Patterson, "Make sure you keep that championship."

About the only person in America who had a kind word for Liston was the heavyweight champion himself, Floyd Patterson. Shortly before their first ring encounter, in September 1962, Patterson asked America to "give [Liston] a chance to bring out the good that is in him." Liston did not reciprocate. "I'd like to run over him in a car," he said of Patterson. On September 25, he just about did. It took Liston all of two minutes and six seconds to flatten the overawed Patterson. Depressed like nearly all of his fellow citizens, black and white, author James Baldwin headed off to a neighborhood bar "to mourn the very death of boxing."

As 1963 BEGAN, America was prepared to celebrate the young miracle worker who could redeem the sport and bring the world of boxing back to life. That year would also see the high-water mark of American liberalism, Martin Luther King's eloquent "I Have A Dream" speech, delivered at the August March on Washington. In that historic event, Ali played no role, nor did his new friends in the Nation of Islam. Not one to mince words, Malcolm X dismissed the historic event as the "Farce on Washington."

SAVE US, CASSIUS CLAY

I remember the night of February 25, 1964, as clearly as I remember the afternoon of November 22, three months earlier.

Raymond, Kenny, and I sat at the kitchen table in my house staring at the radio in front of us. I had retrieved this boxy, off-white, knobless relic from my attic bedroom. Children of the TV generation, we had no practice in this sort of thing—listening to the radio collectively. It was all very awkward.

And tense. As we were learning, radio exercises the mind and intensifies fear in ways that TV never could. I finally understood why my mother panicked when Orson Welles's Martians marched across New Jersey and on to Newark. Now, twenty-five years later, I imagined a terror just as raw in the form of Sonny Liston, and I anguished even through the introductions.

Our hero, Cassius Clay as he was then known, had just climbed into the ring to face Liston, the world heavyweight champ, a seemingly invincible force of pure primal menace. Ali reached my friends and me in ways that only adolescents can be—or need to be—reached. This was no small accomplishment. Unlike some of our more privileged peers, we could claim no special sensitivity in matters racial. In the dwindling pockets of white Newark, such sensitivities did not exist.

Yet for all that, we rooted passionately for Ali. We urged on a black man against all comers, black or white. How could we do otherwise? The man emerged as the coolest of our cold warriors, a transcendent young American seemingly unburdened by history. For all his seeming sangfroid, I worried about Ali deeply. I saw in him then, and still do, some ineradicable innocence, some ineffable softness, the "essential sweetness" perhaps that he had absorbed from his beloved mother, Odessa.

But there was also something else, something unspoken even among my friends. For all his later protestations of blackness, Ali did not seem *black*. In some small part, his color, or lack of it, shaped our perception, but it was much more than that. He showed none of the defensiveness that I sensed among the blacks in my neighborhood and that they surely sensed among us. As in the ring, if Ali had defenses, they were not obvious or orthodox.

Admittedly, I was drawing these conclusions from a distance. But many of those who have known Ali up close have registered a similar impression. His high school classmates talk of him as being a "nerd." Angelo Dundee tells of an unabashed fifteen-year-old who invited himself up to his Louisville hotel room and spent four hours charming him. At nineteen, in Miami, Ali disarmed Dundee's wife and children with his openness and eagerness.

Even at the height of his anti-white posturing in 1969, Ali seems so at ease with Cus D'Amato in their spontaneous scenes for the documentary *AKA Cassius Clay* that D'Amato could be a best friend or favored uncle. This was not unusual. Future heavyweight champ and frequent sparring partner Larry Holmes observes that for all his anti-white talk, Ali always seemed "more friendly with white people than blacks."

In his insightful book, *The Fight*, Norman Mailer describes Ali as "not wholly convincing as a black." One of only a few people in the dressing room with Ali before the legendary "Rumble in the Jungle," Mailer had a good view. "Something in his personality was cheerfully even exuber-antly white," he writes. Joe Frazier says much the same but with a nega-tive twist. "Muhammad just wasn't right as a black man," he tells Stephen Brunt in *Facing Ali.* "He just wasn't right." The fact that Ali would not and, admittedly could not, dance surely confirmed Frazier's suspicions.

Regardless of race, Ali had much less is common with Joe Frazier than he did with the most popular white man of his generation, Elvis Presley. Each in his artless crossover appeal was an American original, a self-created amalgam of black and white Southern culture, a culture so deeply shared between races and so mutually shaped that its origins defy easy analysis.

Both Elvis and Ali were inherently sweet, Southern momma's boys, each with something of a chip on his shoulder—Ali because of race, Elvis because of class. Both achieved too much fame too soon and sought pro-tection in their respective entourages. Not surprisingly, they were fans of each other. When a Chicago reporter asked Ali what he would like to do after the 1960 Olympics, he answered, "I'd like to be a singer like Elvis Presley." Years later he would tell Hauser, "All my life, I admired Elvis Presley." And Elvis admired Ali. Before Ali had regained the champi-onship, in fact, Elvis had him fitted for a $3,000 robe embroidered with "People's Champion," which Ali wore proudly.

Importantly, they were both insecure, painfully innocent, and in need of a powerful mentor. The mentors they found were self-created, self-named hucksters. As it happened, each mentor sought to pull his protégé back within his respective race, to strip him of his hybrid vigor, Elijah Muhammad more aggressively than "Colonel" Tom Parker. Arguably, it is for this reason that Ali rejected the draft and Elvis accepted it in grand style.

At the time, in Newark, we were crawling back into our own racial shells as well. Black and white, we girded ourselves daily for confronta-tion, and there was a world of it to be had. The story is often told of a young black man in the 1930s about to die in the gas chamber, who cries out, "Save me, Joe Louis. Save me." In 1964, in a less dramatic way, we were asking Cassius Clay to save us.

By 1964, our neighborhood had "turned." For several years, new families had been moving in, but these were a new kind of family, families without fathers. If the media failed to distinguish, we did. The tipping point had come on my block when our neighbors two doors down moved out, and three single mothers replaced them with sixteen kids in tow. Soon after, a swarm of astonishingly noisy fatherless children descended upon the Farley's old house right across the street, an absurdly perfect mirror image. To this day, I have nightmares in which I move my own family to such a block and kick off the covers wondering what possessed me to do so.

Not all of the new, impaired families on our block were black. My mother, in fact, worried more about the white ones, especially the family down the street with the two spectacularly slutty daughters just the age of my brother and me. My mother, however, did not know the gyms and playgrounds as I did. On the basketball courts, class had no meaning. Here, all differences devolved down to race, and even the well meaning could sense its uneasy tectonics. The plates were pulling apart, and the divide between black and white was growing. We no longer made friends across it.

"This ain't Mississippi, mother f***er," I was lectured after one rough rebound. Scanning the courts, I could see no more than three whites on the playground out of a hundred. "You telling me something I don't know," I answered, the unwitting ambassador from a "white America" that did not know I existed. Somehow, though, Ali made us forget the playground. It may have all been an illusion, but there seemed to be something larger and more important about him, something almost transcendent, something that could erase the fault lines, chalked in but not yet etched in asphalt.

"Save us, Cassius Clay. Save us!"

I had been following his career faithfully ever since the Olympics. The first seventeen fights had presented no serious problems. For the most part, these boxers were the kind of "tomato cans" savvy mangers feed to their rising stars. The goal is to build their confidence and improve their skills. The best of the opponents, the senescent Archie Moore, Ali knocked out in four rounds just as he had predicted. Thanks to ABC, which had picked up the Gillette *Fight of the Week* from NBC in 1960, I got to watch several of these bouts on TV.

I saw the spring 1963 Doug Jones fight only in replay, and I am glad I missed the original. It was much too close. Sugar Ray Robinson sensed trouble even before the fight. As a morale boost, he sent Ali the often dramatic, always dependable Drew "Bundini" Brown. Brown had worked with Robinson during his glory years as something of a personal cheerleader. From that first day on, Bundini would keep Ali relaxed, happy, well-equipped with poetry, and at least somewhat disciplined.

Shortly after Bundini started, for instance, he asked Robinson to intervene with Ali, who was reluctant to do his roadwork. Robinson called, and Ali responded. He idolized the man until he was told not to. In the Ali myth, Bundini just kind of shows up at his hotel. Robinson has nothing to do with it. He has been edited out once again.

A smallish, tough boxer with a strong New York following, Doug Jones refused to go down when Ali predicted; in fact, he refused to go down at all. The judges gave the fight to Ali. The Madison Square Garden crowd— the first sellout for a non-title fight in more than a decade—did not exactly agree. "This was to be the first of many fights," concedes Pacheco, "where Clay's overwhelming reputation gave the judges a slightly biased view."

The Henry Cooper fight in London before fifty-five thousand frenzied fans was scarier still. A classic bleeder—insiders will tell you that whites cut more easily—Cooper was drowning in his own blood by the fourth round. At round's end, however, he launched his nasty left hook, caught Ali with the most perfect punch he would ever endure, and sent him flying through the ropes. Only the bell saved Ali. When it rang, his handlers led the dazed and wobbling boxer to his corner. What transpired in those next few minutes is the stuff of boxing legend.

Angelo Dundee knew he had a problem on his hands. If he sent Ali back out after just sixty seconds, Cooper would likely finish him off. Needing more time, the ever wily Dundee improvised. He aggravated a small tear in one of Ali's gloves, pointed the tear out to the referee, and demanded a new glove. Although a glove could not be found, and the fight continued, Dundee had gained essential moments for his wounded charge. "If we hadn't gotten the extra time," says Dundee, "I don't know what would have happened." One minute into round five, with Cooper now in need of a transfusion to continue, the ref stopped the fight.

THIS MUCH I could read about, and I did so breathlessly after every fight. I knew less about what was going on behind the scenes. This was a story that Ali's management was not eager to share with the world. It troubled many of them. "He was a ship adrift, rudderless, without a captain," says Pacheco of the young Ali, "but now, listening to the wisdom of the old man, Ali saw the way."

The "old man" was Elijah Muhammad. Pacheco had no use for the man or his "Kill Whitey" mission. As Pacheco observes, Muhammad embraced Ali only because he knew "what a valuable jewel had fallen into his lap." Before cashing in, however, Muhammad had a rather large circle to square.

According to Muhammad, professional sport was a "filthy temptation," as vile as pork. His book, *Message to the Blackman in America*, is filled with admonitions against "the white man's games of civilization," none more corrosive than prizefighting. Muhammad would be forced to resolve this issue, however, only if Ali became champion. After Ali's shaky performances in the Jones and Cooper fights, and with the invincible Sonny Liston looming, this did not seem likely. No one in the Nation gave Ali a rat's chance

No one, that is, save for Malcolm X. "One day this kid is going to be heavyweight champion of the world," he told fellow Muslim Osman Karriem, "and he's going to embrace the Nation of Islam. Do you understand what that could mean?" Untroubled by Muhammad's arbitrary disdain for sport, Malcolm took Ali under his wing. "Malcolm accepted Cassius and loved him like a younger brother," Malcolm's widow, Betty Shabazz, remembers. Ali loved Malcolm back.

The relationship between Malcolm and Elijah Muhammad, however, had gotten dicey. The problem first surfaced in late 1962. Malcolm heard through the grapevine that two of Muhammad's former secretaries, both in their twenties, had sued the sexagenarian for child support. According to the story, these women had borne the Messenger a total of four children out of wedlock.

Malcolm was nothing if not faithful. From the time he entered prison until the time he married Betty twelve years later, he did not touch a woman "because of Mr. Muhammad's influence upon me." He presumed the same principled restraint from his fellow Muslims, Muhammad especially. When he first heard the rumors of Muhammad's paternity suits, Malcolm dismissed them out of hand. Historically, the Nation of Islam had booted adulterers from its ranks. Malcolm refused to believe that Elijah Muhammad, the man who made the rules, would "betray the reverence bestowed upon him."

Still, Malcolm was no fool. As the rumors grew more insistent, he investigated on his own. The secretaries confirmed the tales. When confronted, Muhammad assured Malcolm that he was just "fulfilling the prophecies." He was the modern David, committing adulteries; the modern Noah, getting drunk; the modern Lot, committing incest. Malcolm, however, was the modern Thomas, and he was doubting.

As one of Ali's relatives smartly tells Jack Olsen, the Nation of Islam was surely "the most bendable religion in the world." Following Muhammad's example, Ali would raise the Nation's no-fault moral flexibility to an art. Malcolm was not nearly so flexible. When Muhammad sensed this, he froze Malcolm out. "Hating me," Malcolm said prophetically, "was going to become the cause for people of shattered faith to rally around."

In November 1963, Malcolm handed Muhammad a welcome excuse to isolate him further. After the assassination of John Kennedy on November 22, the Messenger instructed his ministers to keep their opinions about Kennedy to themselves. Malcolm tried to honor the request, but when questioned by the press just a few days later, his instincts got the better of him. He rather famously described Kennedy's undoing as a case of "the chickens coming home to roost." In other words, Kennedy deserved what he got for the CIA's real and imagined meddling in various assassination plots. Malcolm might have controlled the damage had he said no more, but he was never one to bite his tongue. "Being an old farm boy myself," he added, "chickens coming to roost never did make me sad, they've always made me glad."

Until this point, few white people had ever heard of Malcolm X, and most blacks were unimpressed. It troubled Malcolm that in a *New York Times* poll of this period only 6 percent of America's blacks identified him as the country's most influential civil rights advocate. The Kennedy remark, however, made him famous overnight, if a pariah could be called famous. With the Liston match just three months away, Malcolm's companionship did nothing for Ali's already flagging popularity.

Muhammad meanwhile quickly seized on what he called Malcolm's "blunder," silencing him for the next ninety days. Chastised, Malcolm asked Muhammad if he could watch over Ali who was training for the Liston fight in Miami. "You will not in any way be representing us," Muhammad told him, "because it's impossible for Cassius to win." The whole fight, Muhammad believed, would be an "embarrassment to the Nation of Islam."

Malcolm went anyhow—as a "private person." He went because he was fond of Ali, and he believed in him. "Cassius was simply a likeable, friendly, clean-cut, down-to-earth youngster," Malcolm recalled toward the end of his life. He would never call him "Ali." He did, however, encourage him to think of the fight as a modern Crusades, "the Cross and the Crescent fighting in a prize ring—for the first time." The night of February 25, 1964, found Malcolm in a front-row seat, the lucky number seven, cheering wholeheartedly for his protégé.

ALI TURNED THE weigh-in on the day of the fight into theater of the absurd. "Clay was acting like a maniac," said the Commission doctor in charge. The doctor told Ali that his theatrics were speeding up his pulse rate and stirring up his blood pressure, but Ali paid him no mind. Those present believed that Ali was simply scared to death. Ali insists the manic taunting was a psychological ploy. It was likely a little of both.

Whatever his motives, Ali tested unacceptably high on blood pressure. Pacheco and Dundee had to go to his house in Miami to run a second test later in the day. The house was jammed with members of the Fruit of Islam, the Nation's Praetorian Guard. As Pacheco remembers, they were listening to tapes from the Nation "exhorting them to kill the white devils." Says he, "I felt like a Jew at a Nuremberg rally." Pacheco overstates the threat level, but not by much. Ali, in any case, felt right at home. His blood pressure had descended into normal range, and the fight was on.

Sugar Ray Robinson also visited the house. Ali had been calling him every day, sometimes twice a day, for advice. Robinson suggested that Ali fight Liston much as he had fought Jake LaMotta—turn Liston's superior strength against him like a matador with a bull. When Robinson offered to send the fight film, Ali begged that he come with it.

"You must be here for the fight," Ali pleaded. "You must be with me." What Robinson found at the house was "Noise, man. Wall-to-wall noise." At the request of Ali's Louisville sponsors, Robinson stayed with Ali the rest of the day. In Ali's autobiography, Robinson merits one sentence. "Robinson has flown down to be by my side," observes Ali, "but he knows nothing of my plan and is embarrassed by the whole act."

Ali's dressing room before the fight unnerved Pacheco almost as much as Ali's house. Alerted by the Muslims that the white man would likely try to poison his water, Ali sealed his water bottle with tape, signed the tape, and assigned the hapless Rahaman to guard it. "Such was the nuttiness of that evening," says Pacheco.

Ali entered a Miami Beach Auditorium that was only about half full. The seeming lopsidedness of the bout kept many a would-be fan at home—the odds against Ali ranging as high as 7–1 before narrowing. The Muslim presence scared away many more. Even before Ali's Muslim affiliations became apparent, his boastfulness had alienated many of the veteran fight fans who remembered the humility of Louis and Marciano and had come to expect it.

Liston himself was a terrible draw and an unwelcome champion. In an article headlined "King of the Beasts," *Look* magazine described him as a "Negro untouchable, the angry dark-skinned man condemned by the white man to spend his life in the economic and social sewers of the country." This was a hard package to take to market. Ali had intensified the animal imagery by calling Liston "the big, ugly bear." In an inspired bit of promotional mischief, Ali had even set animal traps in front of Liston's Denver house to lure him into the fight.

No one will ever know what went through Liston's mind those next twenty-five minutes. The tight-lipped Liston left few clues, and these are contradictory. Films of the fight, however, will show that he came out guns-a-blazing that first round, looking for a kill. Pacheco had heard talk that he placed a serious bet on himself to knock Ali out in round one. Liston had bet on himself before. This is one rumor that makes sense. It made more sense than the strategy. Less than fully fit, and likely fourteen years older than the youth he had dismissed as a "nigger faggot," Liston all but wore himself out in round one.

Back in Newark, my friends and I were relieved that Ali had survived the first round and then the second. In the third and fourth rounds, we were almost giddy as Ali started dancing and jabbing and fighting his fight. He seemed clearly to be winning both rounds. As Ali returned to his corner, we heard only that he was rubbing his left eye. We did not know how close Ali came to sacrificing his career in the next sixty seconds.

"I can't see," Ali was screaming. His left eye was red and throbbing. Somehow, a caustic solution on a Liston cut found its way onto his gloves and from there onto Ali's forehead from which it had dripped into his eye. "I knew the white man would think of a way to trick us," Bundini was yelling.

"Cut them off," howled Ali, holding out his gloves. "I can't see. We're going home." Dundee refused. "No way," he snapped back. "Get in there and fight. If you can't see, keep away from him until your eyes clear. This is the big one. Nobody walks away from the heavyweight championship."

Had Dundee taken off Ali's gloves, the fight would have been over and possibly Ali's career as well. Instead, Dundee grabbed a sponge and tried to rinse out Ali's eyes. At this, the Muslims near Ali's corner started grumbling, accusing Dundee of putting the "stuff" into Ali's eyes. Angelo's brother Jimmy heard the menace in their voices and rushed up to tell Angelo, who then cleverly dripped the sponge water into his own eyes to show the Muslims how benign it was.

At the bell, Dundee pushed a furiously blinking and protesting Ali into the ring and thereby changed the course of boxing history. "Had he quit like a dog," Pacheco speculates, "not even Malcolm X would have taken him in." As to his future in boxing, Pacheco adds, "He would have been dead in the water."

Still half-blind but nimble as ever, Ali managed to evade the flailing Liston. Referee Barney Felix resisted the urge to stop the fight and award a TKO to Liston as Ali slowly regained his vision. By the end of the round, Ali was himself again. By the end of round six, the fight was even on points. Liston returned to his corner, impassively told his handlers that his left arm was numb, and refused to rise at the sound of the bell. He had no Dundee to push him forward. "What a dreary conclusion," writes Mark Kram. "Liston, of all people, quitting, and Clay trying to quit."

On only one earlier occasion during his brief reign had Sonny Liston been cheered the way a champ expects to be cheered. That was home-coming day at Liston's alma mater, the penitentiary at Jefferson City. On the night of February 25, the inmates listened to the Ali fight as intensely as my friends and I did. Our reactions differed at fight's end. When they learned of his surrender, they filled the night air with howls of outrage and disgust. The mother had thrown the fight! They were sure of it. At my house, we exulted. We didn't want to know any more than we knew. The faithful never do. Ali had won. He was the new world champion. That's all that mattered.

TO A PERSON, Ali supporters believe that their man won fair and square. Ali iconoclasts, like Kram and Tosches, are not so sure. Kram reports that a *Sports Illustrated* colleague saw Liston "with real tears in his eyes" as he approached the ring. He describes a fight in which a phantom Liston took the ring, not the real one, not the most powerful puncher in the western world.

Tosches, Liston's biographer, goes deeper. He speaks to any number of people from the boxing demi-monde, many of whom more than hint at a fix. "The fight was five-and-a-half-to-one here," a Chicago bookmaker tells him, "and by fight time it was down to about two-to-one." For the bookie, the odds told the story. At the last minute, serious money was being laid down on Ali.

"Don't bet," Bernie Glickman told his son Joel before the fight. "There's something wrong. I don't know what it is." Glickman had been one of Liston's early handlers and had visited Liston's camp before the fight.

Many of Liston's friends and supporters felt betrayed not by the loss but by Liston's failure to alert them to it. Had they known, they could have switched their bets to Ali and made some serious money. When Liston's bodyguard, Lowell Powell, questioned his boss's silence, Liston reportedly told him, "With your big mouth, we'd both be wearing con-crete suits." After the fight, Liston's mother and brother reached Liston at his hotel. He simply said, "I did what they told me to do." Again, though, Liston had motive to deceive. Given his history, a dive sounded credible and seemed less craven than a surrender.

Former champ Jose Torres offers arguably the most insightful account of the fight. "Clay worked Liston over like no other fighter ever had," he writes. "Liston's eyes became sad. He lost his mean stare. His legs looked weary; his arms seemed to stop."

George Foreman doesn't buy the idea of a fix either. The Liston he came to know as a sparring partner late in Liston's career was "too mean and too proud" to throw away the championship. Foreman advances a sophisticated and possibly accurate alternative theory. As he tells it, "The fans treated him like dirt." This is true enough. There had been no parades for Liston, no meetings with the president, no cheers from the fans when he entered the ring to defend his title. At the second Patterson fight, in fact, they booed him viciously.

In an unguarded moment, Liston told Foreman that he wanted to beat Ali and could have, but the fans "acted like they didn't want me to." Subconsciously, Foreman suggests, Liston gave the fans what they wanted. As one old friend said of Sonny, "I think he died the way he was born." If so, the first Ali fight was just another nail in his coffin.

AUDUBON BALLROOM

Turning my back on Malcolm," says Muhammad Ali forty years after the fact, "was one of the mistakes that I regret most in my life." To his credit, Ali has come to grips with this tragic misstep, at least partially. His faithful, however, have not. To maintain both Ali and Malcolm X in the same unstable pantheon—an astonishing bit of myth juggling—they have had to gloss over an all but unforgivable act of treachery.

Malcolm X died on February 21, 1965, just four days short of the first anniversary of Ali's surprise conquest of Sonny Liston. Ali's victory in 1964, in fact, greased the wheels then already in motion that would lead to Malcolm's death. Had Ali been wiser, or more mature, he—and perhaps he alone—could have thrown a wrench into the whole ugly mechanism.

When Sonny Liston failed to answer the bell at the beginning of the seventh round, the Honorable Elijah Muhammad had something of a revelation. In a heartbeat, he decided that perhaps boxing wasn't such an unworthy enterprise after all. Immediately after the fight, he called Ali and courted him hard.

At a press conference the day after the Liston fight, Ali announced his allegiance to the Nation of Islam and shared with the world his new name. That name makes for a good trivia question. Despite Howard Cosell's claim to the contrary, it was not originally Muhammad Ali. It was Cassius X. The rejection of "Clay" horrified his parents, especially his father, whose name had been devalued in every sense of the word.

A day later, speaking to five thousand followers at the annual Nation of Islam convention, Elijah Muhammad joyously announced that "Clay whipped a much tougher man and came through the bout unscarred because he has accepted Muhammad as the messenger of Allah." This turnabout dismayed Malcolm and his wife, Betty Shabazz. Shabazz remembers all too well the denunciations of Ali before the fight, the hysteria about how he would "bring disgrace to the Nation of Islam," and on and on. "All of a sudden," she recalls, "they were breaking their necks, trying to get close to the heavyweight champion."

In the Nation of Islam one would receive an "original name"—i.e. an Arabic name—only after mythic founder Master Wallace Fard returned from wherever it was he had gone. Thus, even after his years of dedicated service, Malcolm remained merely Malcolm X. But the Nation of Islam, "bendable" as it was, made an exception for an unschooled twenty-two-year-old in a "filthy" profession. On a March 6 radio broadcast from Chicago, Elijah Muhammad gave the young boxer his new name, Muhammad Ali. In fact, Elijah Muhammad used the name as bait to lure Cassius X away from his mentor, the rebellious Malcolm.

At first, the name did not exactly take. When, for instance, Ali attended a fight at Madison Square Garden soon after his name change, Harry Markson, president of the Garden's boxing program, refused to introduce him as "Muhammad Ali." "We've made so much progress in eliminating color barriers," said Markson at the time, justifying his decision, "that it's a pity we're now facing such a problem, the heavyweight champion of the world preaching a hate religion."

Cosell, that critical interpreter of the Ali myth, claims that he alone acknowledged the new name "instantly." He adds, "I could have cared less what the public's reaction would be towards me." To Cosell, it made perfect sense for Ali to change his name. No "intelligent proud black in the 1960s" would want to keep a "slave name." That Cosell changed his own name from the proudly Jewish "Cohen" to the more ambiguous "Cosell" is explained away as a historical rectification.

As Cosell and others retell the story, it was only brave and tolerant souls like themselves who accepted Ali's turn toward Islam. In 1964, however, Ali did not embrace Islam. He embraced the Nation of Islam, a cult that preached segregation, fantasized about genocide, and horrified the serious civil rights liberals of that era, black and white. "When Cassius Clay joined the Black Muslims," said Martin Luther King, "he became a champion of racial segregation and that is what we are fighting against."

Appropriately enough, one person who did support Ali's conversion was the arch-segregationist Georgia senator, Richard Russell. "Cassius Clay," said Russell from the floor of the U.S. Senate, "in common with 180 million other American citizens, has the right to join the religious sect of his choice without being blackmailed, harassed, and threatened with the severe punishment of being deprived of the heavyweight championship."

In his 1970 autobiography, coauthored by Pulitzer Prize-winning *New York Times* columnist Dave Anderson, Sugar Ray Robinson recounts a conversation from this era that nicely captures the Nation's ethos. As he tells it, Robinson invited the new champ down to Jamaica to serve as a celebrity trainer at a Robinson fight. One night, he and his wife, Millie, were sitting poolside with Ali and his new wife, Sonji, when a shooting star passed through the heavens. Upon seeing it, Ali leaped up and shouted, without a hint of irony, "The white man is destroying the world." He explained to Robinson that only Allah and his Messenger, Elijah Muhammad, could save the world from destruction and pleaded with him to join the saved. As an incentive, Ali continued, the Messenger was prepared to lay $700,000 on him, one dollar from each Muslim in America.

Robinson was unimpressed. He told a chagrined Ali that he would not join the Nation of Islam for $7 million. "You know your slogan—'The white man is a devil, the white devils'—That's not right. You can't live in this world hating people," said Robinson. He reminded Ali that he was a Christian: "All the Christian religions preach love for your fellow man." This message had to have rankled the Black Muslims. It is no wonder they cleansed Sugar Ray Robinson from the mythic account.

Although Joyce Carol Oates blasts the "angry self-righteousness of the conservative white press," the major sportswriters of the era—Jimmy Cannon, Dick Young, Jimmy Powers, Red Smith, Arthur Daley, and Milton Gross—attacked the flagrantly *illiberal* character of the Nation. In a fairly typical broadside, Jimmy Cannon argued that boxing had been "turned into an instrument of hate. . . . Clay is using it as a weapon of wickedness in an attack on the spirit." If the next generation of sportswriters "totally accepted the Ali legend," as the Garden's Markson reported, the sportswriters of that time and place weren't buying. They knew better. In the mid-1960s, liberals openly defended values like God, country, and racial brotherhood and challenged those who did not.

For all the guff coming Ali's way, my friends and I continued to cheer him on. The Nation of Islam had been a force in Newark since the day Noble Drew Ali had founded the prototype mosque in the city fifty years prior. This unusual cult did not bother us the way it did our more enlightened elders. If they saw racism as the source of urban problems, we, like the Muslims, saw the problem as a welfare-driven freefall of family and culture. If they saw the hucksterism at the top, we saw the industry and enterprise of the Muslims at the grassroots.

Then, too, few in our neighborhood were any keener on integration than Muhammad Ali. The concept no longer meant what it had when my family moved to our already integrated block ten years earlier. Fairly or not, it now meant the collapse of property values, the implosion of community, the harassment of children. Just months after we listened to the Liston fight together, Kenny was jumped in Branch Brook Park and had his front teeth knocked out. That was enough for his parents. They sent him to live with his aunt in a soulless, slapdash suburb sixty miles from Newark. They followed him there a year later. Raymond and his family moved away the same year. My friends were not alone. From 1950 to 1967, Newark lost 143,000 white residents, almost a third of its total 1950 population of 438,000.

THE YEAR 1964 proved even more troubling for Malcolm X than it did for us. In the first month or so after the Liston fight, word got back to Elijah Muhammad that Malcolm was still mentoring Ali. This had to stop. Muhammad let Ali know that if he hoped to become a minister, he had to sever his relationship with Malcolm immediately. This he did. "I don't know much about what Malcolm is doing," Ali said when pressed, "but I do know that Muhammad is the wisest."

In the spring of 1964, Malcolm headed for Mecca and Africa. He had hoped Ali could join him, but that was now impossible. Instead, Ali went on his own tour. Elijah's son, Herbert Muhammad, joined him, as did several other Muslims, including Ali's brother, now Rudy X. In one of the more cinematic moments of his altogether dramatic life, Ali crossed paths with Malcolm in a Ghana hotel lobby. Ghana's "life president" Kwame Nkrumah, who had just recently designated Ghana a one-party state, was the first in a long line of tyrants to embrace Ali.

Future Pulitzer Prize-winner Maya Angelou was there with Malcolm and recalled the extraordinary moment. After catching his attention, Malcolm called out to Ali, "Brother, I still love you, and you are still the greatest." Malcolm waited for a response, smiling "a sad little smile." Ali looked hard at Malcolm and shook his head. "You left the honorable Elijah Muhammad. That was the wrong thing to do, Brother Malcolm." So saying, Ali abruptly turned and walked away.

"Did you get a look at Malcolm," Ali told the reporters in his entourage, "dressed in that funny white robe and wearing a beard and walking with that cane that looked like a prophet's stick. Man, he's gone." Malcolm had just returned from Mecca. At the time, that did not impress Ali. "Nobody listens to Malcolm anymore," he scoffed.

That was not quite true. Elijah Muhammad was listening with a thousand ears, and what he heard was troubling. The trip to Mecca did not make Malcolm a civil rights liberal by any means, but it did soften his heart. In embracing "true Islam," he could no longer "make sweeping indictments of all white people" as Elijah Muhammad had taught him.

"I was a zombie then—like all Muslims," Malcolm tells Alex Haley about his life in the Nation. "I was hypnotized, pointed in a certain direction and told to march. Well, I guess a man's entitled to make a fool of himself if he's ready to pay the cost. It cost me twelve years."

Malcolm's honesty was making him no friends in the Nation of Islam hierarchy. Soviet style, Muhammad dismissed Malcolm's criticism as "mental illness." As the year progressed, the Messenger continued to ratchet up the threat level. "The white man has offered rewards for people to lie on the Messenger of Allah," Muhammad observed prophetically in June of 1964. "This hypocrite is going to get blasted clear off the face of the earth." In November of that year, an FBI informant inside a Washington mosque told the FBI that a fatwah had gone out on Malcolm's head. A week later in *Muhammad Speaks*, the house organ of the Nation of Islam, Louis Farrakhan, then Louis X, invited Malcolm to imagine that head rolling down the sidewalk.

The death threats rattled Malcolm, but they did not demoralize him. Treachery did that. "Worse than death was betrayal," he would concede. And no betrayal cut as deeply as Ali's. Ali's public rejection of Malcolm "hurt Malcolm more than any other person turning away that I know of," Betty Shabazz, Malcolm's wife, tells Hauser.

On Christmas Day 1964, in a Boston hotel room, a group of Muslims posing as newsmen severely beat Ali's press secretary, Leon 4X Ameer. Although working for Ali, Ameer had remained close to Malcolm, a risky show of loyalty. Two weeks after the assault, Ameer held a press conference in Harlem's Theresa Hotel. He expressed his fears that Ali might be

killed in "Black Muslim in-fighting" and regretted that the spiritual
sense of the Nation was "just about dead."

Either out of fear or a feudal sense of obligation to the Messenger, Ali
held a press conference at the Theresa the same day. "Ameer's nothing to
me," he said. "He was welcomed as a friend as long as he was a registered
Muslim, but not anymore." When asked whether Ameer should fear for
his life, Ali answered coldly, "They think everyone's out to kill them
because they know that they deserve to be killed for what they did." His
"they" included Malcolm X.

Two days later, at the Audubon Ballroom of all fateful places, Ali told
a Fruit of Islam gathering that the "white press" had deceived Malcolm
into thinking he was the Nation's number two man, and now he was
"disillusioned." Soon after, *Muhammad Speaks* accused Ameer of plot-
ting to kill Elijah Muhammad and ran a "Wanted" poster with Ameer's
picture.

As the death threats morphed into murder plots, Betty Shabazz begged
Ali's intercession. "You see what you're doing to my husband, don't you,"
she pleaded after a chance encounter with Ali at the Theresa. Ali blew her
off, disingenuously raising his hands in the air and saying, "I'm not doing
anything to him."

Two days before his death, and five days after a Muslim death squad
had burned down his house, Malcolm X concluded that "brotherhood"
was the only thing that could save this country. "I've learned it the hard
way," Malcolm regretted, "but I've learned it." As he feared, he had one
harder lesson still to learn.

The fatal plot centered on the Newark mosque. *60 Minutes,* among
other sources, has implicated Nation of Islam leader Louis Farrakhan in
the plot's orchestration, a charge he denies. As the FBI reported, Farrakhan
had driven from Boston to Newark early that morning. He was at the
mosque when several Muslim brothers caught up with Malcolm X at the
Audubon Ballroom in Harlem. They rose up during his speech and
blasted away.

The autopsy report lists fifteen "shotgun and other caliber bullet wounds." Betty Shabazz was there with her four children. "She heard shots," reads the chilling NYPD report. "She pushed the children under the chairs in the box and covered them with her body. She then heard someone say, 'Oh, my God! Oh, my God!'" As Malcolm understood all too well, his own chickens had finally come home to roost. Two soldiers in the Fruit of Islam would later be convicted of the murder.

A week after Malcolm's murder, Elijah Muhammad predictably declined all responsibility at the annual Saviour's Day rally in Chicago. "They know I loved [Malcolm]," he contended. "His foolish teaching brought him to his own end." Sitting prominently behind the Messenger on the platform and affirming his every word was Muhammad Ali.

"Ali threw Malcolm away like a pork chop," says Sunni Khalid, one of the few journalists to see through the myth. "Even today those who really know can never forgive him." Two weeks after that, Ameer called the FBI and agreed to help identify the shooters. He never got the chance. The next day, he was found dead in his hotel room of unknown causes.

For the great majority of Americans, black and white, the death of Malcolm X did not resonate like that of JFK or Martin Luther King. Few, myself included, could tell you where they were or what they were doing when they first heard the news.

The death that I remember most vividly that winter took place four weeks earlier. I attended the memorial service. The deceased was a friend from Boy Scouts, Billy Swaykos. Billy was a few years older than I and much nicer than the neighborhood that produced him. We called him "Rocky." He got the nickname not for his boxing but for his swimming skills or lack thereof. To advance in the Scouts, one had to swim much better than a rock, and so Billy persisted.

It did not surprise me that Billy joined the Army after high school. He learned patriotism in the Boy Scouts as well as swimming. We all did. For all the travails of our neighborhood, we were taught to see beyond it, to understand that our real identity was not as Irish or Italian, or as black or white, but as American. To this day, I am still not sure why we took this lesson to heart so much more deeply than our affluent peers, but almost to a person, we did.

On January 23, 1965, the Viet Cong beheaded the twenty-one-year-old Billy. Unlike Malcolm X, he knew what he was dying for. If not before his death, certainly afterward, I *did* have a quarrel with them Viet Cong.

PHANTOM PUNCH

On July 3, 1964, Herbert Muhammad introduced Muhammad Ali to Sonji Roi in Chicago. It's likely, in fact, that Herbert paid her for the date. He and Ali were just back from Africa, and Herbert thought Ali should "have some fun." As Ali professed, "We Muslims don't touch a woman unless we're married to her." But for Ali, as for Elijah Muhammad, this seemed more of a guideline than a rule. What Herbert did not expect was that his naïve twenty-two-year-old charge would propose to Sonji that very night.

Sonji Clay, as she prefers to be called today, was older then Ali. She had a child at thirteen. And she had no gift for being a Muslim woman, none at all. Her disposition was pure *party* in its best, most dazzling, most feminine sense of the word. Blinded by the light, Ali wed the spirited Miss Sonji in Gary, Indiana, in August 1964. The marriage misfired right from the beginning.

There is little doubt that Sonji loved Ali. Looking back from nearly thirty years distance, she describes the young Ali as precious, sweet, and gentle. "He was a good husband." What troubled Sonji deeply, as it would Ali's other wives, was that she wanted a man "who'd be his own master." That was not the young Ali. His master was Elijah Muhammad. As she would tell Jack Olsen, "They've stolen my man's mind."

The battleground in this marriage was the very topography of Sonji herself. The instinctive Ali liked it painted and exposed, as did Sonji. That was her glory and her strength. The Muslim Ali needed it to be covered and cleansed.

In his autobiography, *The Greatest,* editor Toni Morrison reported word for word a circa-1970 conversation between Ali and Sonji. The feminist in Morrison likely thought this side of Ali needed airing. The Muslim editors may not have realized how badly Ali comes off in this account, which goes on for a heartbreakingly honest twenty-five pages. For no easily understood reason, Ali and his Muslim mates allowed the heart of this scene to remain in the movie version that was otherwise as disingenuous as the book that spawned it.

The two talk about why their marriage dissolved. One highly indicative incident took place in Jamaica at a grand reception for Sugar Ray, to which Sonji wore a snug, orange-knit outfit. "I was vexed over that dress," Ali recalls. At the party, he did not like the way "the devils" were looking at Sonji. "But you bought that damn dress. You picked it," counters Sonji.

That fact no longer mattered. Both Ali and Sonji agree that the approving stares of the white devils had set Ali off. He dragged Sonji past all the gathered luminaries and into the bathroom. "I'm crying and pulling away and you're jerking on me and yelling and you've forgotten that everyone's looking." In the bathroom, he tried to stretch her dress out and ripped it in the process. "So now I'm nearly naked," Sonji recounts. "I'm trying to break away and you're fighting me, pulling on my clothes, slapping me." The movie version of this incident, with Ali playing himself, is hard to watch.

Upon reliving this account, a contrite Ali asks plaintively, "Why couldn't you go along. Why couldn't you?" Sonji's girlfriends could not understand either. "Baby," one of them only half-jokes, "I'd wear a fisherman's net under a deep-sea diver's suit with a Ku Klux Klan sheet and a monk's frock, if I had a husband that rich and handsome and famous, and he dug me wearing it."

What Sonji understood that her friends did not is that clothes were mere symptom of a deeper dysfunction. "I wanted you to be my hero, my god," she tells Ali. But at the time, as both knew, Ali was not his own man, let alone his own master. "You wanted to take this kind of love from me and make me give it to some other man," Sonji explains. "Well, I rebelled against that." That "other man" was Elijah Muhammad.

"I couldn't understand [Ali's] two faces," Sonji informs Hauser twenty years later. "I mean stand up for what you believe and feel and want, but don't do one thing for the Nation and another when you're alone with me like God can't see."

On the eve of the first Liston fight, while still a member of the Nation of Islam, Malcolm X had shared with writer George Plimpton the essence of the Nation's worldview. As Malcolm and the Muslims saw it, Martin Luther King and the other civil rights activists were little more than fools and dreamers. "I am not interested in the dream," he told Plimpton, "but in the nightmare." After four years of relentless molding, the Nation had all but succeeded in turning the upbeat Clay into the paranoid Ali.

TO SEE ONLY nightmare in the mid-1960s there was much that Muslims had to overlook. Malcolm X, for instance, flew often on commercial airliners—"in more planes probably than any other Negro." He had always been treated well and occasionally even commented on it, but if he saw the uniformly sunny and accepting world of air travel as a glimpse into America's future, he never got the chance to say so.

Ali was never comfortable flying, which was one reason why he and his entourage took Ali's bus from Miami to his Massachusetts training camp for the second Sonny Liston flight. As Ali announced, the bus wasn't "flying." It would be passing right through an old South that had not quite yet given up the ghost. This would give Ali a chance to share his nightmare vision with those who needed to see it.

George Plimpton was one of the few reporters on the trip. As night came on, and Bundini grew hungry, Bundini had the bus stop at a shabby, tired diner in a north Florida town called Yulee. When Bundini and Plimpton went in and sat at the counter, the manager sheepishly told him, "Sorry, we have a place out back." Ali, who never left the bus's side, exulted in his friend's rejection, "You damn fool. I tol' you to be a Muslim." His brother, Rahaman, was even more excited: "A man has seen reality, seen re-al-i-ty." Back on the bus, Ali humiliated Bundini to the point of tears. "Tom! Tom! Tom!" he whooped. "You belong to your white master."

Bundini was not one to give up the dream. "I'm free," he cried. "I keep trying. If I find a waterhole is dry, I go on and find another." Bundini did just that. Just across the state line, he asked Ali to stop at a Howard Johnson's. "This is Georgia, Bundini," said a disbelieving Ali. "You haven't been showed?"

The bus stopped. Bundini, Plimpton, and a few of Ali's black sparring partners walked into the Howard Johnson's and sat at a booth. A waitress walked over, looked at them, and said, "You all look hungry." She smiled and passed out the menus. America was changing. The South was changing in a hurry. In July, President Lyndon Johnson had signed the landmark Civil Rights Act of 1964 into law. The act prohibited racial discrimination in public accommodations. Ali and his Muslim handlers had nothing to do with it, and it pained them to see it actually work.

MEANWHILE, IN PHILADELPHIA, the twenty-one-year-old Joe Frazier was laying the groundwork for his own *Rocky*-like career. In fact, Sylvester Stallone lifted elements of Frazier's story for his Oscar-winning movie, including the Philadelphia location, the morning runs through the streets, the culminating jog up the steps of the Philadelphia Museum of Art, and even the carcass-punching.

Frazier, still a teenager, had gotten a job at the slaughterhouse soon after leaving South Carolina. Although the job paid well enough, he "hated being ordinary." At seventeen, much like Ali, he spied a glimpse of a larger destiny at a boxing gym, this one also run by the police. Soon afterward, he had the great good fortune of meeting veteran trainer, Yank Durham, an African American whose own career was cut short when he broke both legs while serving in World War II. Durham guided Frazier, now twenty, to the Olympic heavyweight championship in 1964. In the spring of 1965, Durham assembled a mixed-race Philadelphia investor group, and an extraordinary career was born.

DESPITE HIS CHAMPIONSHIP status, Ali had much greater anxieties than Joe Frazier that spring. In addition to the very real fear of facing Sonny Liston once again, his marriage was in shambles, and his life in jeopardy. On February 21, the night of Malcolm's assassination, a highly suspicious fire erupted in his apartment. Two days later, someone firebombed the Nation of Islam headquarters in New York. As Ali trained for his May rematch with Liston, he had reason to be grateful for the protection the FBI offered.

"The atmosphere surrounding the fight was ugly," reflects sportswriter Jerry Izenberg. Rumors abounded of a retaliatory strike against Ali. There were rumors, too, of Muslim threats against Liston. The stone-faced Fruit of Islam guards were intimidating and everywhere. Although Izenberg would accept Ali as "Ali" long before most of his peers, the Ali of this period unnerved him.

Izenberg recounts an impromptu press conference a week or so before the fight. When a reporter asked Ali if he was worried about Malcolm's "people," Ali snapped back, "What people? Malcolm ain't got no people." Izenberg was one of the few journalists of the period, in or out of sports, to respect Malcolm X. It chilled him that Ali would dismiss the now dead Malcolm so coldly just "because somebody tells you he's nobody."

Held in the unlikely town of Lewiston, Maine, this second Liston fight proved to be more Punch and Judy than the expected horror show. It began much like the one in Miami with Liston stalking and Ali circling and jabbing. Less than two minutes in, while many in the small crowd were still settling into their seats, Liston slumped on to the canvas. "What happened?" Ferdie Pacheco remembers the crowd shrieking as if one. Ali, understanding the ramifications, stood above Liston yelling, "Get up, you bum. No one is going to believe this."

Almost too casually, Liston rolled over on to his back and looked up at the ranting Ali. Celebrity ref Jersey Joe Walcott could not begin the count until Ali headed for a neutral corner, but Walcott was slow to corral him. Meanwhile, boxing historian Nat Fleischer—"a little, wrinkled old man," as Pacheco describes him—ran down to the ring and started shouting that more than ten seconds had expired, and the fight was over. In the midst of all the confusion, Liston had gotten up and resumed fighting. Yielding to Fleischer's authority, although he had none, Walcott stopped the fight. The crowd started chanting, "Fix, fix, fix." Given the circumstances, their outrage seemed more understandable than anything else that had transpired.

Even in replay, the celebrated knock-out punch is hard to see. "I'm so fast, I even missed the punch on TV," Ali would admit. In time, he would come to call it his "anchor punch." Most everyone else refers to it as "the phantom punch." Jose Torres, broadcasting for a Spanish language station in New York, recorded his commentary, and again he was on the money, "a perfect shot to the jaw, right on the button and Liston is down."

When later asked by the California boxing commission why he did not get up, Liston replied, "Commissioner, Muhammad Ali is a crazy man." Liston then made an entirely rational case that a manic Ali, still in center ring, could smack him down as soon as he tried to stand up. Torres makes the equally rational case that Liston feared the Muslims a good deal more than he feared Ali. Whatever the true explanation, it went to the grave with Sonny six years later.

THE MORE INTERESTING fight, the one for Ali's soul, played out later that evening. It unfolded at the hotel in Auburn, Maine, where Ali and his entourage were staying. He and a few of his fellow Muslims were carrying on in the courtyard when Sonji emerged on the balcony and tried to lure her victorious young husband upstairs. Ali's friends objected—they never did like Sonji and her sequined independence—and they persuaded him to stay. "Go to bed," Ali yelled up at her.

Sonji never had a chance. Less than a month later, Ali filed for annulment in Miami. Chief among his complaints was that Sonji refused to follow Muslim tenets as she allegedly had promised. "Someone else made the decision," Sonji tells Hauser. She wanted to fight the annulment, but she feared the consequences. "I wasn't going to take on all the Muslims. If I had, I'd probably have wound up dead."

THAT SPRING IN Newark, the highway department finally got around to buying up the properties in the way of what would become Interstate 280. Our weary house on Myrtle Avenue was among them. We were relieved. By this time, no one else would have bought it. When our next-door neighbors moved out, the midnight plumbers moved in, stripped the place of its copper, and burned the house down, three feet of alley away from us. It was time to go.

The playgrounds had gotten weird as well. A few years earlier, the dominant metaphor had been the civil rights struggle. That I could negotiate. By 1965, however, the indecipherable plot lines of black nationalism had seeped into our pickup games. On more than one occasion, I found my teammates rooting against me, often the only white on the court, occasionally the only white on the playground, even though keeping the court hinged on our victory.

"Give the brotha the ball," one teammate repeated ominously and ironically on a day when I couldn't miss. "He think he better than we are. Give the brotha the ball." Meanwhile, my little sister found herself the recurrent victim of the kind of taunting, hair-pulling attacks little girls inflict on one another. What provoked the attackers was her blond hair, rare in the neighborhood, and a symbol of her oppressive, preteen whiteness. And no matter how bad it got, there was no calling my father any more, or even my big brothers, who had gone their separate ways. We were pretty much on our own.

Forced to move, my mother guilt-tripped the city's Italian police director into finding us a place in one of the city's "better" public housing projects, such as it was. Born in Newark and prepared to die there, my mother remained stubbornly proud of her hometown until the end. There would be no "white flight" for her. She had nowhere to flee to.

NO QUARREL

On April 28, 1967, Muhammad Ali performed the defining act of his career. When the induction officer at the Armed Forces Examining and Entrance Statement in Houston called out his still legal name, "Cassius Marcellus Clay," he chose not to step forward. This gesture followed a year of unsuccessful negotiating, and it secured for Ali a place in American cultural history that he himself never intended or imagined.

More than any other moment in Ali's life, more than all the other moments combined, that day in Houston made possible what the *New York Times'* Robert Lipsyte describes as "Ali's journey from ridicule to beatification."

"Children in this country should be taught forever how [Ali] stood by his convictions and lived his life," gushes the normally restrained baseball great Henry Aaron. Aaron's idolatry hews to the norm. Those who dissent have faced the abuse of the cultural establishment, an abuse transparent even in the casual asides of the sportswriter.

"Today," Jerry Izenberg would inform Hauser twenty-five years after Ali's refusal, "you'd be hard pressed to find anybody—the guy would have to be a dyed-in-the-wool Nazi—who doesn't feel that Ali's stand on Vietnam was understandable and basically justified."

Before slandering his fellow citizens, Izenberg might first have asked whether Ali himself could justify his actions, let alone understand them. This question is not glibly posed. It cuts to the very heart of the Ali myth and demands a serious answer before the canonization process continues.

IN THE MONTHS before the first Liston fight, Louisville sponsor Bill Faversham used his influence to keep Ali out of the service at least until after the fight. This effort had nothing to do with principle and everything to do with dividends. Liston volunteered to help Ali out. "You put him in the ring with me before the Army gets him," he boasted, "and you can bet any amount of money that the Army wouldn't want pretty boy after I finish him off."

Shortly before the fight, Ali took the mental aptitude test as part of the Selective Service process. Consistent with his poor performance in high school—he graduated very near the bottom of his class with a D-average—Ali did not do particularly well on the exam. His I.Q. tested at 78, which put him in the 16th percentile from the bottom. At the time, the Army was recruiting only those in the 30th percentile and above and classified Ali 1-Y, "not qualified under current standards."

As future tests would prove, Ali was not faking. "I only said I was the greatest," he would repeat with something like embarrassment, "not the smartest." In truth, Ali was smart. It is just that he was very nearly illiterate. By all accounts, Ali read painfully and slowly and rarely got beyond the headlines. His writing was more painful still. When older, Ali, like many other functional illiterates, would attribute his problem to dyslexia. In Ali's case, the self-diagnosis may be accurate. Although Ali had learned much of his chatter by rote—"Float like a butterfly / Sting like a bee"—his spontaneous conversations showed him to be much more clever and creative than a 78 I.Q. would suggest.

If illiteracy did not rob Ali of his verbal gifts, it did deprive him of the information he needed to make informed judgments about the world. For an international spokesman on war and peace, the gaps in his knowledge base were frightening. As Jack Olsen reports, he would sometimes shock his friends by not knowing what month it was or how to calculate the number of months separating any two non-consecutive months.

Throughout his life, Ali remained blithely oblivious of the past. Famed black photographer Gordon Parks recounts how he visited England with Ali. In attempting to assess the seemingly more benign British personality, Ali asked Parks, "Have they ever been in any big wars?" This was only twenty years after the bombs stopped dropping. His knowledge of geography was more limited still. "I don't know nothing about Vietnam," he told Parks. "Where is it anyway? Near China?"

In early 1966, with the conflict in Vietnam escalating, Selective Service lowered the bar to include those whose mental aptitudes were in the 15th percentile or higher. That meant Ali. He was not pleased. He immediately had his attorney apply for a deferment based on the financial hardship it would cause his parents, but the request was turned down. Ali was reclassified 1-A.

The *New York Times'* Lipsyte was with Ali in Miami when he first heard the news. "How can they do this to me?" Ali griped. "I don't want my career ruined." Then the phone started ringing, and reporters from all over the country peppered him with questions. Throughout the day, meanwhile, his ever-present Muslim retainers filled his head with the likely horrors of Vietnam, horrors visited not by "Charlie" as in the VC, or Victor Charlie, but by Mister Charlie. "Some white cracker sergeant is gonna put a shank in you," Ali heard over and over again in one variation or another.

Finally, after a day's worth of mind games from his friends and phone calls from reporters, Ali sounded off, "Man, I ain't got no quarrel with them Vietcong." Out of this one chance comment, mindless and peevish, planted by the Muslims, inspired by a little more than a looming inconvenience, a mighty legend was born.

IN 1966, JOURNALISTS, especially the sports journalists, still took patriotism seriously. Almost to a person, Ali's behavior offended them, even the liberals among them like Milton Gross. "As a fighter, Cassius is good," observed Gross, "as a man, he cannot compare to some of the kids slogging through the rice paddies."

Most athletes felt the same way. "I can't help wondering how he can expect to make millions of dollars in this country," asked World War II veteran Jackie Robinson, "and then refuse to fight for it." "He's a guy with a million dollars worth of confidence," affirmed Joe Louis, "and a dime's worth of courage." A month after Ali refused induction, Floyd Patterson visited the Marines at Khe Sanh, in part to show his contempt for Ali.

If the sports pages reflect the culture, they rarely shape it. That happens on the op-ed pages and in the op-ed publications. In the same year Ali came out against the war, so did Noam Chomsky. In a bellwether Harvard speech, the man who would become America's most influential public intellectual read the riot act to his colleagues. "We can hardly avoid asking ourselves," Chomsky preached, "to what extent the American people bear responsibility for the savage American assault on a largely helpless rural population in Vietnam." Chomsky's selective indignation would quickly trickle down, and Ali's would bubble up. When the currents converged, the great part of liberal opinion would be swept away.

In 1966, however, Ali was swimming against the tide of popular opinion. His decision to resist the draft cost him a good deal of fan support and some serious endorsement money. Fifteen years later, a more reflective Ali would tell *Sport* magazine that his "biggest mistake" ever was coming out against the war "too early." Still, he persisted. The Nation of Islam had tightened its grip, and Ali had little room to maneuver. In that same year, Ali's contract with the Louisville Sponsoring group expired. Ali did not renew. The Nation pushed the Louisville people out and moved its own people in. Although keeping Dundee on as trainer,

NO QUARREL

Herbert Muhammad replaced him in the more responsible and remu-
nerative role as manager.

In March 1966, Ali's attorney again appealed for reclassification, and
this time he added a wrinkle: Ali was a conscientious objector on religious grounds. The request was denied. In August 1966, Ali got to make
his own case for reclassification before an administrative judge. Under
oath, he testified that true Muslims like himself "could not participate in
wars on the side of nonbelievers." Like many a judge in and out of the
ring, this one finessed the decision Ali's way. He overlooked the bellicose
history of Islam and contended that Ali was "sincere in his objection on
religious grounds to war in any form."

The Justice Department was not quite so naïve. Its attorneys argued
that political and racial considerations inspired Ali's opposition to the
war. The Kentucky Appeals Board sided with the Justice Department. The
mythmakers who portray these decisions as racist and/or reactionary
miss the obvious. "I don't think the Nation of Islam was a religious
organization at all," confirms Malcolm X's daughter, Attallah Shabazz.
What Ali pulled from the experience, says Shabazz, "was a social and
political awakening."

Malcolm X had made much the same distinction. "The Mohammedan
abroad believes in a heaven and hell," he had told George Plimpton in
1964. "Here, we [the Nation] believe that heaven and hell are on earth,
and that we are in the hell and must strive to escape it." In America, no
other religion of note lacked an afterlife or the discipline imposed by one.
At the time, the display of the Crescent did not make the Nation any more
Islamic than a burning cross made the Ku Klux Klan Christian.

Publicly, Elijah Muhammad kept his distance from Ali on the subject
of the draft. He had to. It was against the law to encourage draft resistance. He had already done time for a related offense. He wasn't eager to
do more. He made a point of telling the press, "Every one of my followers is free to make his own choice."

Privately, however, Muhammad was yanking Ali's chain. If he did not tell Ali directly what to do, he made sure Ali got the message through Herbert. "I know my father didn't want Ali to go in the Army," Herbert admits to Hauser years later. He shared his father's misgivings with Ali.

Howard Cosell insists that on the question of the draft, "Ali bent neither to pressure nor friendly overture," but then he quotes Ali one page later as saying, "Can't talk to you no more, not without Elijah's permission." Cosell comments, "This was simply further evidence of the degree of control the Muslims exercised over him." Unlike Cosell, Ali's no-nonsense Aunt Mary talked out of only one side of her mouth. "He was brainwashed," she would say of her nephew. "He's gonna mess himself up so won't nobody go see him."

Ali heard the Messenger loud and clear, and he was inclined to listen. During this period, in fact, he made no bones about his dependence on Muhammad and the Nation of Islam. "If it weren't for the Muslims," he was not embarrassed to say, "I'd be nothing."

When Hauser writes that the chain of events that would "shake America and place Ali in the annals of United States constitutional law" began when Ali registered for the draft in 1960, he purges from his definitive Ali biography Elijah Muhammad's altogether relevant dealings with the American government in the 1930s and 1940s.

Muhammad, the reader recalls, not only ducked the draft but also conspired with America's Japanese enemy and indirectly with Japan's Nazi allies. "The Japanese will slaughter the white man," Elijah had boasted repeatedly. This was not the kind of mentor from whom one could expect to learn the arts of pacifism or conscientious objection.

Ali surely respected Muhammad, but that respect had to have been tinged with fear. He had seen what Muhammad could and would do to his enemies. Ali did not want to become one. When faced with the draft, Ali chose the least frightening option. There was little courage involved, less principle, and no sign at all of independent thought. He was not "his own master," as his wife Sonji lamented. He was not the "autonomous negro" that Eldridge Cleaver insisted he was in his radical classic, *Soul on*

Ice. Ali belonged heart and soul to what Malcolm X had sadly concluded was a nation of zombies—"hypnotized, pointed in a certain direction and told to march." Ali marched right up to the edge and jumped when ordered.

An encounter with Sugar Ray Robinson illuminates his state of mind in early 1967. When Ali was in New York for the Zora Folley fight, his last before the exile, he called Robinson and asked if he could come see him at his midtown hotel. Robinson obliged. Ali wanted to talk about the Army.

"You've got to go," said Robinson.

"No," Ali answered, "Elijah Muhammad told me that I can't go."

Robinson explained the consequences of his refusal, and Ali answered, "But I'm afraid, Ray. I'm real afraid." When Robinson asked if he were afraid of the Muslims, Ali refused to answer. "His eyes were glistening with tears," Robinson reports, "tears of torment, tears of indecision." In 1970, Robinson had no reason to spin this story one way or another. For all of his misgivings about the young Ali, he describes him as "one of the most likable people I've ever known."

Despite the uninspiring dynamics of his resistance, Ali gave what Mike Marqusee calls a "major boost to the anti-war movement." Ali's status as heavyweight champion removed some of the stigma attached to resisters as being unmanly or cowardly. Even more important, he helped dispel the "lily white image of the movement." The New Left was painfully insecure about its whiteness. Ali provided the bridge to the black experience on the one issue most critical to its young white constituency.

Traffic on the bridge went both ways. The more insightful of Ali's observers understood that the young whites were redeeming Ali as he was redeeming them. In an article written for the British *Guardian,* Thomas Hauser acknowledges that the antiwar movement saved the young Ali from the "ugly" mood of the Nation of Islam just as Ali was adopting "the Nation's persona and its ideology."

Without meaning to, Hauser gives away the game. He argues that "when the spotlight turned from Ali's acceptance of an ideology that sanctioned hate to his refusal to accept induction into the US Army, Ali began to bond with the white liberal community, which at the time was quite strong."

Here the Ali myth was born. Had Ali not become an antiwar symbol, he never would have become a symbol of racial healing either. Ali's manic racial ideology had unnerved the white liberal community. Even after his rejection of the draft, old school liberals continued to despise that ideology. The young antiwar left, however, proved much more flexible, and as Hauser admits, this faction was "quite strong."

In his 1968 classic, *The Making of a Counter Culture,* Theodore Roszak argues prophetically that the pampered young of America had been made "almost nauseatingly much of." Whatever sentiments they might collectively voice were quickly being packaged and commercialized, "*including* the new ethos of dissent." The volume level of this dissent would only grow.

The New Left now had a prominent African American to represent its cause. In an awkward way at least, he fused the two major strains of its ideology—war resistance and an evolving form of civil rights. Indeed, Ali made a more symbolically viable war resister than a civil rights icon. Young whites merely had to imagine that his draft resistance was as inspired and independent as they presumed their own to be. On the civil rights front, the mythmakers had to scrub harder to sanitize his unlovely brand of black nationalism. They had to purge or revise much of Ali's history, particularly his relationship with Malcolm X. This historical cleansing was not planned. The spirit of the age inspired and guided it.

By 1967, according to Marqusee, Ali "had matured into a hero of global solidarity." As proof, he cites a speech Ali delivered that year in Louisville. In it, Ali identifies the aspirations of the Viet Cong with those of African Americans and promises not to let himself become "a tool to enslave those who are fighting for their own justice, freedom, and equality."

In 1967, one could forgive Ali his naïveté about the intentions of the Communists in Indochina. In 1999, one cannot easily forgive Marqusee his willful blindness. So critical is a happily "liberated" Vietnam to the sustaining of the sixties mythology that Marqusee must allow Ali's admittedly ghostwritten agitprop to stand as truth and Ali to stand as truth teller. That Ali knew nothing of the area's geography and history doesn't faze Marqusee. He acknowledges as much openly. What matters is that Ali's "understanding of the moral dimension of the choice before him was now deeply informed." Marqusee declines to reveal just who is doing the informing.

Marqusee's projection of Ali as fellow New Left warrior is standard fare. Sports scholar Michael Oriard sums up the intellectual assessment of Ali's war resistance in pure postmodernism. "Ali," he declares blithely, "was the author of his own narrative." To make such a claim, Oriard has to ignore *all* existing evidence. Indeed, few Americans had less control over their own destiny than the young Ali. "He had a great love for Elijah," Ferdie Pacheco admits, "and mostly he did as he was told."

The man dictating Ali's narrative did not make a very convincing pacifist. From the first days of his involvement with the Nation of Islam, Elijah Muhammad had been preaching and prophesying the violent destruction of the white race. In the years leading to World War II, he had plotted to make that happen. And more recently, he had laid the groundwork—at the very least—for the murder of Malcolm X and for the intimidation and assault of other dissidents. The media, the broadcast media in particular, chose not to know.

ON SEPTEMBER 11, 1964, ABC broadcast the last bout in the Gillette-sponsored *Fight of the Week* series it had inherited from NBC. "For many network executives," writes historian Randy Roberts, "the problem was not boxing's ratings, it was boxing's audience." The members of the audience were the people I grew up with. At the time, the media benignly caricatured them as gruff, unshaven, beer-drinking, blue-collar slobs in the image of the *Honeymooners'* Ralph Kramden. In just a few years, alas, Ralph Kramden would become Archie Bunker.

ABC, like the other networks, saw the future in the baby boom generation just coming of consumer age. I was a member of that audience as well. If ABC took away the *Fight of the Week*, it gave us *My Three Sons* and *Shindig* instead, a dubious trade-off. However, Ali proved to be the link between audiences and generations. "He was perfect for the youth market," Roberts observes, "honest but irreverent, sincere but boastful." For all his unpopularity on the sports pages, Ali's TV ratings continued to be strong.

Under the aggressive leadership of ABC's sports director Roone Arledge, the network cleverly promoted Ali as a fighter/entertainer. It showed the replay of the first Ali-Liston fight on *Wide World of Sports* and creatively packaged it with color and commentary. For the next several years, ABC continued to show Ali's fights either live or in replay. Howard Cosell served as liaison between the audience and Ali. Almost to a person, Ali supporters underestimate how deftly Cosell played this role. His interaction with Ali humanized the boxer at a time when Ali needed all the humanizing he could get.

ABC kept me in touch with Ali. In one form or another, I watched all the fights of his championship reign and cheered him on in each. Even before researching this book, I could have named his opponents from this era very nearly in order. Like all of the Ali faithful, of course, I had to screen out much of the noise surrounding the man lest it undermine my affection. To be sure, Ali more than occasionally put my loyalty to the test and never more so than in his November 1965 fight against likeable former champion Floyd Patterson.

ALTHOUGH ONLY SEVEN years older than Ali, Patterson belonged to a different generation, a more sensitive and appreciative one. He had much to be thankful for. The first ten years of Patterson's life rivaled Liston's in their loneliness and despair. As an eight- or nine-year-old, he would often avoid school and hide in the New York City subways for days on end to avoid contact with humanity.

"I can't remember ever having any fun at all, or even laughing," writes Patterson in his mature and introspective autobiography, *Victory Over Myself*, "until after I was placed in the Wiltwyck School for Delinquent Boys."

The teachers and counselors at this private school in upstate New York turned his life around. His education continued at special public schools in New York designed for kids like himself. "The lost boys," writes Patterson, "put on the road back at the first place, were firmly and understandably directed to a life of useful citizenship at the second." Through a good marriage, his adoption of Catholicism, and close supervision by his manager, Constantine "Cus" D'Amato, Patterson continued to build a career and rebuild his life. Unlike Ali, a stable life and a supportive extended family were not things he could take for granted.

At every turn, Patterson used his growing influence to push for civil rights. Patterson knew much more than Ali did about "my people's fight for the dignity of equality" because he did more of the suffering and more of the fighting, often in small, unseen ways. By the time Ali came of age, much of the fight had already been won. As a case in point, the nineteen-year-old Ali and his friends could buy tickets anywhere in the arena for Patterson's 1961 Miami title defense against Ingemar Johansson only because Patterson built open seating into the contract.

Patterson's psyche, however, was always a fragile thing. His first loss to Johansson threw him into a slough of "blackness and despair" that made him feel like the lost boy in the subway again. The Sonny Liston defeats had much the same effect. Coming into the fight against Patterson, Ali knew this about Patterson—everyone did—and he couldn't have cared less.

In Hauser's retelling, it was Patterson who struck first and hardest in the war of words. Although acknowledging Ali's right to believe what he wanted to, Patterson exercised his own "right to say the Black Muslims stink." His criticisms were more specific and better grounded than the word "stink" might suggest. Mark Kram has called Patterson "a liberal's liberal" in the best sense of the word. Unlike Ali, he went to places like Alabama and Mississippi and lent his moral support. "I do not believe God put us here to hate one another," he argued. "I believe the Muslim preaching of segregation, hatred, rebellion and violence is wrong. Cassius Clay is disgracing himself and the Negro race."

What Hauser overlooks is Ali's ceaseless attacks on Christianity that preceded the Patterson fight. He often referred to it as a "farce" and a "slave religion," one whose primary purpose was "to control black people."

In any case, Patterson's defiance nettled Ali. He promised to punish "this little old dumb pork-chop-eater" and "cause him pain." Ali was as good as his word. Even if Patterson had not wrenched his back early in the fight, he would not have beaten the taller, stronger, younger Ali. Bent over and hobbling and too proud to back off, he was cannon fodder. "Come on America," Ali taunted him. "Come on white America." As tennis great Arthur Ashe would observe, "No black athlete had ever spoken so disparagingly to another black athlete."

Ali let the punishment proceed for twelve merciless rounds. *Life* magazine, usually in Ali's corner, called the fight a "sickening spectacle." The *Times'* Robert Lipsyte, another supporter, compared Ali's style to that of a "little boy pulling off the wings of a butterfly piecemeal." As best I could, I tuned it all out and kept pulling for Ali.

THE ERNIE TERRELL fight in Houston in February 1967 proved a further test for all Ali fans. To strengthen his conscientious objector credentials, the Nation of Islam had begun to describe Ali as a minister and to assign him some ministerial functions at the Houston mosque. A few weeks after the fight, in fact, the *Muhammad Speaks* newspaper would announce that Ali had taken "complete charge" of the mosque while the regular minister was on leave.

Terrell had met Ali in Miami in the early days of his Muslim phase.

They were friends and sometime sparring partners. The laid-back Terrell tells of driving to Louisville with Ali and stopping along the way at a black college to allow Ali to spread his newfound message.

"If you see a Chinaman," Ali told the students who had gathered around him, "you know he comes from China. If you see a Frenchman, you know he comes from France." This was a song and dance that Ali would trot out for many years to come. It culminated with the punchline, "Now, tell me, what country is called 'Negro'?"

This audience proved less pliant than later ones. "I don't know," answered one student wryly, "but I never heard of a country called 'white folks' either." A frustrated Ali grabbed Terrell, and the two promptly hit the road again. Terrell stayed at the Clay house in Louisville and remained on friendly terms with Ali over the years.

When Terrell and Ali signed for the fight, the promoter expressed his wish that both would spend the last two weeks in Houston for promotional purposes. "It's all right with me if it's alright with Clay," Terrell said unthinkingly. Without meaning to, he triggered a reaction in Ali that turned uglier than Terrell could have anticipated. "My name's Muhammad Ali," the champion snapped, and he would drum that name right into him.

Ali was not the only one in a boastful mood that February night in Houston. The top dog of the Cleveland numbers racket held forth at ringside in high bombast. Despite a murder charge back in Ohio, his thirty-fifth arrest, Don King crowed openly that he would beat the rap. As a show of confidence, he bet a crony $3,000 that he would never spend a day in jail.

King had reason to be confident. In 1954, he had shot and killed a man who tried to rob one of his gambling joints. He finessed that one on a self-defense gambit. To say the least, this second murder charge looked more daunting. On a Cleveland sidewalk, in broad daylight, before a crowd of stunned onlookers, using his loaded .357 Magnum as weapon, King had smashed senseless a numbers client half his size.

"Don, I'll pay you the money," said Sam Garrett as he faded into uncon-sciousness. Always resourceful, King had invested $30,000 in an ad hoc eyewitness silence-buying program and figured he was home free.

King figured wrong. The two cops who stopped the beating saw King deliver one last vicious kick to his victim's head. His shoeprints on the man's jaw confirmed the cops' story. The jurors would convict King after only four hours of deliberation and leave him staring down the barrel of a life sentence. As cunning as he was, even King could not have imagined that just seven years later he would be in position to promote the most mythic of all Ali fights, the "Rumble in the Jungle."

That night in Houston, Ali beat Terrell almost as viciously as King beat Sam Garrett. In the early rounds, he fractured the bone under Terrell's left eye. Terrell claims Ali did it deliberately, using his thumb to push Terrell's eye down to the bone. "When the stakes are high," says Terrell, "I guess people do certain things." What no one denies is that the fight was brutal. From the eighth round on, Terrell was all but defense-less, and Ali taunted him without pity.

"What's my name, Uncle Tom?" Ali shouted. "What's my name?" The spectacle sickened even some of Ali's staunchest fans. "He has turned people's stomachs," wrote Milton Gross. "One almost yearns for the return of Frankie Carbo and his gangster ilk," reflected Jerry Izenberg. "If Ali was an evil person that's the kind of person he would have been all the time."

For the would-be conscientious objector, the fight was a public rela-tions disaster. "What kind of clergyman is he?" asked Jimmy Cannon of Ali. "He is against all that ministers pray for in their churches." Said Illinois Congressman Robert Michel from the floor of the House in a memorable *bon mot*, "Apparently Cassius will fight anyone but the Vietcong."

REBELLION IN NEWARK

Nineteen sixty-seven was the year Muhammad Ali confronted the nation with his principles," writes Hauser, "and those in power struck back with a vengeance."

By "those in power," Hauser refers specifically to the political hacks manning the various state athletic commissions. New York State's commission withdrew recognition of Ali one hour after Ali refused induction, and the other commissions followed suit. As Ali would learn, these commissions made it well nigh impossible for him to fight in the United States. "It was an outrage," remembers Howard Cosell, "an absolute disgrace."

As to "his principles," those would prove hard to nail down. Still, the U.S. government treated Ali as gingerly as a nun. In May of that year, a grand jury indicted him only because it had to. As it happened, Ramsey Clark, the most liberal attorney general in the nation's history—there is no close second—approved the trial. "The good thing about it," Clark tells Hauser, "is that there was power on both sides to shape and test the issues." Ali's financial power and popular appeal were to secure him unprecedented due process for a draft case.

Before the trial, Ali and his attorneys came very close to negotiating a compromise in which Ali could perform a role not unlike Joe Louis's in World War II. A Democrat administration had little stomach for a fight with a popular black champ in those volatile times. Its attorneys were eager to compromise. By most accounts, so was Ali. Mort Susman, who headed up the U.S. Attorney's Office for the Houston office, suspected that Ali was very close to accepting a deal, "but some of his advisors wanted to make a martyr out of him."

One of those advisors was Jeremiah Shabazz. "Nobody put pressure on Ali not to go into the Army," he says in something close to parody. "The Messenger might have counseled him regarding what to say and not to say, but the final decision was all his own."

That same Ali relative who described the Nation of Islam as the most bendable of all religions also wryly observed that "when they have got to choose between accounts receivable and the scriptures, they vote for accounts receivable every time." This was not necessarily true. In this instance, Herbert Muhammad, who wanted to keep Ali earning for both of them, lost out to his father, who had a deeper agenda.

In the month before the trial, Muhammad gave a rare and careful interview broadcast over the major radio networks. On the question of whether Ali was being mistreated because he was a Muslim, Muhammad replied, "It can't be anything else. Muhammad Ali is harassed to keep the other mentally sleeping so-called Negroes fast asleep to the fact that Islam is a refuge for the so-called Negroes in America." As Muhammad saw more clearly than his son, the Nation would profit more in the long run if Ali did go to prison.

By contrast, the last place the government wanted to put Ali was in the slammer. Ali admits that its attorneys offered him "all kinds of deals." "Trouble was," Kram reports, "that the Muslims insisted he never be in uniform and never be given a rank." These were demands to which the government could not yield.

In the likely hope of swaying his father, Herbert persuaded retired football great Jim Brown to hold a meeting of black athletes to help Ali sort through his options. Although they could not know what was going on behind the scenes, the athletes came away convinced that Ali was sincere in his faith. "I'm not going because it's against my religion," Ali told the group. At issue, though, was not Ali's sincerity. At issue was the sincerity of the "religion." On matters of war and peace, the Muslims were hardly the Amish. Few other faiths picture the world ending with an aeronautical assault on the white race.

Presenting the government's case at Ali's trial in June was Carl Walker, an African American and Ali fan, who handled all the selective service cases at the time. His very presence should have made Ali and his colleagues understand how grimly anachronistic was their nightmare view of America, but it obviously did not. The jury convicted Ali after twenty minutes of deliberation. The terms were so narrow that it had little option but to convict.

In the penalty phase, the government made the case that the Nation of Islam was "as much political as it is religious." At this point, Ali interrupted politely to say, "My religion is not political in any way." He may have actually believed that, but Elijah Muhammad surely knew better. To him, Ali was a veritable poster child of a political pawn. Despite a plea for leniency by the U.S. Attorney's Office, the judge handed down the maximum sentence of five years. The Messenger had to have been delighted.

That summer, I broke with Ali. It was not the draft resistance that pushed me away. Although I believed the war was just and still do, I was in no position to get high-minded. I had a student deferment at the time, one of the few in my neighborhood. In fact, I was one of only two males from my eighth-grade class of twenty-some to go directly to college. When I blew out my knee playing basketball in my freshman year of college, I had to drop out of ROTC and presumed that the injury would keep me out of the military altogether.

The sequence of events that severed my bond with Ali began in

Newark of all places on July 12. A rumored police killing of a cab driver started a series of scuffles and protests outside of Newark's Fourth Precinct. When broadcast on television, the fracas inspired more protest still, and the protest quickly devolved into riot.

That summer, I was nineteen years old and working at a camp for troubled New York City kids some forty miles from the city. The camp was co-ed, multiracial, and "progressive" in any number of interesting ways. For a young, self-identified Democrat eager to sample the perks of "the revolution" and not at all above its pretenses, the camp seemed a likely place to spend the summer.

When the riot broke out in Newark, my camp buddies and I watched the news on a kitchen TV. Armored vehicles were rolling out of the Roseville Avenue armory a block from where I had grown up. My family, I learned, was bunkered down in our new project. My uncle, a Newark cop, had been in the thick of it from the initial assault on the Fourth Precinct, when he and his fellow officers found themselves holding off an angry mob without helmets, shotguns, or useful riot gear. After a brief reprieve, my uncle would be called back the next day and would stay on duty for seventy-two hours straight. He thought he had seen the worst the world could offer in Korea, where he had been seriously wounded, but in Korea at least you knew who the enemy was.

As to the fate of my father's friends—policemen and firemen and rescue workers—that I did not know beyond what I could see. I was sure, however, that they wanted to be in this war zone no more than Ali wanted to be in Vietnam. They had their duty, however, and I was sure, too, they would do it, even if it meant endless shifts under the threat of sniper fire.

As I watched TV with the camp staff, radicalized urban blacks and preening suburban whites, I understood quickly and clearly that we saw events unfold through different eyes. Where I saw relatives and friends, they saw "pigs." They weren't shy about saying so. It was the first time I had heard that slur within striking distance, and it very nearly came to that. By the time the smoke had cleared, so had my illusions. For my progressive colleagues, however, this was pure opportunity, the Nation of Islam's "nightmare" manifesting itself in all its televised glory.

Within months of the riot, Tom Hayden and Vintage Books had elevated the event into *Rebellion in Newark*. Earlier in the decade, Hayden had drafted the Port Huron statement, the defining document of the New Left. The year before the riots, he and a pal had visited North Vietnam and written a sympathetic account about what they found there. Later, of course, Hayden would marry Jane Fonda and become very wealthy. The winds of change seemed to channel right through him.

In Newark, Hayden imagined a police state and decided this was the rare police state he did not admire. The Newark police, he writes, were the real purveyors of "intimidation, harassment, and violence." The two hundred and fifty black officers—nearly 20 percent of the force—were mere "tokens." That all the police, black and white, struggled and suffered and sometimes fell to preserve their own community mattered to Hayden not a whit.

"Few whites were killed," Hayden assures the reader. These included "only one policeman and one fireman," as if the word "only" offered some balm to the wives or children or friends of the dead. He scolds liberals and conservatives alike for thinking the riot "a form of lawless, mob behavior." No, he says, "A riot represents people making history." Hayden's glib history cost 26 lives and more than a 1,000 businesses, some 167 of them food stores, most of them never to return. From the New Left perspective, people making history was far more interesting than people buying groceries.

After the riots, I knew that if push ever came to shove, the New Left and I would man opposite sides of the barricades. I sensed, too, that Ali would be on their side. When he talked about "fighting for 22 million Americans," he may have counted Hayden among them, but he no longer counted me. He had new white friends now, and they would serve him better than my pals and I, at least in the short haul.

A MONTH LATER, in August 1967, Ali married the seventeen-year-old Belinda Boyd. A principled young Muslim male could not have imagined a more perfect wife. Like everyone else who knew Belinda, Ferdie Pacheco was enchanted.

"Under her Muslim-prescribed floor-length, flowing robes," he reports in near awe, "one could sense a strong, well-formed body. One got the sense of being in the presence of one of the world's great women, one of the world's great beauties." By the time Ali regained the championship seven years later, Belinda was wearing a "George Foreman" button. Ali would betray her and their four children more grievously than he had betrayed Malcolm X and far worse than he had betrayed me. To the shapers of his myth, however, none of it would matter.

BLACK REDNECKS AND WHITE LIBERALS

On October 3, 1968, theatergoers in New York first turned their lonely eyes to the hero of Howard Sackler's new play, *The Great White Hope*. The hero they saw was the revived and sanitized Jack Johnson. They liked what they saw.

From that day on to 2005, when Ken Burns aired his PBS documentary, *Unforgivable Blackness*, America's cultural elite has enjoyed its very own historic black boxing icon. A quick Google search shows thirty-nine thousand references to Jack Johnson, boxer, to Joe Louis's thirty-four thousand, this despite the fact that Louis reigned as champion twice as long as Johnson and thirty-five years more recently. The references are also more consistently positive for Johnson.

Burns, who has long milked the culture for its white guilt content, sees Johnson as "an embodiment of the African-American struggle to be truly free in this country—economically, socially, and politically." He commends him for having "absolutely refused to play by the rules set by the white establishment, or even those of the black community."

Like much of the multicultural canon into which it fits, the Johnson resurrection has a sharp, zero-sum quality about it—Johnson is OK, Joe

Louis is not. Johnson prospers at Louis's expense. Mike Marqusee argues that some unnamed "white people" have forced aspiring black boxers to choose between the two role models: Jack Johnson, the "bad nigger," and Joe Louis, the "Uncle Tom." This "polarity," he continues, has "haunted" the black fighters who followed Louis and Johnson.

Despite his intrinsically sweet and generous nature, Ali chose to play at being Johnson. It is no coincidence that 1967, the year Sackler finished *The Great White Hope*, was also the year that Ali refused the draft. Ali saw himself and was seen by others as the contemporary embodiment of Johnson. In 1969, he ran into James Earl Jones, the actor who played Johnson on Broadway. After mimicking a few of Johnson's lines, Ali told Jones, "You can see it's me. I'm Jack Johnson. Without the white women."

The Jack Johnson theatergoers saw on Broadway, however, was a "shadow of the real thing." So argues historian Randy Roberts in his largely sympathetic biography of the fighter, *Papa Jack: Jack Johnson and the Era of White Hopes*. The real Johnson was cut from a much rougher cloth.

In his presumed fight for freedom, Johnson lived a defiantly hedonistic life. "He did just as *he* pleased," writes Roberts. He married three white prostitutes, had affairs with scores of others, beat at least a few of them to the point of hospitalization, and "openly flaunted his heroic infidelity." He made a fortune and spent it recklessly. He paid bills when and if he felt like it. He drank excessively and drove like a madman before finally killing himself in a car crash at age sixty-eight.

Many black leaders of the era felt that his behavior seriously damaged race relations in America. Booker T. Washington was among them. He regretted Johnson's self-indulgence and his refusal to assume any kind of leadership role. He argued, rightly as it turned out, "that his personal rebellion would result in a more general racial oppression." Roberts also notes that Johnson lacked a "highly developed black consciousness" and that he "made a number of derogatory comments about blacks, particularly black women, throughout his life." His open preference for white women had to have stung the already vulnerable black female psyche.

Many of those who knew Johnson, like Louis and his trainer Chappy Blackburn, had come to resent Johnson's "supreme ego." Writing at a century's remove, Ken Burns does not. "He fought for freedom not just as a black man, but as an individual," argues Burns fatuously. Says Roberts, "It is only from a safe distance, intellectual as well as physical, that Jack Johnson could honestly be admired as a man."

The grievance narrative, of course, focuses not on the wrong done by its hero, but the wrong done to him. There was enough of that. Although Johnson did move prostitutes around the country, it is highly unlikely that the government would have prosecuted a white fighter for doing what Johnson did. And even if Johnson had been a saint, he still would have had to chase the championship, and he would have still caught hell for winning it from a white man.

That much said, Johnson emerged as the world champion of a major sport forty years before blacks were even allowed to play major league baseball. He made extraordinary sums of money. He was well-spoken, well-read, well-traveled, and he lived like a king. Johnson's success, like Ali's, derives from one shared, usually unmentioned variable: They each came from loving, middle-class homes. In fact, they were the only two major heavyweight champions of the twentieth century so blessed. Johnson's home in Galveston, Texas, says Roberts, was one of "solid respectability." Unlike so many of his peers, Johnson went to school where he learned to read and write. His middle-class skills and self-assurance allowed Johnson to negotiate a career that most other boxers, black or white, could not have.

Like Ali, Johnson chose to rebel. The model he adapted, however, was by no means distinctively black. In his tightly argued book, *Black Rednecks and White Liberals*, black economist Thomas Sowell makes the case that this model of prickly, bombastic, and often violent irresponsibility was part of a "centuries-old pattern among the whites in whose midst generations of blacks lived in the South." Sowell traces the roots of this culture back to the lawless border regions between England and Scotland, the so-called "Celtic Fringe," and the largely Scot-populated Ulster region of Ireland. Although white Southern "redneck" culture is not without its virtue, the anecdotal and even statistical evidence for its social pathology—crime, poverty, illegitimacy, illiteracy—is beyond dispute as its influence on the emerging culture of free blacks in the post-Civil War South.

As Sowell notes, intellectuals have been particularly prominent in turning this "black redneck culture" into a "sacrosanct symbol of racial identity." The critical question that he poses is whether the promotion of such a culture does blacks any earthly good, and the evidence strongly suggests that it does not.

Johnson may have turned his back on one model of "white" behavior, but he took on another, more destructive one. To advance race relations in America, he would not have had to grovel, to be a "Tom." He would have only had to check his rebellious instincts and live a decent life. By 1968, however, the very notion of a "decent life" had fallen into disfavor among the thinkers and writers and producers who shaped the culture. They preferred their black heroes anarchic, defiant, and hedonistic. These heroes, Sowell argues, became the "mascots" of white intellectuals, acting out their own imagined resistance to the larger culture. On Broadway, this model may work. On any other street in America, it wreaks havoc.

If Ali never quite convinced himself of his badness, he seems to have convinced Ken Burns and Mike Marqusee, both of whom turned eighteen the year Ali returned from exile to face Joe Frazier. Hauser that year was twenty-four. As they and their peers matured, and the more critical generation of sportswriters faded away, these young critics increasingly seized control of the cultural apparatus and began to impose their tortured perspective on sports.

"These were not boxing fans, they were seekers of the antihero," writes

Mark Kram, the one notable exception to the cultural left's monopoly on the Ali story. "What mattered was Ali's style, his desecrating mouth, his beautiful irrationality so like their music." As if to prove Kram's point, Marqusee wanders into a fifteen-page digression on pop singer Bob Dylan, justified by no more substantial a bond than this: "Both [Ali and Dylan] felt themselves part of a separate culture, wedded to values at odds with America's mainstream."

Ignoring boxing history, these young writers could imagine Joe Louis as an "Uncle Tom." They could presume, too, that the most prominent black boxers between the Louis and Ali eras were "haunted" by a repressive "polarity." And yet this presumed polarity does not even begin to explain characters as distinctive as Archie Moore and Sugar Ray Robinson. "Some styles are slick and creative and imaginative and innovative and others aren't," jazz great and ultimate hipster Miles Davis would write. "Sugar Ray Robinson's style was all of that." Davis, in fact, describes Robinson as "one of the few idols" he had ever had.

In 1968, Ali helped many young whites distance themselves from those implicitly racist "white people" who failed to appreciate people like himself and Jack Johnson. Unable to box while he appealed his draft conviction, he turned to the college lecture tour. Ali spoke at as many as two hundred campuses on any number of topics—black pride, integration, his legal battles.

"He was leading people into areas of thought and information that might not otherwise have been accessible to them," claims the *Times'* Robert Lipsyte. Among those otherwise inaccessible areas were the Nation of Islam's plans for a separate black homeland and Ali's own dread of the "little pale half-white green-eyed blond-headed Negroes" that allegedly resulted from intermarriage. For all that, the assassinations of Martin Luther King in April and Bobby Kennedy in June lent an urgency to the time and a seeming importance to Ali's mission.

Not surprisingly, the one subject on which Ali and the audience truly connected was Vietnam. In late January 1968, Ali had caught an unlikely break. During a declared ceasefire to mark the national Vietnamese holiday of Tet, more than eighty thousand North Vietnamese regulars and Viet Cong attacked six major cities, thirty-six provincial capitals, and twenty-three airfields and military bases throughout the South. At first blush, the attack proved disastrous for the North. The Viet Cong were never again able to muster a serious military threat. The fact they had also executed as many as five thousand civilians in the areas they controlled should have been a propaganda blow as well, but it was not.

By 1968, America's cultural elite had begun to doubt not itself exactly, and certainly not the Viet Cong, but the lesser mortals who comprised America. *The Great White Hope* was a symptom of the doubt. Among the doubters was newsman Walter Cronkite. On February 27, 1968, he gave his famous "we are mired in a stalemate" valedictory on the CBS news. "My God," Lyndon Johnson is reported to have said on hearing this, "if we've lost Cronkite, we've lost Middle America!" Cronkite's announcement made it respectable to protest the war in Vietnam.

College students, with their own futures on the line, embraced the protest now in vast numbers. They began to see Muhammad Ali not as a celebrity ambassador of an oddball cult but an as embodiment of all the virtues they attributed to themselves—wisdom, mercy, justice, and especially courage. Like Ali, like Jack Johnson before him, they too were rebels.

The Ali college crowds were "overwhelmingly white," civil rights activist Julian Bond remembers. "And Ali would have them in the palm of his hands." The students and their sympathetic elders would use the literary-media complex to convince themselves that they were right in their judgment. They would start by suppressing the truth about Tet and would end by suppressing most inconvenient truths about the war, about Ali, and indeed about themselves.

One such truth was the state of Ali's finances. On the lecture tour, he often talked about the financial sacrifices he had endured to protest the war. "We can eat on three dollars a day," he said of his family. "What do I need money for?" What he did not tell the students is that, by his own calculations, he was making an average of $5,000 a week as a speaker. In the way of perspective, the sticker price in 1968 for a four-door Chevy sedan was $2,800. The average home price was $26,000. Even with his legal fees, Ali was living large.

A still friendly Joe Frazier talked to Ali about his Philadelphia-area home during this period. "Clay told me the house he was now living in had a color TV in every room, twelve telephones, and a swimming pool." Bundini would tell George Plimpton that the house actually had twenty-two telephones, two of them and a large color TV next to a bathtub roomy enough to backstroke in. Twelve or twenty-two, Frazier was awed by just how luxurious martyrdom could be.

Frazier, now twenty-four, was quietly and cleverly doing well for himself. He chose to avoid the eight-man tournament that the World Boxing Association had arranged to find a new champion. Instead, he worked diligently on his skills, won all his fights, and waited patiently for a WBA champion to square off against.

The only fighting Ali was doing during this period was in court, and he wasn't winning. In May 1968, a Federal Appeals Court affirmed Ali's conviction. The Court held that Ali was a boxer, not a minister, and thus he did not merit a ministerial deferment. Although there were virtually no blacks on the Kentucky draft boards, the judgment made sufficient sense in itself that only the most edgy could have read it as racial conspiracy.

Ali, in fact, was not the first heavyweight champion to face draft problems. During World War I, Jack Dempsey worked in a shipyard but continued to box. After the war, a patriotic fervor swept the nation and caught Dempsey in its wake. "I was a faker and a slacker and I had to be crucified," Dempsey recalls in his autobiography. The antislacker mania led to an indictment for draft evasion by a federal grand jury, even though Dempsey was now champion. In June 1920, a jury found him not guilty.

Still the "slacker" accusation haunted Dempsey for the rest of his career. When he fought Frenchman Georges Carpentier in New Jersey a year later, the American crowd pulled for the French war hero Carpentier. To get out from under the weight of the charge, the middle-aged Dempsey served in World War II as director of the U.S. Coast Guard physical fitness program, and he later toured the Pacific theater as a morale officer. To his seeming good fortune, Ali chose a more sympathetic time to make his stand.

At about this time, George Plimpton helped organize a writers' committee to support Ali's quest for reinstatement by the various boxing commissions. Plimpton got it into his head that Howard Cosell could add real momentum to this movement if he signed on to the cause. He arranged a meeting at Cosell's ABC office in midtown Manhattan.

"Let me articulate my position," Cosell told Plimpton, sounding for all the world just like he did on TV. "I'd be shot, sitting right here in this armchair, by some crazed redneck sharpshooter, if I deigned to say that Muhammad Ali should be completely absolved and allowed to return to the ring." Cosell would later jump on board, but only when the once lonely cause had turned into a crowded bandwagon.

In August of this incredibly volatile year, the Democratic National Convention in Chicago dissolved into chaos. The old-line liberals and traditional Democrats eventually prevailed, but the moral victory went to the young and the restless. From that moment forward, they would drive the party and, increasingly, define the culture.

MUHAMMAD SPEAKS

In boxing, the most dangerous punches are the ones you don't see com-
ing. Adrift, and in exile, the champ had no way of anticipating the blow
Elijah Muhammad was about to send his way. In the April 4th issue of
Muhammad Speaks, the Messenger let his Nation know that Muhammad
Ali had been stripped of his "holy name." Said Muhammad with calcu-
lated malice, "We will call him Cassius Clay."

Ali had not intended to give offense. Howard Cosell had asked him
whether he would ever go back in the ring, and Ali had merely responded,
"Yea, if the money is right." It had slipped Ali's mind that prizefighting was
a "filthy temptation," one which deeply offended Muhammad, at least on
occasion. "Mr. Muhammad Ali has sporting blood," the Messenger
decreed. "Mr. Muhammad Ali desires to do that which the Holy Qur'an
teaches him against."

Since Muhammad wasn't about to come to the Greatest, the Greatest
went to Muhammad. Advisor Jeremiah Shabazz went along for the ride.
According to Shabazz, the Messenger told Ali that he had no use for a
fool "so weak as to go crawling on his hands and knees to the white man
for a little money." The Messenger had to teach Ali humility. Elijah

Muhammad biographer, Claude Clegg, compares Ali's ostracism to that of Malcolm X along a comparable fault line of "authority, generational issues, and jealousy." Says Clegg, "Arguably, the punishment was meant to be a reassertion of Muhammad's dominion over the Nation—a reminder to followers who had become a bit too enamored of Ali."

What had sparked Muhammad's resentment of Malcolm X was his popularity on campus. As Malcolm would tell Alex Haley, the university was one venue where the ill-educated Messenger felt "unequipped to speak." Like Malcolm, Ali touched many people on his campus tours who were otherwise beyond the Messenger's reach. This did not make Muhammad proud. It made him nervous.

The Messenger had, however, a much firmer grip on Ali than he had had on Malcolm. If Malcolm cried "foul" when squeezed, Ali cried "Uncle." "I made a fool of myself when I said that I'd return to boxing to pay my bills," Ali told a student soon after his suspension. "I'm glad [Muhammad] awakened me." Ali would not abandon Allah or the Messenger.

The timing of Ali's suspension was bad enough to be suspicious. Ali could hardly claim ministerial privilege from a religion that had disowned him. It is possible, even likely, that Muhammad wanted Ali to go to prison. Imprisoned, Ali would justify Muhammad's reactionary worldview and do wonders for the Nation's recruiting, all without threatening his power.

Nevertheless, Ali persisted in his appeals. By 1969, he had come to understand just how much of an icon he had become in the eyes of the left-leaning world. In his autobiography, he talks boyishly about the praise he has received from people like French intellectual Jean Paul Sartre and famed British philosopher Bertrand Russell. Russell's frequent letters gave Ali heart.

"The men who rule Washington will try to damage you in every way open to them," Russell wrote on one occasion. They would do so, he told Ali, because he was "a symbol of a whole people determined no longer to be butchered and debased with fear and oppression." Russell was proving himself a master of the grievance narrative, and Ali was all ears.

Since Russell didn't send checks with the letters, Ali agreed to "box" the forty-five-year-old Rocky Marciano in a simulated, computer-judged match. To prepare for the event, Marciano lost fifty pounds and donned a toupee that made even Howard Cosell's look sprightly. The two filmed seventy-five one-minute rounds over several days and waited for the computer and the film editors to recreate the fight sequence.

The summer that passed between filming and final product was among the most eventful in American history. On July 20, Apollo 11 landed on the moon, the first manned landing ever. On August 9, the Charles Manson family went on its murderous rampage in the canyons above Los Angeles. On August 15, nearly a half million young people gathered in a New York state cow pasture to celebrate their splendid, newly liberated selves.

The news that rocked my housing project that summer was the death of Mary Jo Kopechne. In Senator Ted Kennedy's account, he tried to rescue Mary Jo from his sinking car off the island of Chappaquiddick but failed despite his valiant efforts.

Just a year earlier, the death of his brother Bobby left just about everyone at the project, myself included, dismayed and disoriented. Almost to a person, those old enough had voted for his older brother for president. The behavior of his younger brother, however, had left everyone flat-out disgusted.

To protect his image as a happily married man, Kennedy had made his first seventeen phone calls to lawyers and press agents. Only when he and his cronies had finished crafting their heroic rescue saga did anyone think to call the police. A compliant media asked few questions. After the riots in 1967, the people in my world no longer trusted the media. After Chappaquiddick, they no longer trusted the Kennedys. They were beginning to feel as used and disposable as Mary Jo, and I could hardly blame them.

Not surprisingly, Hauser quotes Ted Kennedy on the subject of Muhammad Ali. Kennedy tells how his brother Bobby followed Ali's resistance to the war, "a commitment they shared." Kennedy then relates how Ali had given Ted a pair of autographed boxing gloves. "He said he hoped the gloves would help me in the fight to knock out injustice," says Kennedy without a hint of irony. The Newark response to this folderol would be, "Yea, right. Tell that to the Kopechnes." Mary Jo, not yet thirty, was their only child. She and her parents had once lived in our project.

Two news events far from home framed that memorable summer for Ali. On May 20, the Paris peace talks began, and soon after, President Richard Nixon announced the first troop withdrawals. From that moment on, America was fighting a rear guard action for which few were eager to volunteer. Three months later—the weekend of Woodstock in fact—I took my Army physical in downtown Newark. I had told my mother to prepare herself. If I passed, I was going. When I shared the news that I had in fact failed, my whole family was relieved. This was not World War II.

The second news event of note began to unfold on September 5, when Lieutenant William Calley was formally charged with premeditated murder for his role in the My Lai massacre of the previous year. When reports of this incident finally broke out into the public, the New Left gleefully ran with it.

My Lai represented for the left not a failing of human nature but the nightmare vision of American imperialism, an example of which antiwar activists had been seeking. Many were now pulling openly for American defeat, "Ho, Ho, Ho Chi Minh, the NLF is going to win." Ali, who strongly discouraged drugs and usually avoided revolutionary rhetoric, was beginning to seem downright moderate. And unlike most war protestors, Ali had at least put his money where his mouth was, a sacrifice that did not go unnoticed even among his critics. History was breaking his way.

Amidst the furor of that summer, few paid heed when a private plane crashed in a Newton, Iowa, cornfield. The date was August 31. Among the three victims was Rocky Marciano, who was traveling home for his forty-sixth birthday party the next day. The *Boston Herald Traveler* rightly eulogized Marciano as "a man whose life style was the legendary American Dream come true." For Marciano and his parents, the paper continued, "The American Dream was real and true and not something to be ridiculed and denigrated."

"Ridiculed and denigrated?" What an extraordinary caveat. Just a few years earlier, the *Herald Traveler* would not have thought to defend the American dream. It would not have had to. No one of consequence was attacking it. Martin Luther King was ennobling it. Ordinary people were living it. In the years since King's "I have a dream" speech, the standard of living had only increased, and the dream had extended its embrace. Like Joe Louis before him, Marciano had celebrated the dream and embodied the shared ethos that allowed America to cohere. In 1969, Muhammad Ali did neither. Partly in recognition of that, a tradition-minded computer allowed Marciano to knock out Ali after thirteen simulated rounds.

If Ali did not honor the dream, the dream was honoring him. After being exiled from the Nation of Islam, his fortunes improved dramatically. According to Howard Bingham, he negotiated a much better speaking deal without the Nation's help. He received $900,000 for lending his name to a new franchise called "Champburgers," and Random House advanced him an extraordinary $200,000 for the autobiography that would emerge as *The Greatest*. How deeply the Nation had been picking his pockets remains a subject of some speculation, but financially, he was hugely better off without its help. This did not go unnoticed.

THE SECOND COMING

When George Plimpton asked Muhammad Ali why he did not sue the boxing commissions that had taken away his title, he drawled, "Aw, they did what they thought was right."

During the years of his exile, Ali distinguished himself by two virtues in short supply among his own supporters—a lack of self-pity and his instinctive tolerance. That tolerance was tested on February 16, 1970, when Joe Frazier knocked out WBA tournament-winner and former Ali sparring partner, Jimmy Ellis, to unify the title. After years of holding firm, *Ring* magazine, the industry's Bible, finally recognized a heavyweight champion other than Ali.

Still, publicly at least, Ali held no grudges. "Joe's got four or five children to feed," he told an interviewer. "He's worked in a meat-packing house all his life and deserves a break. He would have fought me if he had the chance."

In August 1970, Ali arranged a rather remarkable ride with Frazier from Philadelphia to New York, just the two of them, the two undefeated heavyweight champions, taunting each other, talking trash, and catcalling to women on the streets of Manhattan. Ali flicked on the tape recorder for the sake of his autobiography and captured the conversation for history.

Frazier proved as straightforward as he was in the ring. He tells Ali that he "was some kind of inspiration." Just the thought of Ali made him train all the harder. "I had to get to you," Frazier says. "Now here I am. They should allow you to fight, you know what I mean. Taking your license away like they did wasn't justice."

Frazier also did a good job of countering Ali's future alibi. "I don't want no excuses," Frazier tells him. "Ain't nothing wrong with you. Not a thing. You just had a little rest; that's good for you."

Ali, however, was a man permanently on stage. He played to the tape recorder like he did to the camera. He patronized Frazier throughout the conversation subtly enough that Frazier missed much of it. At one juncture, he compliments Frazier for avoiding politics, "Why get caught in something you ain't in?" Then Ali explains why he had to do otherwise. "I saw Negroes getting lynched, and I saw Negroes off with white women when they got rich or famous, and poor black people going hungry."

Frazier could not begin to suspect just how deftly Ali was establishing what marketers call their "positions." To this point, Frazier had not said a bad word about Ali in public. As a proud Baptist, he had no use for the Muslims. And as a proud American, he thought this "a great country worth defending." Still, he generally liked Ali and kept his reservations to himself. When he dropped Ali off on West 52nd Street that August day, he had no idea how ugly things would get and how quickly things would get ugly.

NOR DID THE young George Foreman have any idea of Ali's contempt for him. It's just as well. Ali's remarks would have stung the insecure young boxer. Foreman had turned twenty-one the past January and idolized Ali. Fans remembered Foreman as the boxer who had pulled out a small American flag and waved it as he walked around the ring after beating a Russian to win the heavyweight championship at the 1968 Olympics. In 1968, this was a provocative gesture. Activists had tried to get black American athletes to boycott the Olympics. A few, like Kareem Abdul-Jabbar, actually did. Others, like sprinters John Carlos and Tommy Smith, gave black power salutes on the victory stand.

Foreman wrote off their gestures to the exuberance of the college-educated. "Maybe I was ignorant," Foreman says of his own reaction to the boycott, "but even at its most desperate and violent, the world I'd grown up in hadn't made me mad. I'd never, not for a day, felt inferior to anything or anyone." And just as Ali felt proud and patriotic after winning the gold eight years earlier, so did Foreman.

By 1968, to some people at least, patriotism seemed as delusional as the American dream. Ali was among the more prominent of those people. "George Foreman carried that flag 'cause he was a brainwashed black super patriot," Ali complained to Frazier. "But John Carlos and Tommy Smith, they held up their arms in the sky; their image will go down in history."

ALI WORRIED LESS about Foreman or Frazier in 1970 than he did his main opponent, the various boxing commissions. Although his draft conviction was under appeal, the states still refused to let him fight. As it happened, the first state to buckle was Georgia. This turn of events took much of America by surprise. At the time, Georgia was best known for its governor, the irrepressible Lester Maddox. Maddox had first come to public attention six years earlier when he and his ax-handle-wielding supporters turned a group of civil rights protestors away from his chicken restaurant. Soon afterward, he shut the restaurant down rather than integrate it as now required by law.

In 1967, with an ax handle for a logo, he ran for governor. In the open primary, many Republicans crossed over to vote for the Democrat Maddox, thinking he would be easy to beat in the general. In the general election, however, write-in candidates denied either party a majority. The election then reverted to the solidly Democrat legislature, which preferred a madman to a Republican, and that's what it got.

Georgia may have had a segregationist for a governor, but it had no state athletic commission. Ali's promoters saw the state as vulnerable. Besides, the South was changing almost moment by moment. A black state senator named Leroy Johnson had already emerged as a major player in Atlanta politics. He controlled enough votes to coerce the Jewish mayor of Atlanta, Sam Massell, to let the fight proceed. "Johnson cut himself a piece of the promotion," Ali publicist Harold Conrad admits, "and after that visited Massell to call in his chits." Johnson was also powerful enough to influence Maddox. "We're all entitled to our mistakes," said Maddox of Ali. "I see nothing wrong with him fighting here."

After hearing from his irate constituents, Maddox started to gripe about the fight to the point of calling the slotted fight date "a day of mourning." This was largely for show. The business community in this "city too busy to hate" needed some high voltage event to counter Maddox's reactionary image. As a businessman himself, Maddox could, if not sympathize, at least understand. Although he may be overgenerous in his praise, Angelo Dundee gives the credit to Maddox for making the event happen. The movie, *The Greatest,* does the same. "All it took was politics and money and three years of trying until we worked things out in Georgia," says Conrad.

The fight was set for October 26. The opponent was to be the always-tough Jerry Quarry. Were Quarry to win, he would be thought of as "the greatest White Hope in the history of boxing." Or so Ali believed. "I'm not fighting one man," said Ali in the days before the match, "I'm fighting a lot of men, showing them there is one man they couldn't conquer." Ali's white supporters—and their ranks continued to swell—prided themselves on rooting against Quarry. Unlike their less enlightened brethren, they had long since transcended the need for a great white hope.

If any fight was ripe for rhetorical overkill, it was this one. Yet Ali took it easy on Quarry. In part, it had to do with Quarry's background. Although three years younger than Ali, Quarry and his four brothers lived an early life more like *The Grapes of Wrath* than *Father Knows Best.*

"The first home I had was a tent in Utah," Quarry recalled before accumulated brain damage robbed him of his ability to recall much of anything. "Then we moved to California to work the fields." His father obviously didn't expect much more. He had the words "hard" and "luck" tattooed on either hand.

In his pre-boxing days, Quarry had been making $99 a week changing tires on Greyhound buses. Hard times had stripped him of sentiment. "I wasn't fighting for race, creed, or color that night," he claimed. "I was fighting for money." Quarry was not the only white boxer Ali refrained from abusing. In truth, he spared them all. The deep, soul-wounding abuse he reserved for his fellow blacks. "One of the many paradoxes about Ali," affirms historian Randy Roberts, "is that he embraced an ideology that disparaged white people; yet he was never cruel to white people, only blacks."

Two hugely colorful criminal incidents would define the fight environment, one real and one imagined. The imagined one would be celebrated by the more adventurous of the Ali mythmakers. The real one would be slighted, perhaps even suppressed, by just about everyone.

IN THE RUN up to the fight, Ali and his insiders camped out at Senator Johnson's rural Georgia retreat. One night, a shadowy group of racist gunmen attacked the house. "Get out of Georgia, you black son of a bitch," the gunmen yelled at Ali and his entourage after firing at the house. So, at least, Team Ali claims in the 1977 movie *The Greatest*. In the book, Bundini grabs a pistol and comes out the front door firing. "Here we are!" he yells. "Come on you sonofabitches," and the white men flee cravenly into the night.

The more responsible Ali biographers ignore this story. George Plimpton, who visited the house at the time, did not even know there was a story to ignore. Thomas Hauser, who knows the story exists, glosses over it. By the time Ali gets around to dictating his memoirs in 2004, the story had finally come back to earth. "I started receiving death threats and crank calls," he now recollects more credibly, "saying that I would be killed if I didn't get out of Georgia immediately." Mike Marqusee, among others who stick to the original story, claims that "Ali-haters" fired gunshots outside the house.

In the thirty years between autobiography and memoir, this fabrication thrived unchallenged. Thanks to the book and movie, the Nation of Islam reached literally millions of Ali fans that they could not have reached otherwise. Both media reinforced the bogus Muslim notion that nothing had changed, or in Ali's words, "The black man's condition is the same." The more innocent among the Ali fans came away believing that notion. If bands of evil white men could still routinely prey on innocent blacks, even famous ones like Ali, of course nothing had changed.

This message, repeated often and almost everywhere, locked many of Ali's black fans into paranoia and white fans into a paralyzing guilt. About the only scholars bold enough to confront this corrosive hokum have been African Americans like Gerald Early. Most white scholars and reporters either ignore the distortions or excuse them.

Such literary falsehoods had real life consequences. They shifted black attention away from actual dangers to imagined ones. By 1970, the physical threat to black men in America came not from whites, but from other black men. Although Ali is not to blame, the great surge in American homicide rates almost perfectly coincided with his public career. The homicide rate in 1960 was 4.7 per 100,000 people. By 1980, it had more than doubled to 10.7 per 100,000, the highest rate before or since.

This surge in violent crime hit black communities like a nasty left hook. By 1980, blacks were six to seven times more likely than whites to be murdered. They were nearly twenty times more likely to be killed by a black person than a white. And yet Ali and his fellow Muslims were diverting black attention to the South's vestigial killer crackers. As is often true of generals, Nation of Islam leaders were fighting the last war, but in this case, they were doing so knowingly. Ali's white supporters proved useful allies.

WITH THE EXCEPTION of George Plimpton, no other significant scholar or reporter covered the one crime story that really did spin out of the Ali-Quarry fight. And a hell of a story it is. Had the thieves gotten away clean, this might have provided the basis for a fun Hollywood heist movie. But life imitates art only in films like *The Greatest*.

Given the allure of the Ali return, the "Second Coming" as he immodestly called it, the fight proved to be a powerful draw throughout black America. An impressive array of black politicos, entrepreneurs, entertainers, and athletes descended on Atlanta for the fight. "That night," says activist Julian Bond, "Atlanta came into its own as the black political capital of America." Like all big-time bouts, however, this fight also attracted some of the heavy-hitters from the underworld.

As Plimpton reports, a hustler named William Gordon threw a birthday party for a Harlem character named Tobe at his posh Atlanta house. The party was essentially a front for a sophisticated gambling operation. The pair had set the game up to entertain the high-rollers who had come in from New York City and elsewhere. The night before the fight, the operation went as planned, and a good deal of money changed hands. The night after the fight promised to be more festive still and even more lucrative.

Bundini set the tone for the fight by shouting over and over, "Jack Johnson's heah. Ghost in the house." In his return from exile, Ali was feeling particular kinship with Johnson, who had himself been exiled. After his return from Europe, however, Johnson had lost to the great white hope of the moment, Jess Willard. Ali fared considerably better. He opened up a huge cut over Quarry's eye in the third round, and the referee stopped the fight at round's end.

The outcome of the fight put the sporting men and their women friends in an expansive mood. They headed out to Gordon's house on this second night in high spirits and sensed nothing amiss until they felt the sawed-off shotguns against the back of their heads. Seven hooded men were brandishing them, but these weren't Klansmen. These were gangsters, as black as the guests. They rudely ushered their victims to the basement, stripped them to their skivvies, separated from their valuables, and forced them to the floor.

As the night wore on, the guests piled up. "About a hundred people were packed down in there, some of them lying on top of one another because there wasn't room," writes Plimpton, avoiding the obvious historical reference this imagery suggests. When the gunmen ran out of floor space, they gathered up at least four large pillowcases stuffed with plunder and split.

Almost none of the guests cooperated with the local police. The baddest of them returned to New York with vengeance on their minds. The gunmen had messed with some powerful people. Those people were not about to let this humiliation go unpunished. Shortly after the holdup, an anonymous source called up Atlanta police headquarters. The caller told the lieutenant working the case that he and his cronies were about to spare them a lot of messy detective work. In fact, they had just brought three men "sitting in a Cadillac on Fulton Street in the Bronx" to summary justice.

As Plimpton learned, six of the seven Atlanta gunmen would themselves be gunned down. The seventh escaped death only by executing the sixth, his partner and ringleader, Harlem mobster Cadillac Dick Wheeler. Although at the time Ali aspired to be as "bad" as he imagined Jack Johnson to be, all he had in common with the truly bad Cadillac Wheeler was a Cadillac.

ALL IN THE FAMILY

On December 30, 1970, the deal was signed for what by any objective standards loomed as the fight of the century. Twenty years earlier, sportswriters had overwhelmingly chosen the wild 1923 brawl between Jack Dempsey and the "Wild Bull of the Pampas," Louis Firpo, as the fight of the first half of the century. After having been knocked clear out of the ring in the first round, Dempsey came back to knock Firpo out in the second. By any variable other than the number of knockdowns, that fight would not compare with the drama of the Ali-Frazier fight set for New York's Madison Square Garden on March 8.

ON THE SAME day that the Ali-Frazier deal was signed, an undercover narcotics agent paid a visit on Charles "Sonny" Liston at his luxurious Las Vegas home. He was the last person to see Liston alive. When Liston's wife, Geraldine, returned to the house a week later, she found Sonny long dead, most probably from a heroin overdose. The raised welts on Sonny's back were vestiges of his father's whippings.

Like every other major moment in Liston's troubled time on earth, even his death was shrouded in controversy. More than a few serious people have speculated that he was murdered. This mystery, like the others, went to the grave with Sonny as well. The bronze plaque on his tombstone listed his name and the inscription, "A MAN." Only one of his twenty-something siblings was there to see it.

ALI HAD BEATEN Quarry in Atlanta in October 1970 and the current Wild Bull of the Pampas, Oscar Bonavena, in New York in December. He was ready for Frazier, and Frazier was ready for him. Both were unde-feated. They were inarguably the two best heavyweights since Marciano and Louis, quite possibly the best two of all time. And they were bring-ing to the fight an unprecedented degree of passion.

Ali had launched the war of words. He was relentless and brutal. All that could be said in his defense is that he did not know that his words would have such consequence. By January 1971, Ali had more media power than he suspected. With the winding down of the war and the violent protests it spawned, America's rebels, young and old, had stom-ach only for proxy battles. Ali became their symbolic warrior.

Ferdie Pacheco completely misunderstood the media dynamics. Like many of Ali's faithful, he saw Ali's attacks on Frazier as part of an "act," an attempt to build box office. "For one fight," Pacheco observes, "Joe Frazier became white, the public made him the good guy, the white guy." What Frazier understood better than Pacheco, however, was that the "good guy" in this drama was no longer "the white guy." The white people that mattered, the ones who controlled the switches and toggles of the broadcast media, colored Frazier white at the prodding of Ali, and they did this to insult Frazier. As Ali friend Jim Brown accu-rately observes, the post-exile Ali had become "part of the establish-ment."

In a divided nation, Ali had assigned an unlikely role to Frazier, that of traitor to his race and titular leader of the forces of reaction. With his greater rhetorical skills and his access to an increasingly friendly broad-cast media, Ali painted Frazier into a corner. "Anybody black who thinks

Frazier can whup me is an Uncle Tom," said Ali at the time. "Everybody who's black wants me to keep on winning."

The black media piled on. *Jet* magazine described Frazier as an "unheralded white-created champion." Even more telling was the slight delivered by future *Today Show* host Bryant Gumbel, then writing for *Black Sport*. Gumbel asked in his headline, "Is Joe Frazier a White Champion in a Black Skin?"

For the record, the "French Creoles" Web site proudly boasts of Gumbel's background: his judge father, his middle-class upbringing in the neighborhoods around the University of Chicago, his Catholic schooling, and his graduation from Bates College in Maine, where he sidestepped the civil rights battles then raging to concentrate on sports.

As Gumbel admits, he identified at least as much with Ali as a draft resister as he did with Ali as the symbol of black pride. "In every sense of the word," says Gumbel, "Ali was heroic." In retrospect, at least, Gumbel is savvy enough to recognize that Ali had become a "political and generational litmus test."

Moved to anger by the media and Ali, the hardcore faithful threatened Frazier and his family by mail and phone. The police put a watch on Frazier, his wife, and his children. History had proven that Ali's Muslim colleagues were capable of killing.

Even in Philadelphia, the black community turned against the imagined race-traitor, Frazier. Schoolmates teased his son, Marvis, that his father was an Uncle Tom. "Young blacks bought the whole hog," writes the hard-hitting Kram, "not knowing or caring that the Muslims had [Ali] in a choke collar and leash, taking no notice that he had betrayed another hero of large appeal, Malcolm X."

The taunting of his children cut deepest of all. "[Ali] set out to cut me down, and hurt me," writes Frazier in his autobiography, "the only way he knew how—with his lying, jiving mouth." The irony, of course, is that in almost every meaningful way, Joe Frazier led a "blacker" life than Ali. Most obviously, Frazier was conspicuously darker. He had proud Gullah roots, a black manager and trainer, and an integrated management team.

"I grew up like the black man—he didn't," Frazier would tell *Sports Illustrated's* William Nack. "I cooked the liquor. I cut the wood. I worked the farm. I lived in the ghetto. Yes, I tommed; when he asked me to help him get a license, I tommed for him. For him!" The irony stung. "He had a white man in the corner and those rich plantation people to fund him," Frazier writes bitterly of Ali. "A white lawyer kept him out of jail. And he's going to Uncle Tom me?"

Ali and his supporters abused the people who pulled for Joe Frazier even more than they abused Frazier himself. Fight manager and former sports editor Dave Wolf watched Ali on TV one night with Frazier. "The only people rooting for Joe Frazier," he remembers Ali saying, "are white people in suits, Alabama sheriffs, and members of the Ku Klux Klan." Enraged, Frazier smashed his fist mutely into his hand as he watched. Says Wolf, "It was cruel. That's all."

Wolf's memory on this score is accurate. The image of Frazier fans has not appreciated much over time. "The people who wanted [Frazier] to beat Ali," writes Marqusee in 1999, "were the die-hard racists, the love-it-or-leave-it brigade, the people who resented everything Ali stood for." A more reflective Bryant Gumbel would tell Hauser twenty years later, "Joe Frazier became the symbol of our oppressors."

ON JANUARY 12, 1971, two months before the Ali-Frazier fight, producers Norman Lear and Bud Yorkin premiered a breakthrough TV series whose principal character, Archie Bunker, incarnated all the resentments that Marqusee describes. A risky mid-season replacement, *All in The Family* would go on to enjoy enormous success. It held the number one Nielsen ranking for five consecutive seasons, and a top ten spot for eight.

Like most successful propaganda, the show worked by seducing its viewers, not slamming them. Although "a bigot," as Yorkin readily admitted, Bunker was not "a guy who would go out and burn a cross."

This distinction allowed the audience to enjoy Archie Bunker despite his biases. Many in the audience, in fact, identified with him and pulled for him, the latter a guilty pleasure. My mother certainly did.

Like my mother, Archie Bunker faced the whole range of urban problems without voice or power. Unlike my mother, however, Archie lived in a world where the problems were illusory—or at least were made to appear that way. He was not able to address them, as one TV critic accurately observed, because "the root of the problem is himself." The breakdown of the family, the dramatic surge in crime, the collapse of whole communities, the violent anarchy in inner cities and on college campuses—these were outpourings of Archie's narrow imagination. His creators had rendered him foolish, loveable perhaps, but a fool nonetheless.

"*All in the Family* set out to present an essentially liberal viewpoint," writes Donna McCrohan in her appreciative book-length study of the show, "with a conservative character who is generally wrong and a liberal character who is generally right in their perceptions." In 1971—before cable TV, talk radio, and the Internet—a select few people decided just who was right and who was wrong on any number of issues, boxing included. If they saw themselves reflected in Ali's image, they saw the Frazier fans reflected in Archie Bunker's.

TERRIBLE, TERRIBLE NIGHT

When Joe Frazier left Philadelphia for New York a few days before the fight, five armed detectives escorted him. That is how seriously they took the threats on his life. He and Yank Durham had no sooner checked into their hotel than a bomb threat forced them out. Ali stayed at Madison Square Garden to avoid the brouhaha that would have accompanied any move by him and his massive entourage across town. When Ali made it to his dressing room before the fight, the movie star Burt Lancaster was there to encourage him and shoot a documentary. Bundini kept the atmosphere charged and celebratory. The mood in Frazier's dressing room was much more sober. His manager, two trainers, and a Philly cop doubling as bodyguard quietly went through the prefight preparations. Frazier was all business.

Ali entered the sold-out Garden first. Frazier followed. Mark Kram describes the crowd reaction as a "sonic blast of sound." "The roar was inhuman," confirms Ferdie Pacheco. "It was a primal scream of anticipation. I've never heard such a sound."

The sound shook us to our toes in Gary and stirred the souls of millions more in Indy and Philly and Chicago and Camden and a hundred other burgs in the boxing archipelago. In Ohio's Marion Correctional Institution, Don King listened on his radio. This was the last fight he would have to listen to inside. He had somehow gotten to the judge, and the judge arbitrarily cut his sentence from life to four years, outraging every cop and prosecutor in greater Cleveland. Years later, King would rope Ali into campaigning for this same judge when he ran for the court of appeals.

If Don King could not be at "the Fight," everyone else of note was—Elvis, the Beatles, Ed Sullivan, Diana Ross, Bing Crosby, Ted Kennedy, Count Basie, Hubert Humphrey, Aretha Franklin, Salvador Dali. The great fighters of the past showed up as well—Joe Louis, Sugar Ray Robinson, Jim Braddock, Gene Tunney, Jack Dempsey. Frazier ignored them all. "My focus," he recounts, "was on the jiveass sucker in red velvet trunks."

Niagaras of printers' ink have been spilled on Ali's gifts as a boxer. Even the skeptical Kram gives him his due. "Ali was physical art," admits Kram. He "belonged alone in a museum of his own." Frazier meanwhile had perfected his art in a slaughterhouse. The only museum he knew was the one whose steps he climbed on his morning runs. He compensated for his lack of aesthetics by pure will.

No one in Ali's camp that night, Ali included, had ever seen a fighter more determined than Joe Frazier. Frazier gave up ten pounds in weight, four inches in height, and nine inches in reach. To win, he was going to have to penetrate Ali's long-range defenses. To penetrate, he was going to have to take some serious hits. To survive those hits, he was going to have to bob and weave from the waist, do it repeatedly, and do it all night, an exertion of nearly inhuman persistence and energy.

In the first four rounds, Ali tried to inflict enough hurt on the dogged Frazier to knock the drive out of him, if not knock him out altogether. Frazier took his lumps, literally, and kept on coming. "Visions of King Kong atop the Empire State building deflecting the bullets of the attacking biplanes raced through my mind," remembers Pacheco. Ali was winning the rounds but losing the fight.

In round five, Frazier, still hammering, forced Ali off his toes and into the ropes where he set up shop. "Frazier falls in six," Ali had promised before the fight. Frazier would have none of it. Frazier shot out of his stool at the start of the sixth, shouting, "C'mon, sucker. This is the round. Let's go." In rounds seven and eight, as a form of psychological warfare, Ali started mocking Frazier and playing to the crowd.

"Don't you know I'm God," Ali yelled at Frazier to discourage him.

"God, you in the wrong place tonight," Frazier shot back. "I'm kicking ass and taking names."

In the ninth, Ali let it fly. Students of the sweet science consider it perhaps the most dazzling one-round exhibit they have ever seen. "Frazier's face was falling apart," remembers Pacheco. His resolve, however, was indestructible. If that kind of round could not plunge Frazier "into a well of despair," asks Kram, "what in heaven or hell would— point-blank fire from a gun muzzle?" Ali, who gives Frazier his due in the recounting of this fight, remembers thinking, "Now I know he'll die before he quits."

Pacheco judged Ali the winner of the ten-round fight. The problem for Ali was that this one had to go fifteen. Frazier would not stop. "Hit me, I hit you," Frazier muttered, "I don't give a damn. I come to destroy you, Clay."

The fight turned around in the eleventh. The Ali camp called it the "Gruesome Eleventh." Frazier caught Ali with a wicked, crooked-arm left hook early in the round and sent him staggering to the ropes. "Ali's legs shake," commented Torres from ringside. "He was tagged. That was to the button." Ali survived the round but lost all momentum. By the start of the fifteenth, more people at the Garden were chanting "Joe . . . Joe . . . Joe" than "Ali . . . Ali . . . Ali." "I'd proven I was no fodder for no Cassius Clay fairy tale," remembers Frazier, who understood better than anyone how the Ali myth was being spun.

"The hell of the previous fourteen rounds was meaningless," Pacheco observes. As most saw it, including my friends and I in Gary, the fight hung on the fifteenth. Frazier left nothing to doubt. He cleared the ground with both feet on a looping left hook that caught Ali flush on the right side of his face. "Boom," says Frazier with deadly glee, "and there it was—Mr. Him on his butt, his legs kicking up into the air—the very picture of a beaten man."

In Gary, we watched that knockdown on the large screen from the top of the aisle near the exit. Ali somehow staggered to his feet, his jaw now swollen to twice its size, and stayed upright until the bell. Even Frazier admits that Ali "showed big heart." Big heart or not, no one in Gary doubted the outcome. One angry black man stormed by us at the exit, the depth of his affection for Ali no thicker than his wallet. "Muhammad Ali, my ass," he growled. "That's Cassius Clay."

The decision was unanimous. Frazier raised his hands in victory, thanked the Lord, and with a bloody mouth sneered at Ali, "I kicked your ass." Referee Arthur Mercante thought it the most vicious fight he had ever seen. Mark Kram calls it the "most skillful." And by all accounts, it was the most dramatic. "I was twenty-seven years old, and there would never be another night like it in my life," remembers Frazier. He spent the next three weeks in the hospital.

A more just world would have celebrated Frazier as the "Cinderella Man" of his era: the twelfth child of a rural Gullah family, who hightailed it out of the South on his own at age fifteen, developed his superior strength hauling carcasses in a slaughterhouse, and prevailed over a more privileged, more popular, more physically gifted opponent through an iron display of will not seen before or since.

From the beginning, however, careful observers knew that the story wasn't going to play out that way. "Joe's such a decent guy," veteran black trainer Eddie Futch said of Frazier before the fight, "but when he beats [Ali], Joe is going to go down as one of the most unpopular black champions of all time." Futch was right as rain.

By 1971, Ali held sway over the young people who were quietly seizing the media. Bryant Gumbel was one of them. "It was a terrible, terrible night," Gumbel says of that first Ali-Frazier fight. "I'll never forget it as long as I live."

Gumbel admits that he and his peers felt like "the chosen ones," the ones who had the unique skinny on the way the world turned. What he failed to see at the time was just how influential the chosen ones had already become, and how much more influential they would become in the future. As time passed, they would sing of this fight as just one more obstacle on Ali's heroic road back to the title. And as to Joe Frazier, they would remember him, when they bothered, as roadkill along the way.

Although instinctively gracious in defeat, Ali soon yielded to the dictates of his Muslim puppeteers and began to spin the saga of his loss in politically useful terms. On the Saturday after the fight, Ali told Howard Cosell on *Wide World of Sports* that he was the real winner of the fight. "He was declared the loser," Cosell recalls him saying, "only because of his religion and his attitude toward the draft."

Ali repeated this theme over the weeks and months that followed and started calling himself "The People's Champ." His supporters obliged by picking up the theme and merchandising it. Not content to strip Frazier of his authenticity as a black man, the Ali camp now tried to strip him of his authenticity as champion.

THREE MONTHS AFTER the Frazier fight, Ali prevailed in a fight of even greater consequence, the *United States v. Cassius Marcellus Clay*. On June 28, 1971, the United States Supreme Court reversed Ali's conviction for draft evasion on an 8–0 vote. Most casual accounts of this seemingly unanimous reversal cite it as proof that Ali was "right" all along, a word that pops up with disturbing frequency. Howard Cosell, for instance, would recall the decision as proof of the old adage that "what is popular is not always right; what is right is not always popular." In fact, it proved nothing save that the Supreme Court knew a political hot potato when it saw one.

To qualify for conscientious objector status, Ali had to meet three conditions. The first was that he opposed war in any form. The second was that he opposed war on religious grounds. And the third was that he was sincere. No one doubted his sincerity, however incoherent. The religious status of the Nation of Islam was dubious, but the government attorneys conceded this point. They could afford to. Ali transparently failed to meet the first criterion. Under oath, five years earlier, he had testified that he "could not participate in wars on the side of nonbelievers." Like Elijah Muhammad, he had no objection to war that served a higher purpose. Indeed, Muhammad had cheered on "Allah's Asiatic Army" as it bombed Pearl Harbor and slaughtered innocents up and down the Pacific rim.

On its first pass, with Justice Thurgood Marshall recusing himself, the other eight judges on this liberal court—they would all but outlaw capital punishment and condone abortion within the next year and a half—voted 5–3 to uphold Ali's conviction. For largely emotional reasons, Justice Harlan reversed and threw the vote into a 4–4 tie. This was still not enough to overturn the lower court decision.

Justice Potter Stewart then convinced his fellow judges of the political consequences of jailing a popular black icon, especially given their lack of unanimity. He then contrived a technicality that would exempt Ali but not other Muslims. His fellow judges played along. And the Ali star shone brighter than ever. In 1971, if your name was Muhammad Ali, that's how easy it all was to be "right all along," and it was only going to get easier.

SEED OF THE HYPOCRITE

On January 17, 1973, Muhammad Ali's thirty-first birthday, Lieutenant John 38X Clark of the Nation of Islam's Philadelphia mosque called his teammates together. "Bring your shoes," he told them. Once assembled, the group drove in two cars to nearby Washington D.C. As Clark soon discovered, he had mistimed the project at hand. He and his cronies found it nearly impossible to get a hotel room. Republicans were swarming all over the capital. In just three days, they would celebrate the second inauguration of Richard Nixon.

TO BE SURE, not all of America was quite as enthusiastic. The radicalized left in the Democratic Party had prevailed over the moderate liberals and nominated their candidate for president, George McGovern. Most of those who had protested the war supported McGovern, and those who supported McGovern embraced Ali. Despite their growing influence, however, they were each still allowed only one vote, and McGovern tanked. He carried but one state, Massachusetts.

The magnitude of McGovern's loss shocked this new cultural establishment. Bryant Gumbel compared his despair over Nixon's "crushing mandate" to the way he felt when Frazier beat Ali. He was not alone in his biases. Enough of his media peers shared them to lull *New Yorker* film critic Pauline Kael into her wondrously myopic comment on the McGovern drubbing, "How can that be? No one I know voted for Nixon."

In the meantime, the antiwar ring icon, Muhammad Ali, had not gotten any closer to the championship than McGovern had to the White House. He had won all eight of his bouts since the Frazier loss and would have likely won his ninth had not a proposed November 1972 bout in Johannesburg fallen through for lack of a required letter of credit. "We didn't get into that thing about South Africa," Herbert Muhammad recalls. "That thing" was a widespread boycott of the apartheid state. Bottom line—Ali had not yet persuaded Frazier to give him another shot. In the two years since that first epic contest, Frazier had defended his title only twice, both times against nobodies.

If Ali's career was going nowhere fast, the career of America's second most celebrated Muslim was in high gear. In May 1971, on the way to the NBA's regular season and playoff MVP awards for that season, Lou Alcindor had publicly announced his conversion to Islam and his assumption of the name "Kareem Abdul-Jabbar."

A Nation of Islam apostate by the name of Hamaas Abdul Khaalis had introduced Abdul-Jabbar to Islam when he was still at UCLA. Khaalis had once served the Nation as Elijah Muhammad's right-hand man but, like Malcolm X, grew disillusioned with the organization and quit. Even before Malcolm, he turned to a more authentic form of Islam, in his case a Sunni subset known as Hanafi, and founded his own mosque in New York. Khaalis made few waves in the world of Islam until he managed to recruit Abdul-Jabbar, and his fortunes changed overnight, literally. Abdul-Jabbar bought an expensive home for Khaalis in a black, upper-class D.C. neighborhood known as the Gold Coast, and Khaalis used it as the sect's headquarters.

In early January 1973, some ill-concocted mix of humors—pride, jealousy, revenge—prompted Khaalis to send a series of letters to Elijah

Muhammad, his ministers, and the media. In his righteous anger, he denounced Muhammad as a "lying deceiver" and delighted in exposing the Nation of Islam's founding father, Wallace Fard, as a common crook. Fard still played a key role in the Nation of Islam's mythology. A few years earlier, for instance, Ali had assured Jose Torres that "God talked to and walked with Elijah Muhammad for three years and a half—that was in Detroit, Michigan—then he left."

By Elijah Muhammad's lights, Khaalis was blaspheming, and he did not suffer blasphemers gladly. Ali's coziness with the peace crowd may have lulled Khaalis into thinking that the Messenger had turned pacifist, but as Khaalis was about to discover, he was no Bertrand Russell. The Nation was willing and able to declare war on rogue individuals like himself.

ON THE EARLY afternoon of July 18, John 38X Clark and seven of his fellow Philadelphians paid a house call on the Khaalis manse. They brought their "shoes" with them, locked and loaded. Thinking the Washington house the depository for the Hanafi sect's cash reserves, the Philadelphians expanded their plan to include robbery. This secondary plot inspired them to seize the inhabitants, bind them in the basement, and ransack the house even though the man they had come to chastise, Hamaas Abdul Khaalis, was not at home.

Several of Khaalis's relatives had the terrible bad luck to be at the house that afternoon. One was Khaalis's daughter, Amina. After wrenching her newborn from Amina's arms, Clark made her kneel in a bedroom closet while he taunted her about her father. When she proved insufficiently contrite, Clark shot her in the head. Clark's mujahideen then shoved Amina's ten-year-old brother Rahaman into the same room and forced him to lay on the bed. Over his desperate protests, they shot him twice in the head. They stuffed Amina's two-year-old brother Abdullah into a closet and shot him in the head three times. When a friend pulled up to the house in his car, the gunmen invited him in and shot him dead as well.

Several of the gunmen headed back to the basement where Khaalis's wife, Bibi, was still bound and gagged, and they poured eight bullets into her at point blank range. Amazingly, both she and Amina would live to tell their tales. Upstairs, meanwhile, others in the group filled a bathtub with water. When full, they brought Bibi's one-year-old daughter in and held her under until she stopped struggling. They then did the same with Amina's nine-day-old son. "The seed of the hypocrite is in them," raged one of the holy warriors when questioned as to why the babies had to die.

By nightfall, the eight men were back in Philadelphia. They had found only about $1,000 in cash in the house. Each kept $100 for himself and tithed the rest back to Philadelphia Mosque No. 12. When the story exploded on to the front pages, the Nation of Islam played dumb. Louis Farrakhan claimed that the federal government was behind the murders, and *Muhammad Speaks* dismissed Khaalis as a "modern day Uncle Tom."

In time, the police found their way to James Price, one of the attackers, and he identified his cohorts, six of whom were indicted for the crime. While they were all awaiting trial, Farrakhan gave a national broadcast radio address in which he warned against those "who would be used as an instrument of a wicked government against our rise." He allowed that despite Elijah Muhammad's own merciful disposition, some of the younger Muslims "have no forgiveness in them for traitors and stool pigeons." Price's colleagues got the message. Two of his Muslim prison mates attacked him in his cell, crushing his testicles and ripping open his rectum with a prison shank before hanging him with his own bedsheet. As Karl Evanzz ruefully observes in his book, *The Messenger*, "Price had been mutilated in a way that made Klan violence seem sparing by comparison."

Were it not for Evanzz, a black *Washington Post* reporter, the story of this brutal assault might well be lost to history. Not surprisingly, the various Web sites that chronicle American Muslim history do not mention it at all. Nor do any of the significant Muhammad Ali biographers—with the exception of a brief note by Mike Marqusee. In fact, a Google search reveals not one single reference that ties Ali to the organization responsible for this mini-holocaust.

By 1973, Elijah Muhammad had eased Ali back into the fold after his brief excommunication. Given his identity as a quasi-pacifist and the Nation's most prominent member, Ali should have been called on, at the very least, to denounce an incident in which four children were shot or drowned. The media should have demanded as much. Instead, once again, there was—and is—silence.

IF ALI FANS could ignore or endure events beyond the ring, they would have a harder time overlooking those within. The first blow came on January 22, just two days after the inauguration and four days after the Washington slaughter. In Kingston, Jamaica, the undefeated young heavyweight George Foreman sent champ Joe Frazier crashing to the canvas six times in the first four and a half minutes. It got so bad so quickly that Foreman implored Yank Durham to throw in the towel lest he literally kill his fighter. "For the first time in my career," Frazier confesses, "I'd gotten my ass kicked." Frazier's defeat meant that the next meeting between him and Ali would be little more than a payday.

No sooner had the referee stopped the fight in Kingston than America's most ambitious ex-con rushed into the ring to embrace the new champion. "Don King's body did four years in prison," sportswriter Dick Schaap wryly observed, "but his hair got the chair." Just a year out of prison, King was taking the first bold steps in transforming himself from a short-haired racketeer to a shock-haired boxing impresario. Ali had been instrumental in his rehabilitation, such as it was.

King and Ali had a common friend, singer and songwriter Lloyd Price. In June 1972, King hatched the idea to stage a boxing exhibit to raise money to save a failing, largely black hospital in Cleveland. He prevailed upon Price to recruit Ali, and Ali obliged. King then secured the services of veteran promoter Don Elbaum through a combination of bravado and intimidation. "There's a black hospital that's in a lot of trouble here," he shouted at Elbaum during their first phone contact, "and you and I are going to be the heroes who save it."

The August fight produced a gate of $81,000, the largest ever for a boxing exhibition. The hospital saw $1,500 of it. Within a few years, it had closed its doors. King pocketed a good deal more. In his very first promotion, Don King had shown his distinctive gift for seducing the unwary with the rhetoric of black pride and screwing everyone who got near him.

Ali's participation in this initial King scam, though innocent, was indicative. In a 1975 essay, sportswriter Roger Kahn enthuses about Ali's "simple, spellbinding, eloquent black socialism." Admittedly, Ali did not lack for creature comforts at the time, what with his seven cars including a Greyhound Semicruiser, his homes, his land, and a couple million in handy cash. Beyond meeting his immediate needs, however, he promises Kahn that the rest "would go to the ghettos." He would open bakeries and restaurants, buy buses for Muslim schools and "shoes for barefoot children." As Kahn adds, "He challenged other successful blacks to do the same." And Kahn is just one of the many Ali observers who has gushed about his generosity.

Generous Ali most assuredly was. It's just that so much of his generosity amounted to as little as it did with the Cleveland hospital benefit. Like many who were a product of the sixties, Ali and his faithful seem to have convinced themselves that talk bestowed as much virtue as results. The contrast with previous generations in this regard stands out. In 1950, for instance, Sugar Ray Robinson staged a bout for The Cancer Fund. The Fund received $100,000, $50,000 of it from Robinson, his entire purse.

Robinson also did more than talk about black entrepreneurship. In the 1940s, he opened a highly successful Harlem nightclub. When that prospered, he opened Sugar Ray's Quality Cleaning, Edna Mae's Lingerie Shop, and George Gainford's Golden Glove Barber Shop, all along the same Seventh Avenue block. "All my enterprises were making money," says Robinson without a hint of piety, "and I was spending it." Robinson was also generous to a fault, but instead of shouting that fact from the rooftops, he chastised himself for being a soft touch.

Ali's one-man urban renewal program hinged on his regaining the championship. He faced an unexpected challenge in early 1973, and that came in the form of ex-Marine Ken Norton. In his previous fight, Norton had boxed in front of seven hundred spectators for a purse of $300. Despite Norton's buff physique and good lucks, neither Ali nor his handlers took him seriously. They should have.

In the second round, at least according to Pacheco and Dundee, Norton broke Ali's jaw. Even after learning that the jaw was broken, Ali insisted on fighting. Pacheco knew that the fight should have been stopped right there. But a match against an ex-Marine in a military town like San Diego in the wake of Nixon's landslide carried much cultural weight. "So many of Ali's fights had incredible symbolism," Cosell informs Hauser, and as Cosell could see, this one had more than most.

If Joe Louis fought for America in his most symbolic fights against Primo Carnera and Max Schmeling, Ali fought first and foremost for the Nation of Islam. When Pacheco told manager Herbert Muhammad that the Norton fight should be stopped after the second round, Herbert "did what most indecisive men do: nothing." As Pacheco explains, Elijah Muhammad had entrusted Herbert to "care for, preserve, and nourish the legend," and so he let the fight go on. Ali endured until the end of the twelve-rounder but in vain. Norton prevailed on a split decision.

To his credit, Pacheco does not let himself off the hook. "I also did nothing," he confesses, and neither did Dundee.

For the next several years, long after they knew better, those of influence in the Ali camp would continue to do nothing; nothing that is but urge their proxy warrior into one symbolic battle after another, even after the very real punches had begun to dislodge the illusory symbols in his brain.

RUMBLE IN THE JUNGLE

If there were only to be two figures in an international black national-ist pantheon, Patrice Lumumba would surely be one of them. In June 1960, in the first fresh breeze of liberation, the people of the Democratic Republic of the Congo elected Lumumba their first and last freely cho-sen president.

Immediately after the election, the Katanga province under Moise Tshombe broke away from Lumumba's government, and the democratic enterprise began to crumble. In July 1960, Lumumba made his way to New York looking for support. There he met with the other major black nationalist hero of his era, Malcolm X. Lumumba deeply impressed Malcolm. He would later eulogize him, in fact, as "the greatest black man who ever walked the African continent."

With his Soviet sympathies and his uncompromising style, Lumumba managed to make some dangerous enemies within and without his new country. In 1960, those enemies found their point person in Joseph Mobutu, Lumumba's defense minister. In September 1960, the very same month Ali won his Olympic gold in Rome, Mobutu staged a coup and placed Lumumba under house arrest. In November, Lumumba escaped but was recaptured by Mobutu's troops. They eventually delivered him into the lethal hands of Moise Tshombe with the understanding that he would be permanently removed from center stage.

Ideology fully shapes the death narrative of Patrice Lumumba. Although recent revelations have shown the Belgians to be fully complicit—and they have apologized profoundly—the international left has preferred to blame the CIA, which wasn't. Malcolm X was among those who saw the Lumumba death as one of those infamous "chickens" that had come home to roost in JFK's assassination.

What matters for this story is that Mobutu was as thoroughly implicated in the death of Lumumba as Elijah Muhammad was in the death of Malcolm X. To deny that involvement is to patronize the both of them. Each was capable of murder and competent enough to get away with it. Neither of them needed the help of the FBI or the CIA or the Belgians.

In 1965, Mobutu emerged victorious after an internal power struggle and declared himself president. In October 1971, in a flurry of "authenticity," he renamed the country the Republic of Zaire. This was an odd choice. As a name, "Congo" was true to the area's pre-colonial African roots. "Zaire," however, was a Portuguese corruption of an African word for river. Not content to rename the country, Mobutu forced all of his citizens to rename themselves, and he did the same, now calling himself Mobutu Sese Seko Nkuku Wa Za Banga ("The all-powerful warrior who, because of his endurance and inflexible will to win, will go from conquest to conquest, leaving fire in his wake").

In reality, Mobutu showed an inflexible will only to steal the country blind. The shift from democracy to kleptocracy, however, made him few friends beyond his immediate family. As a way to regain the world's respect, he cast his eye about for the easy fix, and in 1974 he saw the glimmerings of one. The promoter who sold him on this idea just happened to be the one man on any continent who could match Mobutu con for con in his shameless, pseudo-African kleptomania. Don King was coming to Zaire.

How King got to Zaire is a story worth telling. In December 1973, Ali happened to call Don King to console him after Jerry Quarry knocked out a fighter King managed named Ernie Shavers. Ali was feeling generous. In September, he had won a split decision over Ken Norton in their Los Angeles rematch. Although the judges' vote was unnervingly close, Ali was on his way back, and King wanted a piece of that action.

Once again, however, Joe Frazier stood in Ali's way. To get a shot at Foreman and the title, he had to get past Frazier in a January 1974 rematch. As it turned out, the fight proved less lively than the rough-and-tumble that preceded it. When Frazier tried to talk at a press conference at Madison Square Garden to announce the fight, Ali shouted out at him, "I'm sick and tired of you living on my name. I'm gonna whip you like I'm Willie Pep, you Uncle Tom."

"My skin's blacker than yours," Frazier shot back. "Maybe you're really a half breed." Ali would hear none of it. Frazier was the "white man's champ," and he was not about to let anyone forget.

On the Saturday before the match, Howard Cosell invited both fighters to the studio to comment on the first Ali-Frazier bout as it was being shown. Frazier, now managed by veteran trainer Eddie Futch after Yank Durham's untimely death, hesitated to come. As Howard Cosell remembers, Frazier was afraid that Ali "would make personally abusive comments before a national audience," and he knew that the war of words was the one war he could not win. Cosell promised that he would restrict the conversation to the fight. He could no more do that than he could grow hair.

As Frazier remembers, the Uncle Tom reference had "steamed me up." More vexing still, Ali's brother, Rahaman, just ten feet away, was "jiving and heckling" Frazier with his "Amen, praise Allahs" after every Ali punch. Frazier had had enough. Commenting on Ali's swelling jaw, he said, "That's what he went to the hospital for." When Ali pointed out that Frazier had spent a month in the hospital, Frazier replied that he went there to rest.

"That shows how dumb you are," snapped Ali. "People don't go to a hospital to rest. See how ignorant you are." "Ignorant" was the trigger. Frazier would have none of it. He threw his headphones off and jumped up. "Why you think I'm ignorant? Stand up, man."

The ever-protective Rahaman made a move toward the small stage. "You in this too?" Frazier snarled at him. At this, Ali jumped up and grabbed for Frazier who threw them both down off the carpeted platform and onto a cement floor. Rahaman tried to pile on, and a couple of Frazier's people went after him. "Cosell seemed terrified by it all," remembers Frazier friend Dave Wolf, "and Ali looked scared too. At that point, he realized Joe wasn't playing."

For all of Ali's skills in the ring, he had never been in a real fight. Joe Frazier had. "Joe Frazier is not the kind of guy you'd want to fight in the street," says Wolf. "I think Joe would have taken Ali's head off, and that was certainly what he intended to do." Fortunately for both of them, security intervened before any blows could be landed. Each was fined $5,000. Five days later, Ali won a unanimous decision in a fight that was remarkable only for its lack of fury. Without a championship on the line, neither man seemed to have his heart in it.

The Ali victory brought a smile to the face of one Don King. As sensitive as he was to the shift in the zeitgeist, he could all but smell the fight that would make his reputation and his fortune, Ali-Foreman. At this stage, only one man stood in his way, Bob Arum. Arum, a Harvard-educated Jewish lawyer, had promoted Ali-Frazier II and several of Ali's previous fights and had won the trust of Herbert Muhammad.

To this point, King had been a manager, not a promoter. Promoting was a major step up. He was not going to win the bid on the strength of his hand, nor could he bluff his way through. So he played the one winning card that Arum could not, and that was race. In his first meeting with Ali and Herbert, King insinuated that Arum was anti-black, that he had hustled King out of the closed-circuits rights in Ohio for Ali-Frazier II and given them to a white man "who never done boxing before." When that argument failed to turn Herbert against Arum, King started quoting Herbert's father on the necessity of black men helping black men.

Over the next few weeks, he continued his inexhaustible rant. "Consider the monumental magnitude, the symbolic impact," King told Ali. "Your regaining your title would do more for the cause of freedom and justice than anything." King played this hand for what it was worth. He appealed, notes Jack Newfield in his tough-minded book on King, *Only in America*, to the Muslims' sense of "history, liberation, empowerment, and personal redemption." Even before he had the money or a site or even the boxers, King had loaded this fight with more symbolic baggage than any since Louis-Schmeling.

The appeal proved irresistible. Ali and Herbert relented. No fool, Herbert insisted that they would proceed only if King could come up with $5 million for each fighter. Enter Fred Weymer stage right. An international fixer and Nazi fellow traveler, Weymer served as agent for Mobutu Sese Seko. Banned from the United States, Weymer met with King and a few other fixers and financiers in Paris. After much haggling and at least one interracial fistfight, it was agreed that the desperately poor Zaire would put up $9.6 million to secure the fight. Herbert had "no problem" with the choice of Zaire. "For five million dollars," he assured King, "Ali will fight anywhere on the planet."

Although King himself brought nothing to the table but his bravado, he quickly made the fight his own. "All of us in the Ali camp were in favor of Don King," says Pacheco in what may be the first and last positive review ever written about King. Pacheco, in fact, describes King as "one of the greatest promoters in the history of boxing" and adds, incredibly, that "subsequent events have proven our collective judgment correct." What makes Pacheco so valuable an observer is that, as seen here, he imposes no moral judgment on his observations.

When King's patron and partner, Hank Schwartz, first flew into Kinshasa, he was horrified. "This country looked like a shithole," he recalls. Unemployment in the city was close to 50 percent, in the rural areas closer to 80 percent. A dirt road led to the site of the match, a seventy thousand-seat soccer stadium choking on its own underbrush. The stadium had no parking lot. The seats were crumbling. Human feces covered the floor of the dressing rooms. There was no roof over the ring and no microwave connections to the satellite that would make this fight pay. Not to worry, Mobutu told Schwartz. He would simply open the treasury and do what had to be done by fight time.

Mobutu also had a crime problem to take care of. As Norman Mailer tells it, likely with some embellishment, criminals were passing themselves off as policemen and stealing at will. They were assaulting passersby and raping the wives of visiting Americans on the streets of Kinshasa. To instill the fear of God in the criminal class, Mobutu had police round up three hundred of the more notorious criminals and lock them in holding areas under the stadium. Then, without even faking due process, he had fifty of them murdered on site. "The key to the execution is that it took place at random," claims Mailer. The police then released the spared two hundred and fifty back into the population to spread the word: No one messes with this fight.

The one thing that was getting messed with was George Foreman's mind. At a boxing writers' dinner early in 1974, Ali had loudly staked out a position for the unwitting Foreman. "I'm going to beat your Christian ass, you white flag waving bitch, you." Foreman understood there was an element of theater in a diatribe that would have made John Rocker blush, but it troubled him that Ali had "spit the word 'Christian' at me like a curse."

At the time, Foreman had no gripe with the Muslims. Their clean living and self-discipline had attracted him as they had Ali. Foreman had already stopped eating pork and at this "time of great emptiness" was thinking of joining the Nation. The Ali encounter dissuaded him. "I began disbelieving his religious commitment," he says of Ali. "I figured a man who cussed so effortlessly and creatively wasn't exactly God-fearing, at least not in the way I understood or wanted to understand."

Instead, Foreman quietly took his Bible to Zaire. He would need all the help he could get. "This was clearly Muhammad Ali's country," he recalls. On the surface, at least, it certainly seemed to be. "Yea, I'm in Africa," Ali tells the camera in Leon Gast's Oscar-winning documentary on the fight, *When We Were Kings*. "Africa's my home. Damn America." From the visual imagery of the documentary, scenes later recreated in the movie *Ali*, he seems to have charmed the entire country from the children on up. "We were all for Muhammad Ali," one African tells Gast's cameras. "For us he was defending the good cause." Although Ali is oddly quiet about his Zaire experience in his autobiography, most of his chroniclers are not. "Watching Ali in Zaire was wonderful," says Pacheco. "The love, the power he had over [the people]," Pacheco adds, "it was spine tingling."

Years earlier, legendary black photographer Gordon Parks, thirty years Ali's senior, asked himself a question about Ali's appeal that Pacheco and most other observers never did. After walking through Miami with the then twenty-four-year-old champ, and hearing the accolades from the people, Gordon reflects, "I wonder how he could believe that boppish, sycophantic chatter we just heard was 'love.'" As Parks failed to understand, however, in the decade of the 1960s, the currency of "love" had been everywhere devalued.

Of the two boxers, Ali adapted much more readily. He stayed out at the presidential compound in N'Sele forty miles from Kinshasa, and as always, he made himself available to the press and the people. Archie Moore, there in the Foreman camp, thought Ali's act was wearing "as thin as a Baltimore pimp's patent leather shoes," but the media and the locals could not get enough of it. Most of them were openly pulling for Ali.

Foreman was cornered before he ever got to Zaire. "Who is he?" Ali asked of Foreman and then answered. "He is White America, Christianity, the Flag, the White Man, Porkchops." So relentless was the international Ali spin machine that when Foreman arrived the Africans were surprised to see he was black. Ali had once again staked out the "black" position in advance, despite the fact that his entourage was demonstrably whiter and/or lighter-skinned than Foreman's. Mailer describes Ali's reverse racial positioning strategy as "the continuing irony of his career."

Foreman did little to help his cause. The champ took his German Shepherds everywhere, unaware that they were a symbol of Zaire's colonial past. Nor was the young Foreman the gregarious charmer that he would one day become. In Zaire, he was sullen, surly, withdrawn. It was as if he were trying to erase his flag-waving image and flank Ali on the "bad" side of blackness, the Jack Johnson side.

"How do you feel about fighting at three o'clock in the morning?" a reporter asked. "When I was growing up in Houston," Foreman answered without a smile, "I had a lot of fights at three and four in the morning." At the time, Foreman had no gift for the game of blackness. He was what he was. He lacked Ali's deftness, his wit, his feel for the audience. Ali could talk "race" all day long without scaring a soul. Foreman could scarcely open his mouth without alarming a media whose taste in badasses ran to unthreatening poseurs.

No political movement in recent American history so satisfied itself with talk as did the New Left, which, by 1974, was not so new and not so left. Among the phrases to emerge from that period was "Black is beautiful." Ali mouthed it repeatedly, in public at least. Privately, he cut his corners. In Africa, as Pacheco reports, he scoured the countryside looking for a beautiful black girl, but without apparent success. "These girls are too black," he complained. "What they need is a little white blood in them." Pacheco sees Ali's attraction to light-skinned women as an homage to his mother. As Pacheco notes, Belinda, Ali's second wife, also had a "high percentage of white blood," as did Ali himself. Belinda, however, may not have had enough.

Shortly before the September 25, 1974, showdown, a sparring partner accidentally elbowed Foreman in the head and opened a serious gash. The fight had to be postponed indefinitely. When Foreman talked of leaving the country, Mobutu had his passport seized. Foreman had effectively become a prisoner in Zaire, a situation, as Jack Newfield reports, "that further preyed on his mind and mood."

To ease the tension and keep the remaining press and visitors entertained, Don King recruited some high quality cheerleaders, four for each camp. Ali's talent scouts spotted one that had been assigned to Foreman but that they knew their boss would have to have. "Ali was at once smitten," Pacheco reports, "and he negotiated a trade."

Throughout his career, Ali made a point of avoiding white women. He made a virtue of it, in fact. As far as Pacheco and others could see, Ali honored his separatist ideology on the issue of women—at least, that is, if one played by the Jim Crow "one drop" rule. The lovely Veronica Porche had not much more.

"In our family," Veronica told a reporter from the *LA Times*, "it's black, French, Spanish, Indian, and my mother's grandfather was Jewish." The combination was devastating. Lloyd Wells, Ali's designated procurer, called the glamorous and overtly non-Muslim Veronica "one of the most beautiful women in the world." So beautiful, thought Wells, that by comparison, Mike Tyson's former wife, actress Robin Givens, "must look like Buckwheat when she wakes up in the morning."

One night in Zaire, Belinda Ali caught her husband returning to their hotel after midnight with his Creole beauty in tow. "I smacked him good; scratched him a bit," Belinda admits to Hauser. "I would have whupped Veronica worse, but she ran and I didn't know who she was." Veronica was the most obvious reason why the mother of Ali's four children took to wearing a George Foreman button in Zaire.

THERE WAS A second reason as well, a "mystery woman" who had also come to Zaire with the entourage. She goes by the name of Aaisha Ali. Of all Ali's chroniclers, including the otherwise comprehensive Hauser, only Mark Kram tells the sad story of Aaisha. He interviewed her in depth for his 2001 book, *The Ghosts of Manila*.

In the early summer of 1973, soon after Ali's loss to Ken Norton, a pretty seventeen-year-old high school junior named Wanda Bolton visited Ali's training camp at Deer Lake, Pennsylvania, with her mother and brother. In the fall, Wanda was scheduled to attend school in Brazil on an international scholarship. Eventually, she planned to become a doctor like her brother.

The thirty-one-year-old Ali spotted her in the crowd and zoomed in on her. "Have you ever seen a fighter as pretty as me," he asked. Wanda was charmed not so much by his good looks but by his "inner beauty." He put it all on display that day. He showed her a movie, took her horseback riding, and enchanted her thoroughly. Wanda went home elated, "chalking it up as a wonderful memory."

Soon after, Ali followed up with a phone call and asked her to go to Manhattan with him. Wanda's mother understandably objected given that Ali was the married father of four children until Ali offered to take her brother and friend as well. In New York, oddly, they visited Herbert Muhammad at his apartment, and he prophesied, "She'll give you many sons." Says Aaisha perceptively, "Herbert had the same influence over Ali that Colonel Parker had over Elvis."

Ali went through one elaborate ruse after another to see Wanda on her own. Needless to say, the girl's head was spinning. She had never even had a date before. By summer's end, she was pregnant. Her mom, furious, confronted Ali at Deer Lake. He tried to console the mom by telling her that he was going to make Wanda his second "Muslim" wife, but the mom was inconsolable. "She's only seventeen," she screamed. "Her whole life's in front of her."

That whole life did not include graduating from high school. Wanda embraced Islam, took the name Wanda X, learned the domestic crafts, and was eventually accepted by Belinda, who had little choice but to bear up. In due time, she gave birth to a daughter, Khaliah. Later, the Messenger gave Wanda the name Aaisha. "I have no regrets," she tells Kram. "But I have a deep shame and regret for the pain I caused my mother."

Ali brought Aaisha to Zaire but hoped to keep her stashed away. Cassius Sr., who had taken a liking to her, would have none of it. He brought the new mom to a lawn party at which Veronica was also present. "Are you crazy," Ali said to his father. "What you bring her here for?" When Aaisha saw Ali with Veronica, she knew that another eighteen-year-old had won his heart. She would ally with her fellow Muslim Belinda in the battle for his soul.

ONE OF ALI'S great talents as a boxer was focus. As Angelo Dundee remarked on a number of occasions, "He doesn't let anything bother him." No matter what the distractions around him, Ali could screen them out and key in on the task at hand. Still, as the days wore on, Zaire began to wear even on Ali. "I gotta get out of this place," he confided to Norman Mailer in an unguarded moment. When Mailer suggested that he take a few days off and get away, Ali fell back into form, "I'll stay here and work for my people." He was a captive of his own myth, and he knew it.

What Ali did not know, and what no one seemed inclined to tell him, was just how incoherent his myth had become. At one point, Ali jokingly warned Foreman, "My African friends will put you in a pot." His African friends were not pleased. They reminded Ali that such talk is "not in the best promotional interests of a country on the move." The very phrase, "Rumble in the Jungle," coined by Ali and popularized by Don King, dismayed them as well.

Ali's hosts had much to be sensitive about. Mailer marvels at how Mobutu and his henchmen had managed "to couple some of the oppressive aspects of communism with the most reprehensible of capitalism." Images of Mobuto loomed as ubiquitously and as frighteningly as Stalin's or Mao's in their respective heydays. Among these images was a forty-foot photo of Mobutu glaring over the soccer stadium where the fight was to be held.

Mobutu also had the savvy—and the nerve—to build a monument to Patrice Lumumba in the heart of Kinshasa. If Ali ever knew Zaire's history, he seemed content to forget it. "I wish Lumumba was here to see me," Ali tells Leon Gast on camera, "I want to win so I can lead my people."

"History repeats itself," wrote Karl Marx, "first as tragedy, second as farce." The tragedy had occurred ten years earlier when Ali paid homage to a man—Elijah Muhammad—who had encouraged the murder of one of the era's two great black nationalist heroes, Malcolm X. The farce occurred when Ali paid homage to the man who orchestrated the murder of the second, Patrice Lumumba. One can almost forgive Ali his naïveté, but there is no excusing the shapers of his myth. They knew better.

In his autobiography, Ali innocently boasts of the murderous tyrants who embraced him. On his first trip out of the country after the Supreme Court decision, for instance, he flew to Libya where he met Libya's strongman Muammar al-Qadaffi. Ali was seeking financing for a mosque at about the same time Qadaffi was financing the Black September attack on the Israeli athletes at the Munich Olympics. Qadaffi bemoaned "American arrogance" and assured Ali that his loss to Frazier provoked "a day of mourning" in Libya. On the same trip, Ali met Uganda madman Idi Amin, a former prizefighter himself, who "laughed and flexed his muscles" for Ali. In less than a decade of rule, Amin would murder an estimated 300,000 black Ugandans and expel all 80,000 Asians, many of whose families had been in Uganda for generations.

IF ALI'S SMARTS were not readily apparent outside the ring, they surely were inside, especially on the night of October 30, 1974. After the fight, Foreman would claim that his water had been poisoned, and others would claim that Dundee had cleverly loosened the ropes, but Dundee was not that clever, nor did anyone need to sap Foreman's strength. Ali let the ropes do that, and he discovered their power on his own.

Before the fight, Ali talked incessantly about how he would "dance, dance, dance." The press believed him because his own people did. Foreman believed him, too. Ali would repeat the strategy that had worked so effectively against Sonny Liston, a power puncher like Foreman, "float like a butterfly, sting like a bee."

In training, Foreman worked constantly on cutting the ring in half and forcing Ali into the corners and onto the ropes. Once there, he figured he'd wail away on Ali as he had done so effectively on Frazier and Norton. Ali knew this. He also knew that his thirty-two-year-old legs had done just about all the dancing they were going to do. He would have to compensate with a thirty-two-year-old brain that had already absorbed twenty years worth of boxing wisdom.

On the plus side, he had Elijah Muhammad back in his corner. Moments before the fight, Herbert Muhammad entered the dressing room with a word from his father. The reliably bendable Messenger wanted Ali to know that he was fighting for their people and that if he did his best, Allah would be with him. Ali took heart.

As challenger, Ali was the first one to enter the ring. The crowd greeted him with a roar, and he led them in the chant, "Ali Boom-ay-yee." In English, the phrase means "Ali kill him," an unlikely mantra for either a conscientious objector or a religion of peace. "This was his crowd," Pacheco observes. "He was in command." Foreman tried to psych Ali by delaying his entrance ten minutes, but that just gave Ali ten more minutes to pump up the fans. As Foreman sensed immediately, Ali had a huge home court advantage.

The first round went more or less according to plan. Ali danced, and Foreman stalked. Ali surprised Foreman with a few quick stand-up exchanges, but he did not inflict much damage. In the second round, Ali shocked his corner by allowing Foreman to pin him against the ropes. He held his hands up to protect his face, sagged back against the nearly elastic ropes, and let Foreman whack him like a heavy bag.

"Get away from the ropes," Ali's corner yelled. "Get away from the ropes." Their horror was genuine. "When he went to the ropes," Dundee would admit years later, "I felt sick." At the end of the round, Dundee, Pacheco, Bundini—all implored Ali to stay off the ropes. Ali waved them away and said quietly, "I know what I'm doing." Ali had keyed in on the physics of the ring. The inordinate give in the ropes conducted much of Foreman's power right through Ali and out on to the ropes themselves. The give in the upper rope also allowed Ali to lean far back and pull his head out of harm's way.

All along, Foreman had planned to pin Ali against the ropes, but once he got him there, admits Archie Moore, "George didn't know what to do." He just kept crunching away at Ali's arms, and soon enough, he had punched himself silly, the first "dope" snared by the now celebrated "rope-a-dope." By the end of the fourth round, Ali knew he had him. A sharp, five-punch sequence in the eighth caused the champ to jackknife goofily to the canvas. He was up at nine, but referee Zack Clayton waved the fight over. After seven years in the wilderness, Ali had recaptured the heavyweight crown. Forget V-E day or the fall of the Berlin wall. Says Hauser, "No event in history inspired as much global joy."

WE'RE THROUGH

Pacheco speaks often of Ali's "luck," and in Zaire the luck was in the timing. Ali had left for Africa just one month after Nixon's forced resignation over the Watergate affair and two days after his successor, Gerald Ford, pardoned Nixon. "If you think the world was surprised when Nixon resigned," Ali told the Gast cameras on the way to Zaire, "wait till I kick Foreman's behind." Ali's victory and Nixon's defeat, Hauser argues, "seemed to vindicate the [the 1960s] decade." In almost identical terms, leftist Mike Marqusee calls the Ali win "the vindication of a historical epoch." At the time, few seemed to disagree.

In the midterm election held a week after the bout, the Democrats gave the Republicans a comparable whupping, gaining a super majority in the Senate and a 120-plus margin in the House. In their last golden days before the entry of the Internet, talk radio, and cable TV, the major media—the three TV networks, the *Washington Post*, the *New York Times*, and Time/Life—held more sway over American public opinion than they had ever had or would ever again. With a few holdout exceptions, their reporters and producers loved Ali almost as much as they hated Nixon. Ali's moment in the sun had arrived. *Ring* magazine named

Ali "Fighter of the Year." *Sports Illustrated* named him "Sportsman of the Year." Ali also won the Hickok Belt as America's most outstanding professional athlete.

"It is time to recognize Ali for what he is," wrote the *New York Post's* Maury Allen in a fairly routine gush, "the greatest athlete of his time and maybe all time and one of the most important and brave men of all American time." By December 1974, such fulsomeness had become boilerplate in the major media myth mill. With the exception of Joe Frazier and a few aging sportswriters, almost no one with access to the public dared to say otherwise. As to the Frazier fans in the Gary bleachers and elsewhere, few cared what they had to say even if they had a way to say it.

On December 10, Republican president Gerald Ford put his imprimatur on the champ when he invited Ali to the White House. Ford did so as part of his effort to pull the nation together after a highly divisive ten years. A genial middle-of-the-roader, Ford eagerly embraced Ali in the hopes of healing the divisions that Ali and the Nation of Islam had helped create.

"Because of his principles," Ford would tell Hauser, "I firmly believe that as time goes on, Muhammad Ali will be remembered for more than just excellence in athletics." By the end of 1974, the man in the White House proved no more capable of seeing through the Ali myth than the man on the street.

That same month that Ford and Ali made nice, a dovish U.S. Congress, confusing abandonment with peace, washed its hands forever of Indochina. In passing the Foreign Assistance Act of 1974, Congress cut off all military funding to this beleaguered ally, just when South Vietnam needed it most. As Ali succinctly put the case, "South Vietnam, you must do the best you can, because we're through."

This astonishing bit of legislation confirmed the wisdom of Le Duan, Ho Chi Minh's successor. In October, the same month Ali beat Foreman, Le Duan had spoken to the North Vietnamese Politburo about the opportunity implicit in Nixon's resignation. He argued that in Nixon's absence there would be no public will in the United States to enforce the terms of the 1973 Paris Peace Accords. He was more right than he knew.

Although the Tet offensive in January 1968 had been a military debacle for the Viet Cong, misreporting by the American media led to a massive erosion in U.S. resolve. Soon after, the Americans began to disengage, and by August 1972, all U.S. ground forces had been withdrawn. The Paris Peace Accords were signed in January 1973. From then on, whatever ground fighting there was took place between the North Vietnamese Army (NVA) and the Republic of Vietnam Armed Forces (ARVN). U.S. air power and military aid to the Republic guaranteed the peace—at least in the beginning.

By April 1973, however, the Watergate affair had already begun to paralyze the White House, and Congress took advantage of Nixon's distractions to undercut the South. When Congress withheld all funding, the die was cast. Soon after, the NVA began its final assault. By January 3, 1975, its artillery was firing three thousand rounds a day. As NVA General Van Tien Dung told the Politburo conference a few days later, "To fully exploit this great opportunity we had to conduct large-scale annihilating battles to destroy and disintegrate the enemy on a large scale." From mid-March to early April 1975, while Ali trained for the Ron Lyle fight in Las Vegas, the armies of the South valiantly held off the Northern advance before collapsing in the face of major NVA reinforcements.

Meanwhile, the victorious forces of the Communist Khmer Rouge entered the Cambodian capital city of Phnom Penh. This was not supposed to happen. Antiwar activists had long greeted the phrase "falling dominoes" as something of a laugh line. There was nothing to laugh about in Phnom Penh. The Khmer Rouge gave the city's two million-plus residents twenty-four hours to get out of town. As the *Black Book of Communism* reports, the Khmer Rouge intended "the most radical social transformation of all: the attempt to implement total Communism in one fell swoop," and it began with the evacuation of the cities.

Once in the countryside, these "New People" were forced to wear blue clothes while everyone else wore black. Their unelected Communist masters singled them out for starvation and eventually extermination. Realistic estimates put the final liquidation toll at about two million, a quarter of the nation's population. According to the *Black Book*, the Khmer Rouge "was indeed a member of the family," meaning the Communist family. The Vietnamese Communists had exercised the single greatest influence on their development.

In Vietnam, two weeks after Phnom Penh fell, Saigon collapsed following a dramatic and demoralizing siege. When the last Marine pilots reluctantly lifted their helicopters off the embassy roof, they left behind not only thousands of our friends clamoring to flee, but our good faith as a nation. Ali's new buddy in the White House reportedly played a round of golf while the American embassy was under siege. He, too, was something of a jock.

After Saigon fell, the new Stalinist regime in the South promptly sent scores of thousands of its citizens to concentration camps for "re-education" and hundreds of thousands more off to "new economic zones" to work the land. Additional persecution, especially against those of Chinese origin, led to the ethnic cleansing of an additional two million "boat people," many of whom died in their attempt to flee.

The antiwar cohorts, now in control of virtually every major American institution save—barely—for the White House, chose not to notice. They would hold no one accountable for the horrific fate of Indochina, not Ali, and certainly not themselves. Although the South fell three years after American troops left the battle, they would chalk up a big "L" against the U.S. military, give themselves a "W" for wisdom, and glory in their own righteousness for years to come.

THRILLA IN MANILA

The best thing that happened to Muhammad Ali in the turbulent year of 1975 took several years for Ali to understand. On February 25, after forty-one years at the helm of the Nation of Islam, Elijah Muhammad died. At the time, however, the loss unnerved Ali and unmoored him. "Elijah Muhammad was my savior," he said soon afterward, "and everything I have came from him—my thoughts, my efforts to help my people, how I eat, how I talk, my *name.*"

As planned, the Messenger's son Wallace took over. A wiser man than his father, Wallace immediately realigned the Nation with more traditional understandings of Islam. This meant ending the racial posturing, honoring the American constitution, embracing free enterprise, and adopting orthodox Muslim rituals. To signal the realignment, he changed the name of the organization to the World Community of Al-Islam in the West.

This shift did not set well with many Nation members, among them Jeremiah Shabazz, who had helped recruit Ali, and Louis Farrakhan. "There's been a metamorphosis," Shabazz would say of both Ali and the Nation, "and I don't like it." By June 1975, in fact, Ali would tell a reporter from the *New York Times*, "I don't hate whites. That was history, but it's coming to an end." Farrakhan thought otherwise. Within a few years, he would lead a schism against Wallace and reclaim the Nation of Islam banner.

On a personal level, the intervening years were not Ali's best. If he made occasional strides toward racial understanding, he skittered sideways more often than not and occasionally backslid. The death of Muhammad had to have unsettled him, and his revived glory all but overwhelmed him. If that were not stress enough, his infatuation with Veronica Porche undermined his family life. Only in the ring did he maintain his balance, and just barely there.

A month after the Messenger's death, Ali took on the Bayonne Bleeder, thirty-five-year-old liquor salesman Chuck Wepner. Don King promoted the fight. He offered Ali $1.5 million for a match that promised to be no more stressful than a sparring session. As to where King got the money, that, says Jack Newfield, is an "open secret."

Any number of named sources insist that the money came from the criminal underworld. "King wanted to stay in the heavyweight picture," says Bob Arum. "If possible he wanted to control Ali. So he went to some mob guys in Cleveland, and got financing from the mob." Veteran matchmaker Teddy Brenner adds details, telling Newfield that King's slow repayment of the loan almost got him killed. "King went to a friend of mine," says Brenner, "and begged him to cancel a contract put out on his life."

Joe Frazier attended the fight in Cleveland. When he was introduced, the audience hooted and booed. This prompted the *New York Daily News*' old school sportswriter Dick Young to write of Frazier and the Ali fans in the crowd: "He does not appeal to their prejudices, their weakness, the way Ali does. Ali, early on, learned the favorite trick of all demagogues, peddle hatred to a downtrodden people. It is an easy sell." By this time, Young's was a lonely voice.

The fight itself proved more eventful than anyone expected, certainly the bookmakers who did not even offer a betting line. In the ninth round, Wepner stepped on Ali's foot while punching him in the chest, Ali fell over, and referee Tony Perez ruled it a knockdown. With his Rocky-like heart, Wepner pushed Ali into the fifteenth before Perez finally called it off.

Ali was not pleased with the outcome, and he had yet to fully assimilate Wallace's kinder and gentler Islam. Soon after the bout, on *Wide World of Sports* with Howard Cosell, Ali went after Perez. "He's a dirty dog," said Ali. "He's not black and he's not white; he's Puerto Rican. He's more black than white, but he's trying to be white." Perez would have sloughed off the racial slur as other Ali targets had done in the past, but he was not about to tolerate what Ali said next. Referring to a controversial call Perez had made in the last Frazier fight, Ali charged, "He was paid probably by some gangsters or somebody, or he had some money bet on Frazier."

That imprudent accusation provoked eight lawyers to call Perez that very night and launch a $20 million lawsuit. As Perez learned, however, one does not easily prevail over a legend in court. In the middle of the trial, the judge took Perez into his chambers. "I don't see any damage here," he said. "Why don't you shake hands with Ali and forget the whole thing?" Perez was dumbfounded. He refused to back down, but he might as well have. "[The judge] almost told the jury there's no case here," he tells Hauser. The jury agreed. "What happened," laments Perez, "didn't seem fair."

To hype a June 1975 fight against British boxer Joe Bugner in Malaysia, Ali agreed to pretend that this would be his last fight. "I miss my family," he told those gathered at the press conference with disarming conviction. "My life with them is more important than boxing. I want to retire while I'm still on top." If only Ali had believed half of what he said, his life and that of his family would have been incalculably more tranquil.

Unfortunately, he meant none of it. The Ali faithful kept prodding him to fight one more time. Pacheco called the inner core of the faithful "the Ali Circus," and the Circus kept adding new clowns. In negotiating the contract for the third Frazier fight, this one to be held in Manila,

Eddie Futch could not get over Ali's demand for fifty rooms to accommodate the Circus. Frazier, by contrast, needed just seventeen. "It was a horrendous collection of hypocrites and hustlers," says Alex Wallau, then with ABC Sports, "people who had their hands in his pocket and were looking to make side deals whenever they could."

As Ali trained for a third Joe Frazier fight, the unseemly threads of the Ali myth unraveled. The most transparent was the chosen venue for the fight, the Philippines. Once again, a tyrant's money attracted Ali to still another third-world kleptocracy. Despite early promise, Ferdinand Marcos had assumed nearly full power under martial law two years before the fight, and he was not inclined to give it up. He and his extravagant wife, Imelda, spent nearly as much of the country's money on her shoes as they did on the nation's poor.

Mark Kram describes the Marcoses' arrogance as "contagious," and Ali was chief among those infected. Now the "Greatest" once again, he sang the praises of the Marcoses and treated the everyday Asians with imperial hauteur. New to his retinue, for instance, was a body servant from Malaysia named Bala. "He's so obedient," Ali swaggered. "Always saying 'yes sir, no sir.' He'll go fetch anything for you. Even take your shoes off for you."

Ali was less interested in the culture or history of the Philippines than its geography, specifically its distance from the United States. "Ali actually sought the fight," says Pacheco, "because it gave him a chance to be alone with Veronica for six weeks." In perhaps the single most regrettable moment of his public life, Ali brought Veronica with him to meet the first couple at the presidential palace. When Marcos said to Ali, "You have a beautiful wife," Ali did not correct him. "You have a beautiful wife, too," he answered. At the time, the faithful Belinda was back in Chicago with their four children.

Pete Bonventre of *Newsweek* had a dilemma on his hands. His editors had sent him to Manila to do an in-depth feature on Ali. He was tempted to bury the Veronica subplot, but he feared his editors' response if they saw photos of this unaccounted for beauty at so intimate a reception. What made the story newsworthy, Bonventre understood, was not that a boxer had a mistress. Hell, even Chuck Wepner boasted of a stable of willing ladies. What made it newsworthy was that it so challenged the integrity of Ali's public posture as a Muslim. He joined the Nation in no small part to discipline his own behavior.

"When you can live righteous in the hell of North America," Ali told Jose Torres years earlier, "when a man can control his life, his physical needs, his lower self, he elevates himself." Malcolm X's integrity on this issue led to his death.

In the run-up to the Manila fight, Ali had paused to do a curiously intemperate interview for *Playboy* that would appear a month after the fight. In the interview, he continued to make the case for a separate African-American nation and promised that "America don't have no future. America's going to be destroyed." That was still rote Elijah Muhammad. By the mid-1970s, such expressions of national self-loathing had ceased to be provocative. What did provoke in this newly feminized era was his view on sex and gender.

In comparing Muslims to the allegedly war-worshipping Christians, Ali made the point that Muslims "live their religion—we ain't hypocrites." He continued, "We submit entirely to Allah's will. We don't eat ham, bacon, or pork. We don't smoke. And everyone knows we honor our women." As he went on to explain, Muslim men honor their women by keeping them "in the background" and protecting them from the predations of other men, especially white men. "Put a hand on a Muslim sister," said Ali, "and you are to die." When asked if he believed that lynching was the answer to interracial sex, Ali answered, "A black man *should* be killed if he's messing with a white woman."

Belinda Ali was kept in the background, and one could understand if in 1975 she did not feel particularly honored. In the eight years of her marriage, she had put up with a lot. Somewhere along the way, the once shy and respectful Ali had become, according to Robert Lipsyte, "relentless, indiscriminate, and indiscreet." Kram traces Ali's transformation into "an indiscriminate sexual marksman" back to at least 1967, the year he married Belinda.

Larry Holmes, then a sparring partner, saw a lot of this and was not too pleased with what he saw. On one occasion, he brought a good-looking woman to a party only to have Ali swoop down on her and take her away. "Ali was very good at that," says Holmes. "He'd see something he wanted and try to get it." The only time, in fact, that Ali rebuked Holmes was when he suggested that Ali cut back on the womanizing before a particular fight. "Don't you ever tell me what to do," Ali scolded him, and Holmes never did again.

Torres also got an eyeful when Ali came to Puerto Rico to box an exhibition match. One night, Ali and a few of Torres's friends went out on the town to look for "foxes." What makes the story noteworthy is that Herbert Muhammad went with them. Unsuccessful in their quest, the men settled on one veteran prostitute who serviced them all. She told Torres that Herbert, "the son of God," was her favorite—at least until his check bounced.

In a *People* magazine profile from that era, Pacheco described Ali as "a pelvic missionary," meaning one who "bestowed his favors on the beautiful and the ugly alike." Although Ali found no fault with Pacheco's description, "the advance scouts, the procurers" in the Ali Circus were outraged. "We never got him no ugly broad," protested one. By all accounts, the numbers in Ali's "endless stream" of women were Wilt-like, incalculable. "The downfall of so many great men," Ali told *Playboy* in 1964, "is that they haven't been able to control their appetite for women." In 1964, Ali at least appeared to take his faith seriously. Ten years later, he obviously did not.

If *Newsweek's* Bonventre did not know all the details, he knew the general story line of Ali's adventurous love life. "I told it like it was," he remembers, "that here was this complex man with so many contradictions fused into one cosmic personality, and one of his contradictions was his devotion to the Islamic faith at the same time he had a mistress." As is evident in Bonventre's elaborate justification, however, he was incapable of telling it "like it was." The terms of the myth obliged him to elevate Ali's everyday bad behavior into something "cosmic."

Pacheco does much the same thing. "Did Ali have serious affairs?" he asks. "A few. Some pregnancies? A few. Some bastard children. A few." Incredibly, less than ten pages later, he tells the reader, "Ali's life is exemplary."

TV correspondent and former *New York Times* reporter Lipsyte reveals how easy it is to transform the illicit into the exemplary. He tells of interviewing Ali in 1986 when "two teen-aged women" came up to Ali's hotel suite for an autograph. The forty-four-year-old Ali led them off into a sleeping alcove, winked at Lipsyte, and said, "Hey, Bob, just like old times." Lipsyte would share this story at a public conference with Ali present as something of a comic aside. What allows the story to be offered as humor is Lipsyte's unlikely coupling of the word "women" and the word "teen-aged." Ali is not sexually exploiting two black teenage girls, perhaps criminally. He is having relations with two "women."

Unlike Malcolm X, Ali had to test his Muslim faith against the influences of the most sexually permissive era in American history. The media all but encouraged Ali to fail the test, which, of course, he did in spectacular fashion. After those first few years of resistance, in fact, the majority of the media endorsed Ali in almost anything he said or did. Those who continued to see Ali as less than heroic, says Lipsyte, did so only because of "their emotional baggage."

Despite the *Newsweek* story, an indulgent media might also have let the Veronica flap pass without further comment had Ali not made a classic PR blunder. He held a press conference to demand his right to privacy when cheating publicly on his wife. "I could see some controversy in this if [Veronica] was white," said an irate Ali, "but she's not. The only person I answer to is Belinda Ali, and I don't worry about her."

Those last six words reveal just how painfully naïve Ali still could be, even at thirty-three. "I was hurt a lot by what was going on," Belinda confesses to Hauser. "But mostly I kept the hurt inside. That's how we lasted nine years together. But finally it got to be too much." Within twenty-four hours of Ali's public slight, Belinda was on a plane for Manila. Joe Frazier's wife, Florence, and his four daughters just happened to be on the same plane. "She looked mean enough to bite the bumper off a Buick," Frazier reports. "Yeah. Sat there on that long flight just staring ahead, like she was about to go to war."

Go to war she did. Dressed in a flowing white dress and turban, the tall and regal Belinda walked through the hotel lobby in Manila as if she owned it. "The queen herself couldn't have done it better," said one British reporter. Belinda headed straight for Ali's hotel room, blew past a *Today Show* crew, pulled Ali into a bedroom, threw everything she could find to throw at him, and dressed him down royally.

"You tell that bitch," she yelled, "if I see her I'm gonna break her back." She then turned right around, headed back through the lobby, into the waiting limousine, and home on the same plane that brought her. "At that point," comments filmmaker Leon Gast, "people were talking about Belinda-Veronica as much as they were talking about Ali-Frazier." If the futures of the couple's four children were not at stake, this talk might have been more amusing.

For all the hubbub, Ali kept his sights fixed on Joe Frazier. Even before arriving in Manila, Ali had determined how best to undermine Frazier's confidence. "He'd had me as a white man for the first two [fights]," recalls Frazier, "and now he was going to make me a cartoon of a nigger, a knuckle-scraping baboon-man. Gorilla. Frazier the gorilla." Or as Ali phrased it, "It will be a killer and a chiller and a thrilla when I get the gorilla in Manila."

As *Sports Illustrated*'s main boxing reporter during Ali's career, Mark Kram got to see just how unfunny this ritual defamation had become. He recounts one chilling episode before the Manila fight in a gym packed with Ali fans. As Kram tells it, after leading the frenzied crowd in chants of "The Greatest," Ali threw out the word "gorilla" and taunted the audience to respond.

"Joe Frazier," yelled one white guy. "Ape! Ape!" shouted a young blond woman. "Jist niggers," screamed a black guy.

"Ain't that the truth," said Ali to the last comment, dropping to his haunches. "Gorilla," he howled now. "Ugly and smelly." As Ali lurched ape-like around the ring, his fans jeered the mock Frazier much in the way the Parisian rabble might have jeered Quasimodo.

For the light-skinned Ali and his fans, Joe Frazier was both too black and not black enough. "A little old nigger boy from Philadelphia," Ali taunted him, "who never had a thought in his dumb head 'cept for himself." Even if there were an appropriate response, Frazier had no microphone. By this stage in his career, Ali owned the media. The psychic blows from this relentless assault bruised Frazier more deeply than all the punches of all the fights he ever fought. "While the public found it amusing, I guess, and came to view [Ali] as a good guy," remembers Frazier, "I knew different."

Ali and Frazier fought that steamy morning in Manila not so much for the heavyweight championship of the world, reflects Jerry Izenberg, "They fought for the championship of each other." With Ali now pushing thirty-four and Frazier thirty-two, there was not a whole lot of dancing, but there was a whole lot of banging. The two pounded each other with as little give as the mechanical sluggers in a penny arcade.

In the first third of the fight, the crisper-punching Ali prevailed. The middle third belonged to the relentless Frazier. He hit Ali so hard and so often in the sixth that even Imelda Marcos had to look away. "They told me old Joe Frazier was washed up," said Ali as he answered the bell in the seventh. "They lied," said Frazier. At the end of ten, the fight was about as even as a fight could be. "I think this is what dying is like," said an exhausted Ali to his corner after the tenth round. Afraid that Ali was about to call it off, Herbert Muhammad yelled up at him, "You a niggah like him! You gonna quit. Get your ass out there! You hear me."

Frazier did not cut easily, but his face tended to swell. After ten rounds of punishment, his right eye began to close. He had vision problems in his left eye even before the fight. From round eleven on, he was fighting pretty close to blind. Ali zeroed in, but Frazier soldiered on. "The thirteenth and fourteenth rounds were the most epic I have ever witnessed," recalls Pacheco. "They were battles of will. They were fights for survival."

After fourteen rounds, the two fighters returned to their corners utterly spent, with Ali ahead on points. Frazier knew he needed a knock-out. The two had now fought forty-one brutal rounds. Frazier had knocked down Ali only once. Ali had knocked down Frazier not at all. His reputation as "The Greatest" hinged fully on his outlasting Frazier in this final round in Manila. He did. As Frazier tried to stand for the fifteenth, veteran trainer Eddie Futch held him back. "Sit down, son," he told Frazier. "It's all over."

From across the ring, a Frazier assistant was desperately trying to get Futch's attention. Eavesdropping on Ali's corner, he swore he heard Ali say, "I ain't going out there. That man's crazy." But Ali never got the chance to quit. Futch restrained a game but wounded Frazier—"No, no, no, you can't do that to me"—and threw in the towel. On seeing the fight waved off, Ali slumped to the canvas, "the closest thing to death" he had ever experienced. In taking two out of three fights, Ali had proved his courage in the ring. He did so by showing that he could take a punch, a display of valor that would have serious real life consequences. "He's a ghost, and I'm still here," Frazier writes of Ali in the last sentences of his unforgiving 1996 autobiography. "Now let's talk about who *really* won those three fights."

Frazier almost surely represented a part of Ali's own cultural imagi-nation that he needed to suppress. "I had always hated being black," Ali once confessed to Jose Torres, "just like the other negroes, hating our kind instead of loving one another." The Muslims appealed to him in no small part because they addressed the issue of self-hate. They assumed that by projecting that hate outward, at the devils, they could direct the love within, at themselves, a strategy that has never worked anywhere and certainly not with Ali. Malcolm's daughter Attallah understood the strategy well. The Nation of Islam "knocked things down in order to build," she tells Hauser, "and that's not a process that set right with me."

The romanticized Jack Johnson gave Ali the role model he thought he needed. As portrayed, Johnson was both scary and sophisticated. "I grew to love the Jack Johnson image," Ali said after the first Jerry Quarry fight. "I wanted to be rough, tough, arrogant, the nigger the white folks didn't like." But white folks loved him. They loved him because they saw themselves in him. As hard as Ali tried, he did not scare at all. Joyce Carol Oates, among other white Ali fans, believed Ali to be the "black man's black man," but Ali could never quite believe it himself.

Nor could Ali ever convince himself that black was really beautiful. It showed in his choice of women. It showed in his treatment of Frazier and, before him, Patterson, Terrell, Bundini, and the other black sparring partners and hangers-on he routinely humiliated. "He thought [Frazier] was a pure nigger," Aaisha Ali recalls. "He says that Frazier didn't know how to talk, or look good, and that it was insulting if he became the heavyweight champ."

One need not be a shrink to sense that Ali was projecting his own self-hatred onto Frazier and the others. Like many black radicals, Malcolm X included, he was sufficiently light and middle-class to almost imagine himself white. Joe Frazier had no such illusions. He always knew who he was. He did not have to imitate anyone to be rough and tough. He has thus always seemed much more secure in his blackness than Ali.

After the fight, Ali sent word that he wanted to speak to Frazier's son, Marvis. "Tell your father all the stuff I said about him—I didn't mean it," he said struggling to sit up. "Your father's a helluva man." Frazier wasn't buying. Ali may have proven himself in the ring, he admits, but a real man would have apologized to his face. "I don't care how the world looks at him," Frazier would tell Hauser fifteen years after the fight. "I see him different, and I know him better than anyone."

The filtered apology offered by Ali says so much about the man in this first phase of his life: good instincts undermined by bad judgment and worse advice. "Always accessible," Lipsyte calls Ali, "always friendly, always basically decent and helpful." Yes, this was all *basically* true, even if it was not always evident to some essential people in his life. Ali was also clever, charismatic, charming, entertaining, a hell of a boxer, and, in the ring at least, as courageous as any sane man could be.

But did he deserve to be a hero? "The period from 1960 to 1975 claimed many lives and reputations," writes Yale-educated sports scholar Thomas Hietala. "Ali was one of the few prominent Americans who emerged with greater stature at the close of the era than at its beginning." There is no denying the accuracy of Hietala's observation, but there is every reason to challenge the premises on which the observation is based. For Hietala, as for many others, Ali made his reputation on the issue of Southeast Asia. Although admitting Ali's "limited" knowledge, Hietala insists that "Ali instinctively felt that the conflict was too distant and too ambiguous to justify American intervention."

"Instinctively"? In the academy, this passes for scholarship. In the real world, an entirely accessible evidence trail tracks Ali's resistance right back to Elijah Muhammad's venomous racism and his consequent collaboration with the Axis powers during World War II.

America's sportswriters are usually wiser than its intellectuals—and, almost always, better writers. Roger Kahn is a good example of what happens when the former tries to pass as the latter. In 1975, the year Ali would publicly humiliate both his wife Belinda and Joe Frazier and glibly dismiss Vietnam, Kahn would praise Ali for "his crystal sense of the irrationality and the cruelty of the society." "Crystal sense"? Frazier and Belinda and literally millions of Southeast Asians could assure Kahn just how little meaning those words have beyond the uncritical confines of a New York newsroom.

The evidence that Ali deserved an elevated status fifteen years into his public career is, to say the least, elusive. A summing up of this first act, however unpleasant, sheds some useful light both on the young Ali and the generation that made him:

Ali knowingly betrayed Malcolm X, a betrayal that led at least indirectly to Malcolm's assassination.

Ali publicly turned his back on his press secretary, Leon 4X Ameer, which led even more directly to Ameer's death.

When Nation of Islam activists executed five friends and family of the Hanafi sect—four of them children—Ali did not quit the Nation or even publicly protest. True to form, the media did not dare suggest that he should do either.

For at least four years running, Ali publicly degraded Joe Frazier, often along the crudest racial lines. "There's a great honor about Joe," says baseball great Reggie Jackson. "That was evident in the way he fought. And Muhammad ridiculed Joe; he humiliated him in front of the world."

Ali also verbally and physically abused Floyd Patterson and Ernie Terrell, two men who hardly deserved it.

Ali was an unapologetic sexist. "In the Islamic world," he told *Playboy*, "the man's the boss, and the woman stays in the background. She don't *want* to call the shots." He wrote this in 1975, three years into the doomed struggle to pass the Equal Rights Amendment. Feminists still wrestle over this one.

While the black family was under assault, with its rate of unwed births nearly tripling during these fifteen years, Ali was fathering children out of wedlock with at least one teenage girl.

He also was about to leave four of his children without a father in the home after rejecting their Muslim mother for a more glamorous, lighter skinned eighteen-year-old.

Belinda Ali was the second wife he had publicly humiliated. Sonji was the first.

Ali remained an unabashed racist, calling for an American apartheid and the lynching of interracial couples as late as 1975.

In the years that mattered, Ali drove a wedge between the races. This may not have been evident to the cultural elite, but anyone who had been at Gary or like venues fully understands.

He routinely denigrated black heroes who did not share his point of view, Joe Louis, Jackie Robinson, and Thurgood Marshall among them.

He continuously belittled and undermined Christianity, a bedrock of black culture in black America.

Ali shamelessly courted some of the most brutal dictators on the planet: Qadaffi, Idi Amin, Papa Doc Duvalier, Nkrumah, Mobutu, Marcos.

One of those dictators, Mobutu Sese Seko Nkuku Wa Za Banga, was complicit in the death of the black nationalist hero, Patrice Lumumba.

Ali helped launch the career of Don King.

And, oh yes, he rejected his country in its hour of need and expressed no regret at the fate of those millions we all abandoned. The man who compelled him to do so had conspired with the Japanese and cheered them on at Pearl Harbor.

Why the silence about what seems so obvious? Larry Holmes knows the answer. "He wasn't a saint," says Holmes. "But if you tell people something like that they kick your ass. You can't talk bad about Muhammad Ali."

ACT TWO

THE CONSEQUENCES, 1976–Present

FOOTSTEPS

The pleasant, white-bread town of Plainfield, Indiana—about twenty miles southwest of Indianapolis—just happens to be the home of two unlikely institutions. The more likely of the two is the Indiana Youth Center, a euphemistically named prison that had to be some place in Indiana. The less likely is the Islamic Center of North America. That both would be in Plainfield, a town of only twenty thousand, would sound like a plot device from an under-funded movie were it not true.

On March 25, 1995, the two institutions were joined in the national consciousness. On that cool, gray morning a young man in a kufi cap, known to himself at least as Malik Abdul Aziz, left the Youth Center for good and headed off to services at the Islamic Center. According to the *Agence France Presse*, whose reporter was one of the two hundred media people to cover this event, the twenty-eight-year-old Malik met at the center with an odd trio of at least semi-famous people. One of the three was the ubiquitous Don King. King, in fact, had accompanied him from the prison. The second was the "early mainstream rapper" M. C. Hammer, best known for his "Hammer pants." The third was the conspicuously impaired former boxing great Muhammad Ali. After the group offered a prayer of thanksgiving to Allah, Malik stood up and helped Ali into a chair. "He showed a great respect and concern for his brother Ali," said Malik's spiritual advisor.

Malik, better known as Mike Tyson, had just spent three years in the Youth Center for raping teen beauty queen Desiree Washington. "Tyson would follow in the footsteps of Cassius Clay," wrote the *Agence* reporter, "as a former champion forced out of the ring for three prime years of his career who converted to Muslim during his layoff."

Like other reporters, this French fellow was trying a bit too hard to establish the continuity between Tyson and Ali. Still, it was not that much of a stretch. Tyson saw himself as a "further reinvention of this black masculine cool," writes the astute black critic Gerald Early, "a revision of Muhammad Ali."

What Tyson did not understand is that there was no copying the cultural hodgepodge of Ali's identity. This identity was unique to his time and talents and largely unsupported by the traditional pillars of black American life—family, church, school, community, nation. Ali would make the most of this errant life. But as Mike Tyson learned the hard way, he left no footsteps in which to follow.

ON TIME

It was F. Scott Fitzgerald who once said, "There are no second acts in American lives." Fitzgerald surely did not get one, nor have most boxers, certainly not much of one in any case. In this, Ali would prove the exception once again.

In 1976, the nation's bicentennial year, Ali was about to start life over. During that one dramatic year just passed, the four major influences on Ali's life and career ceased to be. Elijah Muhammad died. South Vietnam fell. Joe Frazier retired, and Belinda Ali threw the champ out of the house.

Despite the transformations, the Second Act had yet to take shape. The Circus continued to move from town to town as noisily as ever. There would be bumps along the road. Pacheco, in fact, describes the next three years as "The Bloody Trail to Defeat, 1976–1978," but Pacheco overlooks Ali's more subtle progress as a human being.

Some signs of change were evident in the run-up to a Munich fight in May of 1976 with England's Richard Dunn, the third in a string of easy paychecks since Manila. With Elijah Muhammad out of the picture, Ali fell under the sway of his son, who was much closer in spirit to Ali.

"Wallace Muhammad is on time," he announced on a May 2 *Face the Nation* appearance. "He's teaching us it's not the color of the physical body that makes a man a devil. God looks at our minds and our actions and our deeds."

Ali could also begin to make the kind of gestures that were closer to his heart. One was to give up $100,000 of his purse in exchange for two thousand tickets to be distributed free to American servicemen in Germany. "I didn't go [into the army] because of my religion," Ali explained at the time, all but apologizing to his friends on the left, "but them soldiers are just doing their job." Ali had begun his transition from angry black nationalist to what black sports scholar David Wiggins describes as a "conservative American who favored steady progress for his people within American society." The transition would not be smooth.

At the beginning of the Dunn fight, Ali had stopped circling the ring when the national anthem was played. The NBC cameras showed him standing respectfully with an American flag to one side of him and a white man, Ferdie Pacheco, to the other. This imagery riled the hardliners within the Muslim camp, and they insisted that Pacheco no longer go into the ring before a fight. Ali stood by quietly while Pacheco was being admonished, then took him aside, and told him to forget what he had just been told. "But," adds Pacheco knowingly, "it's not easy to forget the Black Muslims."

Another move that Ali and Herbert Muhammad made was to give the Dunn fight to Bob Arum to promote and not to Don King. Arum was working with an aspiring young black promoter named Butch Lewis. If Ali advanced racial justice as a cause, Don King employed it as a strategy. King did to Lewis what Ali had done to Frazier, undermine his blackness. "Butch Lewis is just an Uncle Tom," King would tell whoever would listen. "He's just a front man for Arum."

Herbert and Ali had good reason to be suspicious of King. Word had gotten back to them that he had quietly put several of those in Ali's entourage on his payroll. "I saw it myself," Ali employee Bahar

Muhammad tells Newfield. "I used to see Don come up to Deer Lake and give guys cash to spy for him." King was gathering information about Ali and spreading disinformation about Herbert. His goal was not just to promote Ali's fights but to manage Ali. It didn't work. "Don tried a hostile takeover of Muhammad Ali, and it failed," adds Bahar. "That's why, to this day, orthodox Muslims don't like Don King. He tried to cheat the messenger's son." King dismissed Herbert as a racial "Judas," but he would soon enough pay for his sins.

Richard Dunn paid for his as well. Ali knocked him down five times before putting him away in the fifth. Ali would fight five more years, another ninety-six rounds in seven championship bouts. He would never knock down an opponent again.

CLOWN SHOW

On September 2, 1976, Belinda Ali filed for divorce. Among her charges were adultery, desertion, and mental cruelty. It was not something that she ever expected or wanted to do. But after the humiliation of Manila, she had little real choice. "I was the hostess; I was the mother," she explains to Hauser. "I cooked. I cleaned. I did all those things; and I was happy doing it because it made him happy." And then, she adds ruefully, "Everything got destroyed."

The summer of 1976 began as badly as it ended for Ali. In a move that appalled even the most tolerant boxing fans, Ali agreed to "fight" Japanese wrestling champion Antonio Inoki in Tokyo for the so-called "martial arts championship of the world." "What was Herbert Muhammad thinking?" asks the slow-to-upset Pacheco. Pacheco lays the blame for the fiasco not just on Herbert but on promoter Bob Arum, he of the "brilliant brain" and the "scant morals."

Ali gamely tried to promote the event as he always did. In explaining why he would win and had to win, he said innocently enough, "I can't let the American fans down." No one paid any attention to this admission given the absurdity of the event, but that he was fighting for the

"American fans" signaled a notable change from his posture two years earlier.

In Zaire, to counter Foreman's flag-waving at the 1968 Olympics, Ali had planned to enter the ring waving a Zairian flag, a UN flag, and a flag representing the Organization of African Unity. So he claims at least in his ghosted autobiography. However fanciful that memory might be, there is no denying his "Damn America" statement to the Gast camera crew upon arriving in Zaire. That was then. This was now. Wallace Muhammad had called for a "new sense of patriotism," and Ali was responding. This was not something he had to force. Whatever else he had tried to be, Ali—in his brave and boastful innocence—was always sublimely American. He was becoming the instinctive Ali of Rome once again.

The fight was an "absurd clown show," as Pacheco accurately puts it. Inoki crabwalked on all fours for fifteen rounds, kicking at Ali. Ali, for his part, threw six punches, only two of which landed. The fight was declared a draw, but Inoki had inflicted a good deal of damage to Ali's legs. He collapsed back at the hotel in the arms of Aaisha Ali who had stayed with him after the departure of Belinda. It was the madness of this whole Japanese experience that persuaded the young mother that she too had to escape Ali's gravitational pull.

Pacheco meanwhile informed Ali that those bruises could easily turn into blood clots and recommended that Ali cancel the Korea and Philippine exhibitions on his itinerary and head home. Ali agreed, but Pacheco confronted Ali with a prediction. "As soon as I am out the door, the boys of the Ali Circus, the Hoovers [as the scavengers were called], will be in here telling you to go to Korea." The Hoovers quickly proved Pacheco right, as did Ali, who let them talk him into continuing.

The leg injuries retarded Ali's training for his first serious fight post-Manila. It was his third bout with the always-formidable Ken Norton. Thirty thousand fans showed up the night of January 28, 1976, in Yankee Stadium. Nearly thirty years earlier, in that same stadium, some seventy thousand fans had shown up to watch Louis defend his title against Max

Schmeling. The crowd at that first fight was different. Most of the men wore coats and ties. There were some rough characters in attendance, no doubt, and some who had spent their last dime to get in, and it's likely that a fistfight or two broke out.

But what happened at Yankee Stadium in September 1976 was unique to its era. Outside, pickpockets and purse snatchers ran amuck. Inside, the crowd hovered on the edge of chaos. "A lot of undesirables crashed the gate," James Anderson, an Ali bodyguard, remembers. "Going from the dressing room to the ring that night was the longest walk I've ever taken." A job action by the police limited security and made much of this mayhem possible, but the general breakdown in order in the decade past had made it almost inevitable. Ali had played his part. A progressive whirlwind had been uprooting one American institution after another, and he had helped steer it toward black America.

Once again, Don King exploited the Ali model. After his failed takeover of Ali, Herbert Muhammad had given this fight to Madison Square Garden to promote. As payback, King recruited activist Al Sharpton to whip up a little local discontent. His palms now as greased as his hair, Sharpton sang King's praises as a hero to "third world youth" and slammed Ali as a race traitor. "His rhetoric says black," charged Sharpton, "but the bottom line reads lily white." Only King could out-demagogue the Reverend Al. In his rather aggressive defense of set-aside capitalism, he called Ali's arrangement with the Garden "a case of the slave hurrying back to the slavemaster."

That night, however, all Ali had to worry about was Ken Norton, and that was worry enough. Norton owned Ali for the first eight rounds. Ali "wasn't the same fighter anymore," recalls referee Arthur Mercante. "His timing was off; he tired more easily. But he was still the best boxer I've ever seen at coming up instinctively with whatever was necessary to win." Against Norton, that "whatever" was clinching, an art that he was beginning to master. Clinching allowed Ali to lean on the opponent and catch his breath. Given his superior height and—increasingly—his superior weight, clinching also allowed him to grind his opponent down. The referee's job was to stop this technically illegal maneuver, but more and more, the referees were quietly urging Ali on.

By the fifteenth, Ali had managed to pull even on the judges' score-cards. Norton's corner men had forgotten that their man was fighting a myth. They told Norton that he was comfortably ahead and that to win all he would have to do was survive the fifteenth. The cautious Norton gave the round away and thus the fight. "If you saw the look on his face," Norton remembers, "he knew I beat him. He didn't hit me hard the whole fight." The judges ruled otherwise, and the boisterous Yankee Stadium crowd booed the decision. "The feeling was," recalls Pacheco, "that Ali's popularity and reputation influenced the judges."

After the fight, Ali confided to Pacheco that if he couldn't beat Norton, it was time for him to quit. Pacheco agreed. "This time I mean it," Ali told him. "I've got to get out of this before I start getting hurt." They both knew that even if he truly meant to quit, he couldn't. Ali would fight for five more years.

RUNNING DRY

On June 19, 1977, just three months before he would fight the dangerous Ernie Shavers in Madison Square Garden, Ali married the lovely Veronica Porche in a civil ceremony in Los Angeles. Afraid that Ali would quickly get bored on their Hawaii honeymoon, Veronica invited Ali's best man, Howard Bingham, to come with them. The threesome arrived on a Monday evening. Ali did grow restless, despite Bingham's presence, and they were back home Wednesday afternoon. The fact that the couple already had a ten-month-old daughter took some of the traditional thrill out of the occasion

As the Ernie Shavers fight approached, the Muslims in the Ali camp started to wear on Pacheco. They had gotten it into their heads that the good doctor was going to fix the fight by doping Ali. What triggered their unease was Pacheco's refusal to accept payment for his work. "Their ghetto logic," says Pacheco, "was that I must be getting paid by somebody." The more paranoid among them pleaded with Herbert not to let Pacheco give Ali the usual cortisone injection before the fight, and Herbert obliged them. He brought in his own mystery concoction for Pacheco to use instead. Knowing how Ali hated confrontations, Pacheco took him into a locked bathroom and laid out his options: either he accept the cortisone or fight with unnumbed hands because Pacheco was not about to inject him with an unknown substance. Common sense prevailed.

Madison Square Garden president Harry Markson was not so lucky. On the way to the Garden that September night, Ali had somehow accumulated fifty or sixty hangers-on. They showed up together at the employees' entrance. When Markson hustled down to meet them, Ali demanded that either the whole swarm be admitted free, or the fight was off. Markson explained that even standing room was sold out, but the champ wasn't listening. Just hours before the fight, he turned and walked off into the night. Angelo Dundee had to chase after him. Ali finally settled for twenty free passes.

That night, before a sold-out Garden and a huge national TV audience, Ali out-boxed and out-clinched the hard-punching Shavers to win a unanimous decision. As it happened, Ernie Shavers traced his later embrace of Jesus Christ back to this defeat. Without meaning to, Ali was harvesting souls for the Lord.

On the way to victory in the Shavers fight, Ali took a ton of punishment. To prepare himself for the body blows, he had let his sparring partners whack away at him in training, but his sparring partners could hit. The damage was becoming evident.

The day after the fight, a New York Athletic Commission doctor shared the results of Ali's lab work with Pacheco. Ali had not performed this badly on a test since the draft. The tests showed early signs of kidney damage. The head work didn't look so great either. At the urging of his colleague, Pacheco tried his damnedest to get Ali to quit. He sent separate certified letters explaining the lab report to Ali, Veronica, Dundee, Herbert Muhammad, and Wallace Muhammad. None of them responded, not by phone, not by mail, not any which way. "Ali was a gold mine playing out, a well running dry," says Pacheco. "The Muslims refused to see it; I did not." Pacheco quit the Circus.

ONE QUICK SUBWAY ride away from Madison Square Garden, young Mike Tyson was terrorizing the good citizens of Brooklyn. At the time of the Shavers fight he was living on the streets of Brownsville, robbing stores with his homies, holding up gas stations, mugging his neighbors, whatever. Typically, it was Tyson who held the gun. He was eleven years old. He'd been at it for a year.

Even then, Tyson was precociously strong. He'd take on kids five or so years older, and he knocked any number of them cold. "They would jab and jive like Ali," writes Jack Newfield, "and Tyson would rush in and land his punch of natural power." As he grew older, and became a serious student of the sport, Tyson would style himself after Rocky Marciano. "He broke their will," Tyson would say reverentially of the great Marciano.

MIDDLE CLASS VALUES

O n the night of September 15, 1978, some sixty-three thousand people wound their way into the New Orleans Superdome to see Muhammad Ali take on Leon Spinks. They would spend nearly $5 million for the privilege, the largest live gate since Tunney beat Dempsey fifty-one years earlier.

What made the fight against Spinks so compelling was that it was a rematch. Seven months earlier, the ex-Marine and Olympic light heavyweight champ had been fed to Ali like a Christian to a lion. He had had only seven professional fights to that point. He was not ranked among the top ten. Ali, thirty-six at the time, had been too embarrassed to even talk up the fight. He did little in the way of training, a lot in the way of eating.

"I gave away the first six rounds figuring he'd tire out," recalls Ali, "and then it turns out it was me that got tired." Pacheco was there to give color commentary for CBS. "I felt helpless watching the ghost of Ali take this beating, lose his title to an amateur pretender," he remembers. "It was shameful, degrading, and sad." Ali lost in a split decision that should have been unanimous.

As always, Ali proved to be a good sport at the post-fight press conference. He credited Spinks with fighting a tough fight and never quitting. "You can't just go and die because you lose," he added. "I did my best." Privately, however, he was tormented. A day after the fight, a friend, who was staying with Ali in Chicago, found him up and running at 2:00 A.M., punching the air while he ran and shouting, "Gotta get my title back. Gotta get my title back."

Only an ex-champ knows what it feels like to lose something as all-defining as the heavyweight championship of the world. Floyd Patterson wrote with particular sensitivity on the subject of loss, a subject that obsessed him. "You've got to be able to feel what it means to be somebody—to belong—and then suddenly you don't belong," he observed sagely at age twenty-seven, "and you wonder whether you were ever meant to be a human being other people could look up to."

In no other sport is a single defeat so consequential. In boxing, the loss of a championship fight can very well mean the loss of a meaningful career. "Step into the wrong punch and your chance at the big bucks can go up in smoke," confirms Larry Holmes. "You can go from champion to a perpetual opponent in a blink, your purses shrinking to chump change." Rare is the boxer who has any other skill of value to fall back on. In lingering beyond his moment, Ali was not the exception. He was the norm.

"Leon Spinks borrowed my title," Ali told reporters before the rematch, and Spinks seemed eager to give the title back. He spent those seven months between fights in emotional freefall. He partied hard, smoked dope, drank moonshine, got busted on a cocaine rap, disappeared for days on end, and attracted just about every leech not fixed in the Ali firmament. He trained for a total of about ten days. "I want everybody to love me," Spinks told one reporter in inner city-accented sixties argot, "but I gotta be me. I'm a ghetto nigger; people shouldn't forget that about me." As for Ali, he trained harder than he had since Manila.

The bout itself proved less exciting than a Spinks night out in the French Quarter. The infighting in Spinks's corner was more explosive than the fight in the ring. "Objectively speaking," Howard Cosell recalls, "it was a terrible fight." His skills seriously diminished, Ali relied on his middle class values to pull him through—his focus, his discipline, his patience, his smarts. If such virtues don't make for great TV, they continued to produce results. "He just held a lot," said Spinks, who never quite got it, "and I had a lot of things on my mind." Ali won a unanimous decision and regained the title. The Circus wasn't over yet.

IN BROOKLYN, MEANWHILE, young Mike Tyson caught a break. The police nabbed the twelve-year-old swiping a purse, and the court sent him to a boys school upstate. Although his life would parallel Floyd Patterson's in some interesting ways, including their respective upstate exiles, Tyson was a much rougher customer. He had no fear of God and no father in the home. In Brownsville, by 1978, few boys had either. Having reached critical mass in the city's increasingly mean streets, these wild children committed crimes that would have shocked even the young Floyd Patterson.

When Tyson arrived at the Tryon School, the counselors diagnosed him as "violent, depressed, and mute." They remember him as the most difficult kid in the thirty-five-kid cottage reserved for the baddest of the bad. To complicate matters, Tyson was also the strongest. By thirteen, he could bench press 220 pounds and beat up the guards almost as easily as his fellow residents. He was headed for a gangster's life, and then, just like in the movies, they put the gloves on him.

DISASTER IN THE DESERT

Only Joe Louis held the heavyweight title for more consecutive years than Larry Holmes, and only Louis successfully defended his title more times. He "was a splendid champion who dominated an era," writes Newfield of Holmes. And yet, for all that, Ali's former sparring partner got painfully little respect.

The reason is not hard to figure. "You just don't have the charisma," Howard Cosell ungenerously explained to him early in his career. What Cosell meant is that Holmes had less charisma than the guy he was following. "I was not Muhammad Ali," Holmes admitted, and the fans would not let him forget it. On the night of October 2, 1980, he had the chance to face the man he was not in the one place where charisma counted for nothing, the ring.

Holmes was born the same year as George Foreman, 1949. Although he grew up in "the poor part" of Easton, Pennsylvania, the nature of his poverty reveals just how prosperous America had become. "We lived with no air conditioning in the summer," he recalls painfully, adding, "the only comfort we got was from a store-bought fan." He also talks of watching the TV show, *The Millionaire*, and yearning for the man with the money to show up at his door. Sonny Liston, the titleholder just fifteen years earlier, had grown up in a hotter part of the world without electricity, let alone a television or an electric fan. If he complained, no one bothered to listen.

That much said, Holmes was one of twelve children abandoned by a roving father. He did not have it easy. He credits his loving mother, Flossie, and a supportive community for pulling him through. As with Frazier and Ali, it was the Police Athletic League that introduced him to boxing. He saw it as a way out and up. His seventh-grade education wasn't going to get him into Harvard.

Still, Holmes always managed to find decent work. By thirteen, he was driving—illegally, of course—his own car. By the time he was sixteen, he had bought a brand new Plymouth Road Runner. Soon after, he got a job driving a truck at triple the minimum wage. Boxing wasn't the only way out of poverty for an uneducated black kid like Holmes in the 1960s. It was simply the most promising way, "a chance to make money, a chance to build a life, the best chance I would have."

Lacking Ali's sponsors and Olympic gold, the road to success for Holmes was a good deal longer and less secure. In the swirl of the Ali Circus, no one paid him much mind. He was twenty-six before he fought a name contender. Few saw how much he wanted to succeed and how hard he was willing to work to do so. In 1975, Holmes quit the Circus for good. By that time, he felt confident that he was better than Ali. Ali may have felt the same.

To speed his path to the top, Holmes made a move that he would soon come to regret. He signed on with the "dirty, rotten Don King." As with every other black boxer in his universe, King used and abused Holmes. "Not only was he out to bleed you dry," says Holmes, "he also thought he could run your life like a plantation massah." Lost for words to describe their dealings with the man, many young boxers pulled their metaphors from *Roots* or *Mandingo*.

When Holmes took advantage of a King grand jury investigation to move his business to Bob Arum, King warned Holmes convincingly, "If you do, I'll have your legs broke." From then on, Holmes packed a pistol when he did his roadwork. Still, he hung tough with Arum and managed to win a share of the heavyweight title—the World Boxing Council (WBC) crown—by beating Ken Norton in Las Vegas in June 1978.

Ali meanwhile was making lots of noise about quitting. After beating Spinks for the World Boxing Association (WBA) title in September 1978, he told a reporter, "None of the black athletes before me ever got out when they were on top. My people need one black man to come out on top. I'll be the first." In June 1979, Ali ended whatever little suspense there was by agreeing to give up his WBA title. Hauser speculates that a $300,000 payment from Bob Arum greased the decision. Arum apparently wanted to promote a fight for the vacant crown in South Africa.

To keep busy, Ali made a TV movie called *Freedom Road* in which he played a freed slave who rises to greatness. He had still not quite reconciled himself to freedom for females. "Someone's got to wear the pants and someone's got to wear the dress," he told the *Washington Post* that July. "There isn't going to be any equality."

To further his movie career and Veronica's social ambitions, he moved his family to a mansion in Los Angeles—"the most luxurious residence that any heavyweight ever owned," says Hauser. The only problem was that Ali was close to broke. He had spent most of his millions on his L.A. digs, his ex-wives, his children, the Hoovers who sucked him dry, sundry freelance hucksters, and a string of bad business deals. "Ali should be richer than Bill Cosby," investment advisor Gene Dibble tells Hauser, "but he let anybody and everybody into his business, and signed his future away in the dark." The "simple, spellbinding, eloquent black socialism" about which Roger Kahn had sung never got much beyond the simple, spellbinding handout stage.

With the exception of Pacheco, most of those around Ali blame Herbert Muhammad for the meltdown. "He completely messed up Ali's potential," says Jeremiah Shabazz of Herbert. Adds Dibble, "I think Herbert was first and foremost interested in Herbert." But there was blame enough to go around, and in the final analysis it was Ali who undid his own potential. He signed on to so many bad deals, in fact, that his very signature lost its value. Business held little charm for Ali in any case. For a man who could scarcely read, write, or calculate, it had to be intimidating. Like so many suddenly retired athletes, he was growing unsure of himself. An opportunity to use skills that he had mastered—or at least thought he had mastered—presented itself in early 1980.

A few years prior, Ali had told the *Washington Post* that when he got out of boxing, he hoped to "put on a coat and tie and be the black Henry Kissinger." President Jimmy Carter took him at his word. Following the Soviet invasion of Afghanistan in December 1979, America had chosen to boycott the 1980 Moscow Olympics. To line up support for the boycott, Carter dispatched the black Kissinger to black Africa.

Unfortunately for both men, Carter's grasp of world affairs was no firmer than Ali's. The black African nations understood the difference between a celebrity goodwill tour and a serious diplomatic mission even if Carter did not. The Ali visit did not amuse them. "Would the United States send [female tennis star] Chris Evert to negotiate with London?" asked a clear-eyed Tanzanian official.

Ali lacked the wherewithal to explain the logic behind his own mission or the reason why America had not backed Africa's antiapartheid boycott of the previous Olympics. He knew nothing about various revolutionary movements on the continent or the Soviet role therein. "They didn't tell me about that in America," he conceded at what may have been the most awkward press conference in recent diplomatic history. "Maybe I'm being used to do something that ain't right."

By any measure, the mission was a disaster. Says friend Howard Bingham, "I guess [Ali] thought he was a diplomat, and it kind of hurt when he found out he wasn't." No matter how old or out of shape, Ali knew he was a better boxer than ambassador. He was also learning something about who he really was and where he belonged. "There's no place like home," Ali said upon returning, "especially when home is America."

His restlessness and dwindling resources inspired Ali back into boxing. After some back and forth on choice of opponents, it was agreed that Larry Holmes would be the surest payday. Since beating Norton, Holmes had prevailed in seven straight title defenses, none of his opponents going the distance. He was emerging as the boxer of his generation, but he still lacked the cachet that an Ali fight could give him.

Don King had somehow wormed his way back into everyone's good graces. He first proposed Egypt as the site, but Holmes would have none of it. He could just imagine how long a ten count could be in a Muslim country even if they had invented Arabic numerals. The parties settled on another desert site, closer to home, Las Vegas and Caesar's Palace. Ali was to get $8 million and Holmes $2.5 million. "One more fight and I can be set for life," Ali said at the time. "Where else can I make that kind of money in an hour?"

Despite the impressive hourly rate, not everyone thought a Holmes fight was worth the risk. In his own recounting at least, Don King was among those who tried to dissuade Ali. At the time, King informed boxing writer John Schulian that he agreed to put the deal together only upon Ali's insistence that the fight was "for equality and justice, for the future of our children." Although King was surely lying about his own motives, he may have accurately described Ali's. The champ was still enchanted by his own mythic self. "Ali wanted to be Ali one more time," affirms Pacheco. "To bathe in the love and adulation of his public while everyone listened to him in rapt attention."

Dr. Pacheco was the most adamant and influential of the naysayers. "Ali should not try to come back," he said repeatedly and publicly. Pacheco argued that Ali's organs had been abused over the years and would be subject to even greater abuse in a fight at this age at this level. "Even Ali is human and subject to the laws of nature," he insisted.

When the debate over Ali's health grew more heated, the Nevada State Athletic Commission mandated a trip to the famed Mayo Clinic for Ali. The Mayo doctors observed evidence of "some difficulty with [Ali's] speech and memory and perhaps to a very slight degree his coordination," but for reasons unknown, they downplayed the problems. That was green light enough for the Nevada Commission, which promptly approved the license, and the fight was on.

Helping Ali get medically ready was Herbert Muhammad's personal doctor, Charles Williams. Pacheco had first encountered Williams in Zaire and even then had serious doubts about his competence. In Las Vegas, Williams gave Pacheco all the more reason to doubt him. A few weeks before the fight, Williams diagnosed Ali as having a hypothyroid condition and put him on Thyrolar.

"It was stupid to think he was going to win," Williams admits to Hauser. "I just wanted to get him in good enough shape, and sure enough, he looked good." The Thyrolar seemed, at least, to help Ali deal with his weight issues. So did the amphetamines he was taking. In reality, these drugs did little more for his weight than the hair dye did for his gray, but the hair dye wasn't likely to kill him.

Longtime friend and advisor Gene Dibble saw through the makeover. He had observed Ali since before the Liston fight and sensed that something was seriously wrong. It did no good to talk to Angelo Dundee. Dundee had long since lost whatever control of Ali he once had. The Muslims often shut him out of critical meetings. Dibble understood that he would have to convince Herbert. He tracked him down in the hotel lobby, and Herbert blew him off. He told Dibble that he had no idea what he was talking about.

Despite all the noise from the Circus, Holmes stayed impressively cool and focused throughout the prefight hype. When Ali tried to rattle him with a ritualized insult, Holmes would finish his sentences for him. As Ali's sparring partner for three years, he had heard them all before.

If the patter was old and worn, so was the boxer. "The man was slower than Heinz ketchup," recalls Holmes. For the Easton Assassin, it was like going after a piñata with the blindfold off. "Ali had no spark," says Holmes, "no energy. He was a shell of himself." All Ali had was his mouth. Altogether out of character, as Holmes knew, Ali showered him with one vile epithet after another.

Holmes responded by pounding away surgically at Ali's body. It was "like watching an autopsy on a man who's still alive," said Sylvester Stallone, who was at ringside. It was that bad. "It wasn't a fight," says Hauser. "It was an execution." Herbert sat with his head down for half the fight. He couldn't bear to watch. Although he was reporting on the fight, Jack Newfield could not watch either. Ali had come to carry "so much meaning" for him that he had to turn away.

Only Ali's pride kept him on his feet. "In between rounds," says Holmes, "I sat on the stool and prayed I wouldn't have to hurt him." Finally, after ten skull-rattling rounds, Herbert nodded to Dundee, and Dundee told the referee, "That's all."

Bundini pleaded for one more round, but the usually reserved Dundee harshly rejected his plea, and the "Disaster in the Desert" came to its whimpering end. Holmes walked across the ring in tears and kissed Ali. "I respect you, man. And I love you." Ali was too dazed to comprehend. "They sacrificed Ali," a still outraged John Schulian would tell Hauser a decade after the fight. "That's what it was, a human sacrifice for money and power."

By "they," Schulian was referring to the Ali Circus, particularly Herbert Muhammad and Don King—King above all. Schulian calls Ali "one of the great symbols of our time" and regrets the tarnishing of that symbol by people who "didn't care one bit about the things he stood for his entire life."

Schulian does not specify what those "things" might be. Newfield takes a stab. As he sees it, Ali "symbolized change, rebellion, and liberation in an era defined by those qualities." Those may be "qualities," but they are not values. For Newfield, finally, Ali symbolized little more than the era itself.

In a similar vein, sports scholar Michael Oriard reads the young Ali as a "true multicultural text." He argues that in watching the first troubled act of Ali's life, the years before 1976, "we Americans, in all our diversity, were able to find important values." Individuals who did not find those unspecified values—perhaps half the nation—were apparently too diverse to qualify for Oriard's universe of "we Americans."

Mark Kram makes the clever and painfully accurate comparison between Ali and Chauncey Gardiner, the amiable but clueless protagonist of Jerzy Kosinski's *Being There*. Ali's amorphous nature helped make him as attractive a symbolic vessel as Gardiner. One could imagine that vessel full of whatever content he chose. "Ali has that power," writes the always-observant Torres. "He changes people. He blinds people. Many times you see what Ali wants you to see and not what is there."

What was not "there," and never really was there, was an angry black man or an antiwar revolutionary or an international ambassador of peace. What was there all along was one very good, very innocent, self-deluding boxer. For the Holmes fight, as in many others, Don King manipulated the manipulators. He parodied Ali's "equality and justice" rhetoric and pocketed the results.

True to form, King shortchanged Ali after the highly profitable Holmes fight by $1.2 million. Ali sued King in return. Knowing that a public squabble with Ali was bad business, King devised a plot that was perversely admirable in its grasp of human fragility. To start, he invited Jeremiah Shabazz to his Manhattan office. The Muslim minister had helped lead Ali to Islam twenty years prior, and Ali trusted him. When Shabazz arrived, he saw $50,000 in cash in a suitcase sitting on King's desk. As King explained, that money was for Ali—provided he first sign a waiver dismissing the suit. King knew the weakness boxers had for hard cash, and, in this regard, Ali was just another boxer. King sensed Shabazz's own weakness for cash and, as Shabazz admits, exploited it to recruit his services. Shabazz got the signature, and Ali got the suitcase. He had given up a settlement of more than $1 million for $50,000 in cash.

IN THE SUMMER of 1980, while Ali was training for the Holmes fight, Jose Torres and his friend Jack Newfield took a ride from New York to the small Hudson River town of Catskill, about one hundred miles north of the city. This was the home of the legendary Cus D'Amato. Years ago D'Amato had rescued Torres from the slums of Ponce, Puerto Rico, and before that he had rescued Floyd Patterson from the slums of Brooklyn. He managed them both to world championships.

D'Amato now maintained his own boxing gym above the town's police station. Torres and Newfield had come to check out D'Amato's newest protégé, a fourteen-year-old phenom first spotted by guard Bobby Stewart at the nearby Tryon School for Boys. Stewart had once been a pro boxer and knew of D'Amato's gym in nearby Catskill. He invited D'Amato to Tryon to take a look. D'Amato watched the then thirteen-year-old throw a few punches and said, "That's the heavyweight champion of the world. If he wants it, it's his."

So impressed was D'Amato that he soon took the boy home to live with him. D'Amato shared a sprawling fourteen-room house at the end of a winding dirt road overlooking the Hudson with his longtime companion and sister-in-law, Camille Ewald. Also living in Catskill was Cus's trainer friend, Kevin Rooney, and some of the other young boxers in the D'Amato fold, Mike Tyson the newest and youngest among them.

When Newfield first met Tyson, his social skills were still primitive. Newfield describes him as "withdrawn and sullen," though he seemed to be warming up to D'Amato. Physically, he was only about 5'6"—he would never reach six feet—but he weighed about two hundred pounds of pure fury. When Newfield watched the young Tyson work out, he saw "a manchild prodigy puncher."

D'Amato, however, had long been of the belief that a boxer's character was more important than the power of his punch. He worked with

Tyson, as he had with other young boxers, on instilling traditional virtue: hard work, self-discipline, self-denial, independence, integrity. With Tyson, he was starting from scratch. The boy had learned almost nothing nice in his first fourteen years and a whole lot of nasty. There were no guarantees that D'Amato could turn him around.

TRAUMA IN THE BAHAMAS

For many of the Ali faithful, 1981 began like a nightmare and ended even worse. On January 20, Ronald Reagan was inaugurated president. Fifteen years earlier, Reagan had personally intervened to keep "that draft dodger" from fighting in California, and he was not likely to apologize. Unlike his predecessor, Reagan still saw the virtue in fighting Communists head on, and he wasn't about to high-five those who had avoided the fight.

Even with Reagan in Washington, only bad news came out of California. Ali held a press conference to wash his hands of it. "A guy used my name to embezzle $21,000,000," he admitted, then joked, "Ain't many names that can steal that much." For the investors and employees of Wells Fargo Bank, the joke fell flat.

The scam had its origins years earlier when "Harold Smith"—his real name was Ross Fields—met Ali while he was touring Smith's Tennessee State University. A classic hanger-on, Smith got involved with a sprinter named Houston McTear and parlayed that involvement into one of the cheaper seats in the Ali Circus. One day while discussing various sprinters with McTear and Smith, Ali chanced to say, "Harold, wouldn't it be something if we could get all these niggers together and find out which one really is the fastest."

The result was the Muhammad Ali Invitational Track Meet in 1977. McTear won the premium sprint event, and Marvin Gaye won the celebrity dash. The thirty-five-year-old Ali finished next to last in the celebrity event, edging out Tony Orlando. The relative success of that event led Smith to start a Muhammad Ali Amateur Boxing Team, and that in turn led to Muhammad Ali Professional Sports (MAPS), with 25 percent of the profits going to Ali.

The only one as clueless as Ali in this deal was Smith himself. By using Ali's name, he was able to seduce an insider at Wells Fargo to open the spigot for MAPS. Smith began to promote fights after a fashion, offering huge sums to fighters and getting little in return save for his extraordinary "line of credit" at Wells Fargo. At his trial, he defended himself by claiming that he was running the program for purely altruistic motives, as though that were excuse enough. In reality, the sham glory of orbiting in Ali's universe was the likely inspiration.

Smith persuaded Ali to come to his closing argument and lend his magic to the proceedings. Easily bored, Ali spent most of the time fidgeting and playing with the little girl sitting near him. The jury wasn't impressed. They convicted Smith of thirty-one of thirty-two counts. Well-versed in the art of the exculpatory, Smith admits to Hauser that he may have been "guilty of something" but was sentenced to prison only because "I'm a nigger and I got caught being involved with the wrong people."

"Like I always say," Joe Louis had ventured boldly many years before, "and some people don't like it, first thing black people do when something goes wrong is to say, 'It's 'cause I'm black.'" In Joe Louis's time, that rationale was often justified. By 1981, it rarely was. In a racially recharged environment, however, it made for a useful weapon.

At the time of Smith's trials, Louis was facing a graver trial of his own. He was dying. The heart that had served him so well in the ring was giving out. His longtime friend Frank Sinatra flew Louis to Houston to have the famed Michael DeBakey perform surgery, which Sinatra paid for, but it was to little avail. Louis died on April 12, 1981, at the age of sixty-six. On April 21, as a result of President Reagan's intervention, he was buried with full military honors at Arlington National Cemetery.

"I was privileged and will always be grateful to have had Joe Louis as my friend," said Reagan on his passing. "All of America mourns his loss, and we convey our sympathy to his family and friends. But we also share their pride in his professional achievements, his service to his country, and his strength of heart and spirit."

LIKE HAROLD SMITH, Dr. Charles Williams had mastered the art of denial. Despite a definitive ruling by UCLA that he had misdiagnosed Ali and maltreated him—Pacheco calls his treatment of Ali "almost criminal"—Williams refused all blame. "At UCLA, when they checked Ali, they didn't find any evidence of a thyroid problem but that's because I'd corrected it," he claims with scary defiance. "I'm positive I was correct."

Other Ali advisors, however, accepted the UCLA findings and ran with them, right to Ali. They tried to persuade him that the Thyrolar caused his undoing against Holmes, not his age or his diminished skills, and they were making headway. The Circus was beginning to close in on the ringmaster.

If there was any one factor that prodded Ali to his last fight, it was his felt need to continue speaking to his international audience. "People tell me not to fight," he told the New York Times that year, "but they are at the foot of the wall of knowledge and I am at the top." The Ali myth was in the process of claiming one more victim, Ali himself.

At the time Ali was so conspicuously unfit that even Nevada didn't want the fight. When its State Athletic Commission began hearings on an Ali license, Ali took his business elsewhere. Not finding any interest from theater promoters or the networks, Ali and the Circus settled on a low-rent venue in Nassau in the Bahamas. For an opponent, they scaled down to a troubled young Jamaican named Trevor Berbick, who had recently managed to hang in for fifteen rounds against Larry Holmes.

The Nation of Islam, indirectly at least, had taken over the promotion of the fight. A Nation member, James Cornelius, was the prime mover and shaker. Before getting into the promotion business, Cornelius had been honing a career in larceny and bank fraud. He had nine arrests on his résumé and at least one conviction for theft.

In early December 1981, the irrepressible Don King flew into Freeport demanding his slice of the action. He claimed that he had an option on the three Berbick fights after Holmes and squeezed Cornelius for $100,000 and possibly more. If he did not get it, he threatened to block the impending fight with an injunction. This was one of those rare moments when King seemed to be within his rights.

Cornelius thought otherwise. He and several large Muslim gentlemen paid an early morning visit to King in his room at the Bahama Princess Hotel. "I hear he was begging and pleading," Jeremiah Shabazz recounts with obvious relish, "but the brothers gave him a sound thrashing with broken teeth and blood all over." Cornelius told King to leave the island immediately, or he would kill him, and this King promptly did. He checked into a Miami hospital with a broken nose, missing teeth, a badly cut mouth, and a seriously bruised ego.

Wondrously brazen, King then flew up to New York to file a complaint against Cornelius with the very FBI agents who were then in the process of investigating King's illegal activities. He recounted the beating in such grand style that he had the agents laughing out loud. He told the agents that as the Muslims were beating him he managed to slip two of them $200 each, and the one turned to Cornelius and said, "I think we done enough." Said King to the agents, "I knew my money was working for me already."

"Don King is one of the dirtiest rottenest pieces of scum that ever lived," Shabazz reports to Hauser, then says in the very next breath, "On a couple of occasions, he gave me some bucks to bring Ali to him, and I'm ashamed to say, that's what I did." It was *after* the King beating, in fact, that King used Shabazz to buy off Ali with the suitcase full of cash. What keeps the observer from despising King is his skill at conning the con men. He may have been evil, but he was an evil genius.

The Princess Hotel beating proved to be the more interesting of the Bahamian fights. The Ali-Berbick bout misfired from the get-go. The promoters could not find keys for the ballfield where the fight was to be staged, a bell for the ring, or extra gloves for the preliminary fighters. These misadventures pushed the main event two hours behind schedule. From the opening cowbell, the 236-pound Ali put up little more resistance than an underpaid sparring partner. All three judges gave the fight to Berbick.

Ali had long boasted that he would not end his career the way Joe Louis did. He did not. Louis was two years younger at the end than the thirty-nine-year-old Ali. He fought a valiant last fight against Rocky Marciano in Madison Square Garden with the whole world watching.

Gracious as usual at the next day's press conference, Ali told the few media in attendance, "No excuses this time, but at least I didn't go down. No pictures of me falling through the ropes, no broken teeth, no blood. I'm happy I'm still pretty. I came out all right for an old man. We all lose sometimes. We all grow old." And that was it, the end of the road, the last stop for the Ali Circus. The Ali myth, however, still had legs. It would just take a while to find them.

AS IT HAPPENED, Joe Frazier fought his last fight in December 1981 as well. He didn't need to. When he retired in June 1976 after a loss to George Foreman, Frazier was set for life. He had invested wisely. He also had enough to keep him busy. His eleven-piece ensemble—the Smokin' Joe Frazier Revue—played some of the better clubs in America. The Joe Frazier Gym in North Philadelphia continued to turn out quality boxers. He also owned a restaurant—Smokin' Joe's Corner—and a limousine service. On top of all that, he amused himself with a dozen or so different vehicles, everything from a Harley to a Rolls Royce.

And despite a love life as chaotic as Ali's, he had stayed with his first wife for some twenty years, and they raised their many children strictly and well. Several of his sons and nephews, in fact, trained with him. The most notable of the bunch was his son Marvis, who would go on to fight both Larry Holmes and Mike Tyson. In training with his relatives, Frazier worked himself into shape enough to give boxing another go. "I loved the combat," Frazier says with conviction. He fought ex-con Jumbo Cummings to a draw on December 3, 1981, and heeded his family and friends when they told him that "the smoke was just about out." After that uneasy December, neither he nor Ali would ever fight again.

DURING THE EARLY years of his career, the fate of Newark tracked with Ali's in terms of chaos and turbulence but not in terms of success. Four days after Ali's comeback fight against Berbick in December 1981, I signed on as a deputy director for Newark's thousand-employee Housing and Redevelopment Authority, allegedly under a reform administration. As I quickly learned, Newark's much-discussed "comeback" proved no more successful than the "Trauma in the Bahamas." Appropriately perhaps, the city went ahead and renamed one of its more troubled streets "Muhammad Ali Boulevard."

As fate would have it, I worked on the same block as my friend, Kenny, now a fire captain. I spent more than a few lunchtimes at the firehouse, eating their hearty food and swapping Newark horror stories. As the most visible symbols of authority in the racially troubled decade or so past, the firemen had more than their share.

I had a few of my own. My assignment for the summer of 1982 was to "take back" Hayes Homes, the housing project at the epicenter of the 1967 riot. My boss, a Philippine woman whose idol was Imelda Marcos, brought her Byzantine, third-world skills to the job. To embarrass a politically wired foe within the administration, she had starved this desperate, ten-building high-rise of all maintenance and management assistance for six months. In the interim, the gangs and the squatters had the run of the place. The police from the 4th Precinct across the street patrolled in groups of three when they patrolled at all.

When I went in with an armed bodyguard that first day, I found nine of the ten buildings in almost unbelievable disrepair. The kids had set fires in the garbage chutes. The fires burned out the electric eyes on the trash compactors so the chutes were useless. The elevators were all down as well. The women in the projects—there were almost no men, at least not on anyone's lease—occasionally threw the garbage down to the next landing rather than walk it down ten or so flights. To negotiate the dark and filthy stairwells, the light bulbs having long since been snatched or smashed, they wore miner's caps with lamps on them. The caps also protected their heads against the batteries that kids threw at passers-by from the windows.

In nine buildings out of ten, the flies ruled. They bred in the garbage, water-soaked from the occasional fire, and buzzed as loud as a weed whip. In the entryway of some buildings, they formed a palpable screen that one had to wipe away to pass through.

Then there was the tenth building. And there was the maintenance man, he too named Muhammad. I do not know what Muslim sect he belonged to. I do not know if he was being paid. But I do know that when my boss pulled out the maintenance staff, Muhammad refused to abandon his tenants. He persuaded them to abide by the guidelines he suggested, and they did. Almost miraculously, in the midst of the chaos, the building remained clean, safe and orderly. If Newark was looking for a Muslim to name a street after, one who honored the ideals of the movement, they could have found a real hero much closer to home.

YOUNG REPUBLICAN

Trevor Berbick rates two major asterisks in boxing history. He was the last man to face Muhammad Ali in the ring and the first reigning champ to fall to Mike Tyson.

Twenty years and a world of trouble later, it is easy to forget how brightly Mike Tyson's star once shown. Writing for the *Village Voice* in 1985, the usually tough-minded Jack Newfield said of Tyson, "He has overcome every adversity to redeem a wayward life and become a role model to a generation of lost youth." Writing a year later, Joyce Carol Oates predicted that Tyson would be "the first heavyweight boxer in America to transcend the issues of race."

As preposterous as her prediction now sounds, Oates wrote with some justification. Starting with his first professional fight, a one-round knock-out of Hector Mercedes in March 1985, Tyson attracted highly enthusiastic and largely white audiences, especially on his home turf in upstate New York. Jose Torres writes of Tyson fans arriving by the busload in Glens Falls, New York, for a 1986 fight against James "Quick" Tills. "Glens Falls transformed itself into a huge carnival," reports Torres, "and every one of the mostly white faces was rooting for their favorite son."

Starting in the Joe Louis era, white fans had shown themselves capable of rooting for black boxers, even in fights against white boxers. What Torres finds remarkable is that "every one" of the white fans pulled enthusiastically for Tyson. This was new. Ali had had this potential a generation earlier but chose instead to narrow his audience to the ideologically like-minded.

Tyson's popularity derived in part from his extraordinary skill and single-minded ferocity. Few fight fans can resist a wunderkind. Tyson also benefited greatly from the myth of "Cus and the Kid." Early in his career, D'Amato's management partners, Jimmy Jacobs and Bill Cayton, consciously promoted the myth to soften the contours of Tyson's still rough-edged persona. The formula proved irresistible to fight fans.

Skeptics like Gerald Early and others are inclined to puncture the myth by pointing out D'Amato's potentially exploitative interest in Tyson and his seeming indifference to Tyson's personal problems. Tyson, for instance, was not well enough socialized to survive the Catskill public schools. He had to be tutored at home. Still, whatever its imperfections, "Cus and the Kid" had a more solid grounding in reality than did the Ali myth. D'Amato's friendly Catskill clan was all the family Tyson had or knew, and the members of that family came to matter hugely to him. "My life begins here," the nineteen-year-old Tyson would tell future biographer Phil Berger.

Nor was it a simple affair to transform this feral street child into even an ordinary adolescent. "At first," Camille Ewald tells Berger, "Mike was very rebellious, very angry. He wouldn't listen. But Cus spent hours and hours explaining everything." Tyson does not dissent. "In the beginning," he says, "if I got upset, I'd get nasty."

Early and others suggest that D'Amato would never have taken Tyson in were he not a boxing prodigy, and he likely would not have if for no other reason than he was seventy-five years old at the time. Tyson himself sensed the fragility of the arrangement. During his amateur career, he desperately feared losing lest it mean his exile from the D'Amato Eden.

A video crew once picked up the young Tyson crying before an amateur bout in his truly poignant search for reassurance. "I've come a long way, remember," he pleaded. "Everybody likes me . . . I'm proud of myself." There may have been something in D'Amato's gruff character that prompted this insecurity. His first great protégé, Floyd Patterson, was equally anxious about defeat. Ali, on the other hand, always knew that at the end of the fight his mother and father and brother—and later, half the known universe—would love him regardless of the outcome. Tyson had no such guarantee.

For all its limitations, Tyson's improvised family was more genuine than many a natural one. In 1984, D'Amato signed on as Tyson's legal guardian. When Tyson's mother died back in Brooklyn, Tyson asked Camille if he could call her "mother," and she happily obliged. Until D'Amato died of pneumonia in November 1985, Tyson would introduce Cus and Camille as his mother and father. Tyson's affection for D'Amato was on full display at D'Amato's funeral. "I never knew what love was until now," the nineteen-year-old sobbed to Camille. "He taught me so much."

Although the "Cus and the Kid" myth had an obvious racial angle, it did not depend on race to work. By the 1980s, the media were a little squeamish about its implicit paternalism. The myth was no longer quite the "narcotic" Early suggests it to be. More powerful and more universal was the bridge between generations and traditions, what Early calls "the age-old myth of the coach-athlete friendship." Had the older mentor been a Morgan Freeman type—a Yank Durham, an Eddie Futch, or an Archie Moore—the myth would have played just as well, perhaps better. At the very least, the arrangement would have been less vulnerable to the racially inspired predations of Don King.

A year after Cus's death, Tyson journeyed to Las Vegas to fulfill his prophecy. With Jimmy Jacobs as manager and Kevin Rooney as trainer, Cus was still "in the house." Having had Jacobs's film library at his disposal, Tyson proved himself an ardent student of boxing history. Oates suggests, in fact, that he patterned his look, especially his "savagely short" hair, after Jack Dempsey. In style, given his limitations in height and reach, he patterned himself after Marciano and Joe Frazier.

Trevor Berbick never had a chance. Tyson took the fight to him from the opening bell and defined the ring experience in his own terms. "He created the pressure, and my guy didn't react to the pressure," Berbick trainer Angelo Dundee would say of Tyson after the fight. "He throws combinations I never saw before." In round two, one of those combinations sent Berbick to the canvas. A brutal left hook to the head moments later sent him to the showers. Writes a thrilled and optimistic Joyce Carol Oates, "The post-Ali era has finally ended."

THREE DAYS BEFORE the Berbick-Tyson fight, Muhammad Ali started a new era of his own when he married Lonnie Williams. In a very real way, he was circling back to where he came from and who he once was. Lonnie had grown up across the street from Ali. Their mothers were best friends. Fittingly, the wedding took place in Louisville at the home of former Louisville mayor Harvey Sloane, who also performed the ceremony.

That Sloane was white no longer seemed a matter of significance. "All men are brothers—black, brown, red, or white," Ali had recently told the *Washington Post*. "None of that devil stuff. We used to [believe] that at one time, but [Wallace] saved us from that."

Three months before, Ali had put to bed the most discouraging period of his life when he and his third official wife, Veronica Porche, divorced. Although Ali had to have been difficult to live with, Hauser can find no one to say a good word about Veronica. Ali and Belinda's daughter, Maryum, sums up the consensus from within the Ali camp. "I was always worried about my father with Veronica. She was like a stage wife," says Maryum. "I knew that when my father stopped fighting and the bright lights and money disappeared, Veronica would be gone." And gone she was, and with their two daughters, Hana and Laila. Their departure left

Ali heartsick. True to form, Ali dispensed with a stringent prenuptial Veronica had signed and gave her the greater part of his estate.

That estate unfortunately was considerably less than it might have been thanks to a continuing series of spectacularly bad deals. Perhaps the one that was most indicative of Ali's oversized ambitions was the creation of the Muhammad Ali Financial Corporation, the officers of which were authorized to negotiate a fantastic hundred-billion-dollar loan to build three hundred mosques and one hundred thousand low-income housing units.

AT ABOUT THE same time Ali was imagining the Muhammad Ali Financial Corporation, George Foreman was building the George Foreman Youth and Community Center in Houston. The very tangibility of Foreman's accomplishments during this period serves as a useful contrast to Ali's whimsical schemes.

In the way of background, the twenty-eight-year-old Foreman experienced "a deep pull from God" after losing to Jimmy Young in 1977. "In a split second I was dead, over my head, under my feet," Foreman recalls. "And I just said, I don't care if this is death. I still believe there's a God." That recognition changed everything for Foreman. "I was rescued out of nothing," Foreman continues, "alive in that dressing room again, with blood flowing through my veins, screaming Jesus Christ is coming alive in me."

Unlike the Nation of Islam, Christianity provided a useful role model in the person of Jesus. Foreman needed one. His young life had been a sullen, self-absorbed disaster. After his come-to-Jesus moment, Foreman turned timidly to street corner preaching. As his confidence and his audience grew, people began to take his conversion seriously. Once he found his footing, Foreman turned his attention to a problem he knew something about, namely wayward youth.

To save the kids for the Lord, however, he concluded that he first had to save them from the streets. "I just wanted to keep them around and keep them out of trouble," Foreman recalls. In 1984, he and his brother opened their youth center in Houston.

In 1986, uneasy about asking for donations and needing to fund his center, the now thirty-seven-year-old launched the most improbable comeback in the history of sports. "For ten years, I didn't even make a fist," says Foreman. "I didn't box. I didn't try to box. I was done with it. I was a preacher. A happy, fat preacher." This fat, happy preacher was about to take his act on the road. On several occasions along the way, Foreman tried to convert Ali, but without apparent success. "Hey," Ali told Foreman, "if God wants me to change. God will tell me. God will call me."

WHETHER OR NOT God was doing the calling remains to be seen, but Ali was certainly changing. Much of that change was physical and increasingly obvious. His wife Lonnie tells of seeing Ali upon a 1982 return to Louisville, stumbling as he walked and slurring his speech. He was also despondent. A sales representative for Kraft Foods and an MBA student, Lonnie made the bold decision to move to Los Angeles to look after Ali, even though Ali was still married and living with Veronica. That Veronica knew about Lonnie's move and consented says much about her interests and the state of the marriage.

Ali was changing in other ways too, ways that few people saw or chose to see. He traces his hour of enlightenment to "around 1983." It was only then that he became a "true believer." Always more honest than the mythmakers around him, Ali sheds needed light here on his own reality. Before this moment, he confesses to Hauser, "I thought I was a true believer, but I wasn't. I fit my religion to do what I wanted. I did things that were wrong, and chased women all the time."

This is a stunning admission. It should inform the rest of the Hauser biography and all Ali biographies. Told honestly, these accounts should read like the *Confessions of St. Augustine* or the *Autobiography of Malcolm X* or even the George Foreman story. They should tell a story of a life that was largely squandered on race hatred and sexual exploitation until the protagonist is blinded by the light on his own personal road to Damascus.

"I conquered the world, and it didn't bring me true happiness," Ali admits. "The only true satisfaction comes from honoring and worshipping God." The guardians of Ali's myth, however, can write no such story. To do so, they would have to concede that Ali's opposition to war was no more principled than his stance on extramarital sex. Were they to question his value system, they would have to question their own. Few among them were as willing as Ali to do so.

His chroniclers prefer to write his story as one of seamless virtue. In the retelling, the moment of self-awareness comes in the early 1960s and enlightens all that happens thereafter. Any subsequent incidents that might challenge the myth of the proud, black, independent Muslim hero are typically edited down to the nub or ignored. In 1965, of course, Ali put his still embryonic myth to the test by betraying Malcolm X. In 1984, he put his mature myth to an even more severe test when he publicly supported Ronald Reagan and even attended the Republican National Convention.

This should not have come as a shock. A majority of voters in forty-nine states—Massachusetts and New York included—voted for Ronald Reagan in 1984. An overwhelming majority of those Americans like Ali, who both worshiped God and paid high taxes, supported Reagan. In his devotion to God and in his avoidance of drink and drugs and even dance, Ali could have fit right in with the "Moral Majority."

Hauser is very nearly alone in even breaching the subject of Ali's Republican affiliations, and he does so with unintentionally comic effect, to wit, "Then another problem arose." Hauser admits that Ali supported both Reagan and later Bush, as well as a number of other Republican candidates, most notably Utah Senator Orrin Hatch. Reagan Attorney General Edwin Meese, a liberal *bete noire*, went so far as to call Ali a "great patriot."

This turn of events "saddened" at least several of those that Hauser interviews. Andrew Young, UN Ambassador under Jimmy Carter, "bemoaned" Ali's support for candidates "whose policies are harmful to the great majority of Americans, black and white." Said Democrat activist Julian Bond at the time, "I don't know why he's doing it."

Hauser finds a useful explanation in the manipulations of an attorney and hustler named Richard Hirschfield. He makes the case, which Hirschfield denies, that Hirschfield imitated Ali's voice in making phone calls to support a wide range of policy initiatives, most of them minor. Hauser may be right, but that still does not explain Ali's appearance at the Republican National Convention.

Hauser leaves the vague impression that Hirschfield must have manipulated Ali into his seeming Republicanism as well, but this is a subject that Hauser and the other mythologists leave alone. How, after all, could a man with Ali's "crystal sense of the irrationality and the cruelty of the society" now be supporting causes "harmful to the great majority of Americans"?

The answer to this question is fairly obvious. Outside the ring, his only area of true authority, Ali had long been vulnerable to the most transparent of hucksters. "Ali has always been managed by someone else," says Wilfred Sheed, an early and insightful biographer, "and perhaps he always will be." If not more independent, the Ali who emerged in the summer of 1984 was at least more true to himself than the earlier incarnations. At a fourth of July celebration in Washington, for instance, Ali publicly scolded Louis Farrakhan for an ongoing series of threats and insults against Jews. "What he teaches is not at all what we believe in," said Ali boldly. "We say he represents the time of our struggle in the dark and a time of confusion in us and we don't want to be associated with that at all."

Ali's spirit may have been reviving that summer, but his physical health was not. The year 1984 brought some disquieting news. Despite signs of slurred speech as early as 1978 and increasing trouble even walking by the early 1980s, the medical establishment could not find anything technically wrong with Ali.

In September of that year, Ali underwent a comprehensive series of tests at Columbia-Presbyterian Medical Center. The tests showed, as Dr. Stanley Fahn admits to Hauser, "post-traumatic Parkinsonism due to the injuries from fighting." Although Ali intuitively believes he caught most of that damage from Joe Frazier in Manila, Fahn argues that it was accumulated over time. Had the diagnosis been made earlier, it could have warned Ali off those last few fights. By then, the condition had already dimmed his reflexes and left him, in fighter argot, "shot."

Sugar Ray Robinson, who boxed too long and died too young of Alzheimer's, offers a knowing glimpse into this inevitable short circuiting: "I can see a jab coming, and I can't block it, and I can see an opening to land a jab but by the time my brain sees it and recognizes it, the opportunity is gone." Ali was finished as a fighter at least three years before he stopped. Although Pacheco does not necessarily blame the Circus members for pushing Ali past his prime, he objects "strenuously" to their shared self-deception: "He has Parkinson's disease; boxing had nothing to do with it." As they all know, Pacheco insists, Ali does not have Parkinson's Disease, and boxing had everything to do with his current condition.

BEAVIS AND BUTTHEAD

On the night of March 23, 1988, Jose Torres and a grieving Mike Tyson took a long therapeutic walk through the streets of Manhattan. Tyson was mourning the death of his manager, Jimmy Jacobs. A longtime running mate of Cus D'Amato, Jacobs had died of leukemia that morning. The only family that Tyson had ever felt a part of was coming unglued, and so was he.

Tyson's new family, wife Robin Givens and her gold-digging mom, offered no solace. Only five weeks into the marriage, Tyson did not trust either one of them. He did trust Torres. A spiritual son of D'Amato, Torres served as something of a big brother to Tyson. On this night, Tyson needed all the big-brothering he could get. He rested his head on Torres's shoulder and cried openly. He was a coward, he told Torres. If he had the guts, he would take his own life.

After putting Tyson to bed, Torres went home to his own Manhattan apartment only to be awakened by a 6:00 A.M. phone call. The man who would replace D'Amato and Jacobs as Tyson's surrogate father was making his move. "What time are they going to L.A.," asked the spectacularly shameless Don King of the Tysons. "What airline? What airport? What flight number?" King was launching what Newfield calls "the hostile takeover of Mike Tyson." He had tried with Ali and was determined to succeed with Tyson. If he had to lay the groundwork at a funeral, so be it.

King made the plane on time but did not mix with Tyson or the Jacobs' party. It was no secret that Jacobs never trusted King and had warned Tyson to steer clear of the race-baiting brigand. By 1988, Jacobs and others in the fight crowd knew well just how shamelessly King had plundered the fighters in his charge, one after another, and none more so than Tim Witherspoon. The one-time heavyweight champ had recently sacrificed whatever future he had to file suit against King, the man who "destroyed everything that I tried to be."

In the era between Ali's fall and Tyson's rise, King had seized all but absolute power over heavyweight boxing, and true to the axiom, absolute power corrupted him absolutely. While King was promoting Witherspoon's fights, his stepson Carl King was managing Witherspoon, and both were stealing him blind. If he wanted to get good fights, Witherspoon had little choice but to accept the arrangement.

On January 17, 1986, King rewarded Witherspoon for his fealty with a WBA title shot against Tony Tubbs. The date marked Ali's forty-fourth birthday, and Ali was there to watch. King had chosen this date and an Atlanta venue not for Ali's sake but to celebrate the legacy of hometown hero Martin Luther King on the first nationally recognized holiday in his honor. No memory was too sacred for King to exploit.

The title bout highlighted a program that featured several promising young heavyweights, all of whom, incidentally, were controlled by Don King. The Reverend King would not have been pleased. These up-and-coming black boxers had only slightly more occupational freedom than those who fought for their masters' amusement in antebellum Georgia. Indentured to King, they had little to fight for, and they showed it with one sluggish performance after another.

In the title bout, Witherspoon outlasted the aptly named, 244-pound Tubbs in a fight so boring that fans periodically chanted "Ali, Ali, Ali," as if hoping for a resurrection. Given his status as challenger, Witherspoon did not expect much in the way of payday, and King honored his low expectations. It was the next fight, the title defense in England, that promised serious payback.

The money was there. HBO paid King $1.7 million to deliver the champ. A manager, who was someone other than King's son, would have gotten Witherspoon $1 million of that money. The Associated Press was reporting an anticipated payday of $900,000 for Witherspoon. The crowd of forty thousand in Wembley Stadium augured well for a healthy return. When Witherspoon knocked out hometown hero Frank Bruno in the eleventh round, he was ecstatic. That was "the greatest moment of my life," Witherspoon remembers. "I was the happiest man in the world."

Returning back to his hotel at dawn, still elated, Witherspoon had an unexpected and almost magical encounter with his longtime idol, Muhammad Ali. Ali, who knew more than a little about Don King, hugged the young champ and whispered ominously in his ear, "I know you're not gonna get all your money." Ali had learned the hard way, and Witherspoon was about to. Three weeks later, he received a check for $90,094. Bruno, the challenger and loser, got his check for $900,000. Jimmy Binns, WBA counsel, tells Newfield, "I know for a certain fact Don King made at least a two-million-dollar profit on the Witherspoon-Bruno fight."

More than one hundred lawsuits have been filed against King. In early 1987, Witherspoon, feeling unmanned by the plundering, filed still another against both Don and Carl King, this one a $25 million suit accusing them of fraud and conflict of interest. Five years and a few death threats later, King settled with Witherspoon for more than a $1 million. "Don's specialty is black-on-black crime," Witherspoon would tell Newfield. "I'm black and he robbed me, so I know this is true."

Almost alone among the heavyweights of his era, Tyson had been spared Witherspoon's fate. The D'Amato management team of Jacobs and Bill Cayton, both Jewish, had kept Tyson beyond King's grasp. He remained a genuine free agent and a very wealthy one. As he plowed through one King fighter after another on the way to unifying the title, Tyson had made a literal fortune—$48.5 million in less than two years as champion—and his managers had secured it honestly.

In March 1988, with Jacobs dead, King honed in on the Tyson mother lode. At the Los Angeles funeral home, where Jacobs was laid out, King made his play for a disconsolate Tyson in front of the very casket. "Don was leaning all over Mike," one of the pallbearers reports. "He wouldn't let [Tyson] get away from him. Mike was weeping and Don was hitting on him."

To get to Tyson, King had to get through the grasping Givens and her mother and the no-nonsense Torres. Given Torres's obvious affection for D'Amato, King avoided his usual anti-white line and tried to corrode his sense of justice with an anti-Semitic rant. It didn't take on Torres. It did on Tyson. Soon enough, he would be referring to his managers as "Jews in suits."

Torres tried to strengthen Cayton's defenses against King, but Cayton, now seventy and aloof by nature, had almost no feel for the cultural forces that were soon to undo him. Tyson friend and chauffeur Rudy Gonzalez explained the mechanics behind those forces in an eye-opening *Ring* magazine article. According to Gonzalez, King went to work on Tyson's friends just as he had on Ali's—in this case, a darkly comic pair of deadbeats named John Horne and Rory Holloway. Critics, and they were many, would refer to them as the "Beavis and Butthead" of boxing.

On one occasion, after picking up the two at Don King's offices in a Tyson limo, Gonzalez quietly switched on the limo's communication channel and eavesdropped on their conversation. "Can you believe that nigger [King] gave us one million in cash just to get the nigger [Tyson] to the table?" Horne exulted. "I can't believe it! I can't believe it!"

Once under contract with King, the pair squeezed the racial concentrate out of every conflict in Tyson's highly conflicted life. Givens, equally keen on forcing out Cayton, stirred the racial juices as well. By June 1998, just three months after Jacobs's funeral, King had prodded Tyson and Givens to break Tyson's binding contract with Cayton. Three days later, Tyson was still able to focus his fury and knock out Michael Spinks within ninety seconds to unify the heavyweight crown. Earlier that year, he had demolished both Larry Holmes and Tony Tubbs. He should have been on top of the world, but that world was spinning wildly out of control.

Horne and Holloway oversaw the spin. They relentlessly pumped Tyson full of angry rap music and an unending racial rant of their own. The white man was "evil." Cayton, "the white man," was exploiting him and stealing his money. The white man was "enslaving us again," and they were not going to let him get away with it. As to women, white or black, the pair reinforced what the hip-hoppers were insisting—females were interchangeable, disposable, and there for the taking; romance was for chumps.

On the edge of madness, Tyson wrecked a Bentley in May, broke a bone in his hand during a Harlem street fight in August, crashed a BMW in September, and got drunk almost daily and fatter by the hour. In late September, he sat by passively while Givens accused him of being a manic depressive and a bully before Barbara Walters and a national TV audience. In early October, police broke up a domestic dispute between the unhappy pair, and later in the month, Givens stormed out of their $5 million New Jersey mansion for the last time and filed for divorce.

Givens proved useful to King in estranging Tyson from his white management. But with Givens gone, he wanted all of Tyson. He hired one of the nation's best divorce lawyers to represent Tyson. He cut Tyson off from his old friends in the D'Amato camp like Torres and trainer Kevin Rooney. He even moved the young boxer into his Ohio mansion. There, he gave Tyson a book that he had given many of the young fighters in his charge, *Countering the Conspiracy to Destroy Black Boys*. The book advanced the proposition that a tax-supported system had been put in place with no larger goal than to destroy African-American boys. The entrepreneurial King did the same but without tax support.

At the end of October, Tyson agreed to partner with the insistent King. A month later, in something of a PR burlesque, godfather King had Tyson baptized in a Cleveland church with Jesse Jackson assisting. Tyson hit on one of the girls in the choir immediately afterward and took her back to his room. A few days later, Tyson fired his long-time trainer, old D'Amato hand Kevin Rooney. He had already fired assistant trainer Steve Lott. Indifferent to the niceties of contracts, King squeezed Cayton out and began promoting Tyson's fights.

King's bravado was breathtaking. In just six short months, "Team Tyson" had erased the D'Amato tradition. From here on in, King, Horne, and Holloway would run Tyson's life, and they would run it into the ground. Tyson had just turned twenty-two years old. And although he did not quite know it yet, his career was heading downhill.

"What's amazing," writes Newfield, "is that Tyson was willing to buy into an anti-white worldview, since all his own life experiences with whites in boxing had been positive." The reader of this book will not think Tyson's flip amazing at all. Ali had helped make racism respectable. In assessing Tyson's career for the *New York Times*, Robert Lipsyte makes an unassailable point. "Let us never forget," he writes, "that it was Ali who brought Don King into the boxing tent, and supported his use of the race card to squelch criticism."

King had taken Ali's misbegotten rap and commercialized it. If Ali was sincere, King was not, and his cynicism made him all the more lethal. Ali abandoned racism as he and the society matured, just as Malcolm X had before him. King and the other race hustlers—Jesse Jackson and Al Sharpton among them—had no more reason to abandon racism than they did any other viable promotional gimmick— Christianity, Islam, patriotism, whatever. Racism still worked. It opened doors. It scared prosecutors. It cowed promoters. It secured contracts. It coerced young men like Mike Tyson into depending on "liberators" like Don King. Under King's tutelage, Tyson, the man who transcended race, would soon come to see race as his biggest burden.

"It's very difficult being black," Tyson would tell writer Pete Hamill when in prison, implying that his race was the reason he was there in the first place. The absurdity of that notion does not make it any less scary or sad.

Throughout 1989, Tyson was left to train himself, and he did so halfheartedly. The most aggressive workout Tyson would get that year was in the backseat of his limo with Beavis and Butthead procuring the female sparring partners. "He began to act like a gangsta rapper," Newfield regrets, "instead of Joe Louis." For all his distractions, Tyson still had stuff enough to dispose of Frank Bruno in February and Carl "Truth" Williams in July. He was not sure who was managing him, and he didn't quite care.

The one looming fight that did keep Tyson at least halfway focused was with Evander Holyfield, a powerful, unbeaten contender from Georgia. In large part because he did not control Holyfield, King had other ideas. He saw a way to extract a few easy million out of Tyson by sending him to Japan to fight the little-known Buster Douglas. When Tyson protested, King and company leaned on him. "It was as if they held some special power or control over him," says Gonzalez, "which could take away his will to resist whatever they wanted to do."

Under pressure from King, Tyson's resistance quickly eroded, and Team Tyson was off to Japan. Always alert to the possibilities, King hustled Tyson every which way he could and paid him off in geisha girls. Tyson found little time to train, but that was not a great problem as it would not take much training to dispatch journeyman Douglas. The one Las Vegas bookie that ran any kind of action on the fight had Douglas listed as a 42 to 1 underdog.

Although King had finessed promotional rights for both fighters, he rooted openly for Tyson. But with no D'Amato or Jacobs or Rooney or Torres or Lott to guide him, Tyson seemed lost when he fell behind early in the match. Team Tyson had little advice to offer and even less technical help. They had neglected, for instance, to bring the salve necessary to treat Tyson's closing left eye.

Still, at the end of the eighth round, Tyson was able to channel his rage and knock Douglas down. Not badly hurt, Douglas slammed the canvas with his fist in self-disgust, followed the ref's count, and was on his feet and boxing at nine. At the end of the round, King went berserk, yelling at the ref that the fight was over, but clearly it was not.

In the tenth round, Douglas knocked Tyson down, the first time in Tyson's career. He did not get up. *Time* magazine called the knockout "the biggest upset in boxing history." When the fight ended, Ali phoned Hauser, then at work on his autobiography, and said, "Do you think folks will now stop asking if I could have beaten Tyson in my prime?"

An hour after the fight, King met with the officials of the WBC and the WBA trying to persuade them that Douglas was down for longer than a nine count in the eighth round and the decision should be reversed. Although the argument was absurd on the face of it, the wily King coerced the officials into suspending recognition of Douglas as champion. The media outcry, however, caused these same officials to rethink their decision.

Given his post-fight hysterics, the Douglas camp was in no mood to hear King out when he tried to dictate the terms of Douglas's next fight. Douglas sued King to get out from under his option, and King sued back. Esteemed New York columnist Murray Kempton would describe King's suit as the first attempt in the twentieth century to enforce the Fugitive Slave Act.

King quickly made life hell for the rebellious boxer. In his public relations campaign to regain control of the new champ, King went on the black radio stations in Douglas's native Ohio and attacked Douglas for choosing a white manager and promoter over him. He wrote checks to the NAACP and to the wife of then director, Benjamin Hooks, and got Hooks to come to Ohio and endorse King. He even lured Douglas's father to help in the campaign against his son.

The propaganda was working. It started turning Ohio's black community against its erstwhile hometown hero. Dispirited by the whole affair, Douglas showed up at his one and only title defense weighing a tubby 246 pounds and was gasping for air by the second round. Evander Holyfield knocked him out in the third.

"He talks about the black fighters he's helped, and it's bull," said Douglas's black trainer J. D. McCauley within King's earshot. "The fighters he's helped I can name them, and they're all digging ditches right now." Buster Douglas would soon enough join them.

DO ANYTHING

In 1991, Simon & Schuster published Thomas Hauser's comprehensive oral history, *Muhammad Ali: His Life and Times* "*With the cooperation of Muhammad Ali.*"

I read it when it came out, and I recall feeling shocked and dispirited. Ali had drifted out of my consciousness over the years, but unlike Joe Frazier and several of my friends, especially the veterans, I bore no particular grudge. So much of the information was new to me, and much of it struck me as disturbing—especially the tales of wives and children left behind.

When I began research on *Sucker Punch*, I knew that this oral biography was the place to start. Not remembering the author, I keyed in "oral history" and "Ali" and kept coming up with "Thomas Hauser." The reviews for the Hauser book, however, spoke of it as a "hagiography" or something nearly as worshipful. I thought there had to be another oral history because the one I had read was highly critical. No, as it turned out, Hauser's book was it. The details of Ali's life that seemed damning to me at the time were a matter of indifference to most reviewers and many of those interviewed by Hauser. And although Ali has come to regret much of what he did as a young man—certainly on the questions of race and sex, if not on war and peace—most of his supporters feel no obligation to do the same.

The leftist Anglo-American Mike Marqusee is an interesting exception. He describes the public association of blackness, boxing, and violence against women as an "historic legacy for which Ali must share some blame." That legacy was dramatically reinforced by the events that unfolded in the early morning hours of July 19, 1991, in room 606 of Indianapolis's Canterbury Hotel. There, Mike Tyson concluded a long day of unashamedly crude sexual behavior by raping eighteen-year-old Miss Black Rhode Island, Desiree Washington.

Fifty years from now, the Ken Burns of his generation will produce a new rendition of *Unforgivable Blackness,* in which a mostly white, middle American jury railroads Mike Tyson for no real crime other than being a black man. The producer will portray Tyson, like Jack Johnson, as "an embodiment of the African-American struggle to be truly free in this country" and commend him for refusing "to play by the rules set by the white establishment, or even those of the black community."

Up close, of course, Tyson looks no better to his contemporaries, black or white, than Jack Johnson did to his. The Indiana jury convicted Tyson not because he was black but because he was guilty. If there were any mitigating circumstances, it was the "historic legacy" that Marqusee alludes to.

That legacy, however, derives in no small part from the decade that Marqusee celebrates, the 1960s. For the first time in American history, the gatekeepers of the cultural establishment openly endorsed sexual experimentation. The revolution that began with Kinsey in 1948 and took hold with acolyte Hefner in the 1950s finally blossomed across all strata in the 1960s. One myth of the sixties is that this blossoming had no lasting negative consequences. Desiree Washington and thousands of other young women like her might beg to differ. Even if he had wanted to, it is unlikely that Ali could have held back this tide. Unfortunately, given his vast personal appeal, especially among young black men, he went with the flow.

FLOYD PATTERSON'S *Victory Over Myself* gives some sense of the tragic difference between the culture that Ali helped create for Mike Tyson and the one that nurtured Patterson. The young Floyd Patterson began courting Sandra Hicks in the summer of 1951, forty years before Tyson launched his "courtship" of Desiree Washington with the less than charming "I want to f*** you."

"I made sure I was always clean and dressed properly," Patterson remembers. "I'd be careful about the things I said and the way I talked." Despite his profound poverty, Patterson immediately impressed Sandra as "a gentleman." Patterson was particularly sensitive about her Roman Catholicism. "I wondered," he recalls, "if her belief in the Catholic faith didn't make her what she was." So inspired was he by her example that he started formal instruction.

As his amateur career progressed, Patterson began to get his name in the paper. As much as he respected Sandra's mother, "one of the kindest women in the world," she put little stock in Patterson's growing celebrity. She "didn't want Sandra's name associated with mine unless I had serious intentions." The twenty-year-old Patterson proved his good intentions in 1956, first in a civil ceremony and later that year in a religious ceremony after he had completed his instruction. "She had led me to the Church and given me a goal to work hard for," Patterson writes. "She had given me a real purpose for living."

The culture reinforced the Pattersons in any number of ways. As the young couple prepared for their wedding, one of the songs they heard most often was Frank Sinatra's smash hit, "Love and Marriage."

> Love and marriage, love and marriage
> Go together like a horse and carriage

DO ANYING

> This I tell you brother
> You can't have one without the other
> Love and marriage, love and marriage
> It's an institute you can't disparage
> Ask the local gentry
> And they will say it's elementary

If the Pattersons inclined to more soulful music, they could always tune in to Sam Cooke, Ali's own favorite, who stressed the primacy of marriage in his number one, 1957 classic, "You Send Me."

> At first I thought it was infatuation
> But woo, it's lasted so long
> Now I find myself wanting
> To marry you and take you home

In 1964, when the twenty-two-year-old Ali was courting his first wife, Sonji, the culture continued to reinforce this message, and Ali responded. By all accounts, he, too, was respectful around women and gentlemanly. That year the couple listened to songs like the Dixie Cups' hit, "Going to the Chapel."

> Going to the chapel
> And we're gonna get married
> Going to the chapel
> And we're gonna get married
> Gee I really love you
> And we're gonna get married
> Going to the chapel of love

Ali's generation drove this kind of music from the marketplace, and Ali played his own mindless part in the debasement of the sentiments behind it. The sixties mythologists, the ones who celebrate the early Ali as cultural icon of that charmed decade, are reluctant to challenge the notions on which that mythology was based. One is that sexual freedom enhanced the culture. That this freedom quickly deteriorated into license and misogyny, especially among the more vulnerable populations, passes largely unmentioned. Writers are more likely to blame D'Amato for Tyson's bad behavior than they are an ideologically driven breakdown in the culture.

Yet Patterson and Tyson have stunningly similar backgrounds. This includes thirty or so preteen arrests in a Brooklyn ghetto, a redemptive exile to an upstate boys home, and a career guided from an early age by Cus D'Amato. The difference between the two boxers' behavior was, in no small part, generational. The culture of Patterson's generation reinforced his better angels. The culture of Tyson's mocked his.

When Mike Tyson turned on the radio, he got another message altogether about love and marriage. If the number one pop hit of 1964 was the Beatles' "I Want to Hold Your Hand," the number one hit of 1991 was Natural Selection's appropriately titled "Do Anything."

One of the few hits of the Tyson era to mention marriage was Too Short's "I Ain't Nothing but a Dog," released on the popular album *Shorty the Pimp* in 1992, the year Tyson was convicted of rape. Its message is painfully typical, reflecting a corruption of both values and language. What follows are some of its more printable lyrics.

> I ain't with no marriage and a wedding ring
> I be a player for life, forget about a wife
> She just ain't my type
> Cause I mack each hoe and get richer
> And if it ain't like that then I forget ya

Robin Givens and Desiree Washington and most of young America, black and white, male and female, have grown up listening to comparable music. It is both symptom and cause of an ongoing inner city melt-down. There are young people in Brooklyn's ghettos today who have never even been to a wedding. There are whole blocks where no one has a married father in the home. The Patterson courtship, which was nor-mative in 1956, would today be newsworthy.

THERE WOULD BE no easy redemption for Mike Tyson. On March 26, 1992, he told Judge Patricia Gifford, "I didn't come here to beg for mercy. I expect the worst. I've been crucified." He offered no apology to Desiree. The judge sentenced him effectively to six years in prison with the poten-tial of parole in three, a sentence that was neither harsh nor lenient.

Once incarcerated, Tyson educated himself after a fashion and con-verted to Islam, which did not, to him at least, offer much in the way of restraint. "In Islam," the imprisoned boxer would tell writer Pete Hamill, "there's nobody who can put you in your place." The only one that could judge him was Allah. Tyson liked the leeway.

In prison, Tyson got a tattoo of Marxist madman Mao Tse-tung on his right bicep and tennis star Arthur Ashe on his left—the only one of the planet's six billion inhabitants to have that combination, as Hamill informed him. When Ashe's widow learned of the tattoo, she asked if one could sue a body part.

On the outside world, Bill Cayton continued to press his suit against Don King. Cayton caught a break when King's accountant, Joe Maffia, agreed to comply with a subpoena. Maffia, whose name belies his African-American identity, had grown increasingly disgusted at the "financial rape" of Mike Tyson. When the details of Maffia's affidavit were reported by Mike Katz of the *New York Daily News*, King counter-punched in predictable fashion.

"You're just like the cops who brutalized Rodney King," he shouted at Katz over the phone, adding gratuitously, "Why don't you write about Desiree Washington? She's black on the outside and white on the inside."

The Reverend Al Sharpton supported King publicly—he was being paid to—but he brought copies of the affidavits to Tyson in prison and encouraged him to be "an independent" when he got out. This got Tyson to thinking about an old D'Amato warning. When young Tyson would tell Cus that he'd sell his soul to be a great fighter, Cus would answer: "Be careful what you wish for, 'cause you might get it."

There to buy Tyson's soul on the cheap when he was released from prison in 1995 was none other than Don King. The always-dependent Tyson again signed on. He was twenty-eight years old at the time, the same age as Ali when he returned from his forced three-and-a-half-year exile. Comparisons abounded. "Tyson has politicized his prison experience in much the way Malcolm X did," wrote Gerald Early as Tyson began his comeback. "But there is also an echo of Muhammad Ali in Tyson's insistence that the white system tried to break him but could not, in the end."

Tyson smashed through his first four opponents without breaking a sweat, and in the process regained the WBA and WBC titles and earned some serious money. At the same time Tyson was making his comeback, Evander Holyfield was making his. In 1994, Holyfield had to give up boxing because of a diagnosed heart condition. One day, while watching TV evangelist Benny Hinn, Holyfield felt his heart heal. Incredibly, the Mayo Clinic confirmed this impression, and the born-again Holyfield was back in business.

On November 9, 1996, he and Tyson met in the ring for the first time. Malcolm X had described the first Ali-Liston fight as a battle between "the Cross and the Crescent" with the unlikely Liston cast in the role of Crusader. On November 9, 1996, Evander Holyfield was assigned that same role, and he played it a good deal more credibly. Both he and Tyson had come a long way since the postponement of their planned first fight five years earlier. But the thirty-four-year-old Holyfield had come further.

Although Holyfield entered the ring as much as a 14-1 underdog, he placed great faith in his ultimate Corner Man. "I prayed in training," Holyfield said at the time. "I prayed in the ring. I prayed when I was fighting." He would need all the help he could get and seemingly got it. Thirty-seven seconds into the eleventh round, the ref intervened and spared Tyson, the Muslim wannabe, any further persecution.

It was the June 1997 rematch, however, that would forever define Mike Tyson. Having lost the first two rounds, and angry over Holyfield's head-butting, Tyson removed his mouthpiece and came out for the third with malice on his mind. In a clinch, he chomped off the rim of Holyfield's right ear and spit it out on the canvas. Warned, but not satisfied, he bit into Holyfield's left ear. The judge disqualified him and ended the fight. The religion of peace had no more pacified Tyson than it had Osama Bin Laden. Forever after, fight fans would think of Tyson first and foremost not as a rapist but as a borderline cannibal.

Ever helpful, Muhammad Ali hoped to smooth over the problem by inviting Tyson and Holyfield to a face-to-face meeting at the end of the Ali Cup amateur tournament that September. "Evander Holyfield and Mike Tyson standing together in unity," said an Ali spokesman, "is a tremendous show of support for amateur boxing and respect for the ideals of Muhammad Ali." Unfortunately, neither Tyson, nor Holyfield, nor any other young boxer, had a clue as to just what those ideals might be.

If Ali thought he could talk out Tyson's problems, his African friends knew better. "Black America can only improve its lot the way other minorities and disadvantaged people have done," Ugandan newspaper editor Charles Onyango-Obbo wrote after the fight. "By sending their kids to school; making sure they stay there; keeping their families together; saving up money and investing it; and creating wealth within the community. Biting off other black men's ears or raping black women cannot be the inspiration to a winning future."

As to Don King, he was last seen at the 2004 Republican National Convention. "I'm a Republicrat," he told a CNN reporter. "I'm for whoever's going to be doing something for the upward mobility of America, black and white alike." When asked if he had voted for President Bush in the 2000 election, the ever-elusive King replied, "I'll have to go back and check my notes." As King himself said often enough to be a mantra, "Only in America!"

DIVINE INTERVENTION

Those who believe in the great good humor of God and the glory of the American dream had to have felt vindicated November 5, 1994.

That night in Las Vegas, the undefeated, twenty-six-year-old champion Michael Moorer climbed into the ring for just another payday. He faced an overweight, over-the-hill comedian, who had not fought in eighteen months and had lost when he last fought. In fact, sensible people everywhere thought the challenger deranged for getting into the ring at all against the powerful Moorer.

Never fast, George Foreman at forty-five put the slug in slugger. He may have been the slowest fighter to get a title shot, in any weight class, ever. Early odds against him ran about 4 to 1 before a collective last-minute sentimental surge by thousands of other fat, bald guys pushed the odds against him down to 2 to 1.

For the first five rounds, the Foreman money looked like a sucker bet. Moorer won those rounds easily. In the sixth, Foreman connected with a couple of solid rights, but Moorer finished strong, and Foreman's left eye was closing. Moorer continued to carry the fight in rounds seven through nine.

And then something happened. The reader can call it what he will—a stroke of luck, a second wind, or divine intervention. In the tenth round, the middle-aged fat guy took control. He started swinging hard and landing. Nearing the two-minute mark, he smote the stunned champion with a right to the forehead. As Moorer backpedaled, Foreman popped him with a soft left and then a right to the chin that could have KO'd a horse. Moorer hit the canvas like a sack of oats, and he wasn't about to get up. As soon as he was counted out, the preacher-boxer got down on his knees and prayed. After twenty years, George Foreman was champ once again.

In winning the championship, Foreman had earned a fair amount of money for his ministry, but he was just getting started. The Salton Company introduced the George Foreman Grill a year after the fight in 1995. It was the most inspired product endorsement in marketing history. The amiable Foreman sold seventy million of his grills before Salton decided it would be wise to buy out his interest for $137 million.

In his seemingly miraculous comeback—as preacher, as pitchman, as heavyweight champion, as husband, as father—Foreman had fulfilled the potential that he had shown in the 1968 Olympics. He had fully connected with Middle America. It would not be Ali. It would not be Tyson. It would be the improbable George Foreman who first transcended race in the ring. When ordinary Joes, black or white, saw George Foreman, they saw themselves. This most definitely included the guys at Gary who sat in the bleachers and like-minded souls across America. One suspects that they would have been among the first to rush out and buy a George Foreman Lean Mean Fat-Reducing Grilling Machine.

MADE IN NEW YORK

MY HERO is a well-intentioned, nicely produced, not-for-profit educational Web site that recognizes young people's needs "for positive role models in our society." There is nothing radical about it. It does not post any stories "that promote hatred, violence, or prejudice." As such, it captures the Ali myth perfectly pickled and preserved and passed down to the young for easy consumption.

College student Jaime Marcus wrote the MY HERO profile about "the greatest champion of all time." Marcus did so with good style and with about as much accuracy as most Ali biographies, especially the youth-oriented ones.

As Marcus tells the story, "white America" could not handle young Cassius Clay's audacity in declaring himself "The Greatest." "These same Americans" grew more "enraged" when Clay traded in his "slave name" for a Muslim name. The media "vilified" Ali for his refusal to find quarrel with the Viet Cong.

After sacrificing three and a half years at the peak of his career for his principles, Ali's return to the ring was a "spectacular one." That return began not with the Frazier fight of 1971 but with the Foreman fight of

1974. For Marcus, the "Rumble in the Jungle" transcended lesser sporting events because of "its social impact." As to the nature of that impact, he quotes Ali. The fight was "about racial problems, Vietnam, all of that," says Ali. The trip to Africa also had a "lasting effect on Ali himself," rendering him more compassionate. Afterward, Ali donated millions to charities, "not bad for a man maligned for his religious affiliation."

Unfortunately, Ali was "stricken with Parkinson's disease." As in the past, he did not let this misfortune "stop him from being free to do what he wants." Throughout his life, Ali showed that sport "has the power to change social values" and that a "black man can stand up to social oppression."

For Marcus, it seemed altogether fitting that Ali would be chosen to light the torch at the opening ceremony of the Atlanta Olympics in 1996 and that the wildly but typically inflated "3 billion television viewers" would watch.

Ali seemed the "perfect choice" at the *New York Times* as well. Columnist George Vecsey was sitting in the stadium with two *Times* colleagues. The culturally sensitive Vecsey takes care to tell the reader that one was a black male and the other a white female. When the three saw Ali "shining on that platform," they threw high-fives at each other in recognition of the "audacious perfection" of it all.

"Somewhere along the line, even to most of white America," writes Vecsey, "Ali stopped being a frightening symbol of a 'foreign' religion and a menacing black man." He ceased to frighten, Vecsey reminds the reader, not because white America had matured but because Ali had physically deteriorated. The *Times* reader understands, of course, that Vecsey was never prey to such unseemly fears. Nor were his colleagues. He knew, as they knew, that their high-fives would find a welcome landing on the palms of any *Timesman*.

The folks at the *Times* would not have thrown high-fives for George Foreman. If he had won the hearts of Middle America, he had lost theirs seven Olympics ago when he pulled out that tiny American flag. They preferred the angry theatrics of the gloved fist. Besides, no self-respecting *Timesman* would ever admit to buying a George Foreman Lean Mean Fat-Reducing Grilling Machine.

These folks would not have high-fived for Evander Holyfield either. As an Atlantan and an Olympian and a once-and-future heavyweight champ, Holyfield had a lot to recommend. But like Foreman, he was too publicly Christian. There was not a whiff of Jack Johnson about him. And who knows, he might have prayed on the public dime.

Given that the unstated theme of the Atlanta games was "look how far we've come," the Committee had one ideal choice as torch bearer. This athlete grew up a stone's throw from the Georgia border, willed himself out of poverty, won an Olympic gold medal, and never threw it away. When others demeaned his country, he defended it. When others mocked his skin color or his lack of education, he put his head down and kept on smokin'.

Unlike other heavyweight champions who squandered their winnings, this fighter invested his wisely and raised a great family on it. As a symbol of southern potential and American progress, the Committee could not have chosen better than Joe Frazier. The media would have had a chance to atone for their neglect, if not outright abuse, and Frazier would have had a chance to purge the rage from his soul. So thoroughly, however, had Ali undermined Frazier in the public eye that the thought surely never crossed the Committee's mind.

Not surprisingly, the impetus to make Ali the Olympic torch bearer came out of New York. Dick Ebersol, then president of NBC Sports, takes full credit. He had his "people" make a taped package about Ali for the Atlanta Olympic Committee, including a *60 Minutes* piece from rival CBS. This was necessary, Ebersol recalls, because the locals did not have "a real fundamental appreciation of Ali beyond his being a boxer."

President Bill Clinton was one Southern white who did not need a prompting from New York. The myth of the sixties had smoothed his path to the presidency as surely as it had smoothed Ali's to these

Olympics. He, too, had no quarrel with the Viet Cong. He, too, manned the front lines of the sexual revolution. Better still, he had racially transformed himself to become, in the words of Toni Morrison, "our first black president." After all, wrote Morrison in a much-discussed *New Yorker* article, "Clinton displays almost every trope of blackness: single-parent household, born poor, working class, saxophone-playing, McDonald's-and-junk-food-loving boy from Arkansas."

The fact that Clinton lived a young life that was completely segregated and downright luxurious for his time and place—he had his own bathroom—mattered not a wit. The sixties had allowed both him and Ali to recreate themselves. The same aging baby boomers that had nurtured the Ali myth nurtured his, the facts be damned. He and Ali were mythic brothers, born of the same imagined revolution. Had Ali, the older brother, not done the heavy lifting on Vietnam, America would never have elected a draft-dodger president. This, Clinton well knew. And so, after the ceremony, when he put his hands on Ali's shoulders and said, "They didn't tell me who would light the flame, but when I saw it was you, I cried," the president was very likely telling the truth.

What Clinton did not understand, however, is that Ali had moved beyond the spirit of the sixties. He no longer sexually exploited young women. He no longer spoke divisively on the issue of race or religion. He took his belief in God very seriously. Indeed, it had become for him "the most important thing in the world." If he still prided himself on his Vietnam stand, it was likely because he did not know enough not to. And unlike so many war protestors of his generation, he nursed no simmering grudge against flag and country.

Ali had circled back around. He had become once more the sweet, sensitive, God-fearing son that his mother raised, the only difference being now that he toted a Koran instead of a Bible. What forced Ali to mature in ways that Clinton never has was his physical condition. Muslim or not, he had a cross to bear, and he bore it gracefully, without seeming complaint. Ali had reemerged as an icon of suffering or, as Vecsey writes, our "fragile legend." Like Pope John Paul II, whose Parkinson's symptoms mirrored his own, Ali pulled the right message from his public suffering and turned it into a public good. "God gave me this physical impairment," said a chastened Ali, "to remind me that I am not the greatest. He is."

One can forgive Joe Frazier for not knowing this or caring. As he could plainly see, the media were eager to canonize Ali for all that he was and had ever been, even the "ungrateful scamboogah" who had undermined his career and cheapened his entire existence. With his Christian sense of justice, Frazier expected contrition before canonization, publicly and abjectly, but it was not forthcoming.

And so when Ali bent over the cauldron to light the Olympic flame, Joe Frazier rather wished he'd fall in. The reader of this book will understand why.

AMERICA THE BEAUTIFUL

The last day of December 1999 found Muhammad Ali at a site that disturbed some of his faithful. He was ringing in the new millennium as the guest of the New York Stock Exchange.

Midnight of that fateful day found Ali in Washington D.C. dining in high style on beluga caviar, lobster, and foie gras. "That," says Thomas Hauser in a November 2003 piece for the British *Guardian Unlimited*, "saddened a lot of people."

The more radical among the faithful had been saddened by Ali's presence at the Olympics themselves. "The South's afrostocracy slapped a coat of make-up on the past," writes African-American historian Jelani Cobb of the Atlanta games, "and held it up for world consumption." Increasingly afterward, from Cobb's perspective, the mass marketers co-opted Ali's erstwhile radicalism and turned it to their own profit. Cobb was not alone in this sentiment.

Hauser, the most influential of Ali's chroniclers, has come to feel the same way. Although Hauser considers the Olympic torch-lighting a "glorious moment," he admires little of what Ali has done thereafter. He would elaborate on this in his 2005 book, *The Lost Legacy of Muhammad*

Ali. "Ali today seems to be blatantly for sale," Hauser regrets. He quotes several of Ali's more prominent chroniclers to confirm the point.

"He's safe; he's comfortable," says Robert Lipsyte of the contemporary Ali. "He's another dangerous black man who white America has found a way to emasculate."

"Ali is being reduced to serving as a mouthpiece for whatever ideas and products those with influence and power want to sell," affirms Mike Marqusee.

On this point, Hauser is only slightly more generous, "Ali makes his own decisions, but those decisions are based on how information is presented to him."

Yes, that is true, but that has always been true. Elijah Muhammad captivated Ali with some highly intriguing information, little of it honest or accurate. The antiwar movement did the same. Ali served as a mouthpiece for both movements, understanding neither. Hirschfield, Orrin Hatch, and the Republicans used Ali as well. So, for that matter, did literally scores of sundry hucksters, Don King most notably. The Atlanta Olympic Committee made its own persuasive pitch to Ali. Hauser must have done the same to get Ali's blessing on the book.

If corporate America has Ali's ear, that should not surprise. He is aging, infirm, and as deserving of a stressless swan song as the next man. Besides, he has always lived comfortably and often much better. In hoping Ali would have spent that storied New Year's Eve at "a soup kitchen or homeless shelter," Hauser shows that he has been overexposed to the myth he had helped create. Had Ali ever spent a New Year's at a homeless shelter? Had Hauser?

Hauser is a much better collector of dots than a connector of the same. He treats the corporate makeover of Ali as a unique event, as if Ali had never been made over before. "Sanitizing Muhammad Ali and rounding off the rough edges of his journey," he writes, "is a disservice both to history and to Ali himself." This thought astounds the reader. The New Left and the media it spawned, Hauser most notably, have been sanitizing Ali for the last forty years. Through a highly selective editing of his life, they transformed an incoherent young boxer, his head pumped full of hateful nonsense, into what Hauser is still calling "a gleaming symbol of defiance against an unjust social order."

It took Ali finally to transform himself. At the 2002 NBA All-Star Game in Philadelphia, Joe Frazier recognized the change. The two men stood together at courtside during the playing of "America the Beautiful." Joe, in fact, kept a hand under Ali's left arm to support him. "We sat down and made up," Frazier told Rich Hofmann of the *Philadelphia Daily News*. "Life's too short. He said his apology and I accepted it. Let's bury the hatchet please."

SO MUCH POTENTIAL

I caught up with my friend Kenny as I was researching this book. He is still on the Newark Fire Department, now as a chief. We have stayed in touch over the years, but since our shared listening experience of the first Ali-Liston fight we had not talked about Ali. As we drove up to a takeout fish joint by Barnegat Bay, I offhandedly asked him which fighter he pulled for in the first Ali-Frazier fight.

"Ali," Kenny said. "He was just too cool and too good a boxer to give up on." His answer surprised me. We tend to track closely on cultural issues, if anything, he to the right of me. The view from the back of a Newark fire truck spawns little in the way of liberal sentiment.

"But you know, Ali had so much potential to pull this nation together when it really mattered," Kenny added without prompting.

"And he did just the opposite."

ABOUT SOURCES

No life in human history has been as thoroughly documented as Muhammad Ali's. He has inspired multiple thousands of articles and literally hundreds of videos and books, at least a dozen of those books for the youth market alone.

To this point, however, no book on Ali has mined this vast library. Sportswriters typically rely on their own observations, as do those participants in Ali's life who have written books about him. *Sucker Punch* is the first book to exploit the mother lode of existing Ali data in a dispassionate way.

Two books convinced me that, despite the vast library, the life of Muhammad Ali had to that point escaped serious scrutiny. One was Mark Kram's acerbic *Ghosts of Manila: The Fateful Blood Feud between Muhammad Ali and Joe Frazier* (Harper Collins, 2001). The second was Karl Evanzz's *The Messenger: The Rise and Fall of Elijah Muhammad* (Vintage Books, 2001). Reading these books almost back to back a few years ago started me on this project. Rereading *The Autobiography of Malcolm X* as told to Alex Haley (Houghton Mifflin, 1965) confirmed my suspicions that the real relationship between Ali and Malcolm and the Nation of Islam had gone largely unexplored.

Any serious book on Ali begins with Thomas Hauser's authorized oral biography, *Muhammad Ali: His Life and Times* (Touchstone, 1991). Hauser interviewed nearly two hundred individuals whose lives touched Ali's either directly or indirectly. One limitation of Hauser's book, however, is that many of those interviewed speak more positively of Ali to his authorized biographer than they might (and sometimes do) in other contexts.

The books that helped this project most, as will be obvious, are those told in the first person by the people who knew Ali. The most insightful of these are Ferdie Pacheco's *Muhammad Ali: A View from the Corner* (Birch Lane Press, 1992), Jose Torres's *Sting Like a Bee: The Muhammad Ali Story* (Abelard-Schuman, 1972), and George Plimpton's *Shadow Box* (G.P. Putnam's Sons, 1977). Also helpful in this regard were Norman Mailer's *The Fight* (Vintage, 1975), Howard Bingham's *Muhammad Ali's Greatest Fight* (Robson Books, 2000), Howard Cosell's *Cosell* (Pocket Books, 1974), and Angelo Dundee's *I Only Talk Winning* (Contemporary Books, 1985).

Of great value are the autobiographies of those boxers whose lives and careers intersected with Ali's. None of these is as valuable as Joe Frazier's *Smokin Joe: The Autobiography* (MacMillan, 1996), but a surprising close second is Sugar Ray Robinson's *Sugar Ray: The Sugar Ray Robinson Story* (Viking, 1970). Others that proved helpful and entirely readable are Archie Moore and Leonard Pearl's *Any Boy Can: The Archie Moore Story* (Prentice-Hall, 1971), George Foreman and Joe Engel's *By George: The Autobiography of George Foreman* (Touchstone, 1995), Larry Holmes's *Against the Odds* (St. Martin's Press, 1998), and Ken Norton's *Going the Distance* (Sports Publishing, 2000). Of great merit in and of themselves are Joe Louis's *Joe Louis: My Life* (HBJ Publishing, 1978), Floyd Patterson's *Victory Over Myself* (Bernard Geis Associates, 1962), and Jack Dempsey's *Dempsey* (Harper & Row, 1977).

Ali's own autobiographical efforts are discussed at length in the text. These include *The Soul of a Butterfly: Reflections on Life's Journey* with daughter Hana Yasmeen Ali (Simon & Schuster, 2004) and, more notoriously, *The Greatest: My Own Story* (Ballantine Books, 1975). These works are not particularly reliable as fact but they are revealing as a state of mind.

Of the scores of books about Ali by outside observers, a few stand out. Most helpful was Jack Olson's *Black Is Best: The Riddle of Cassius Clay* (Dell Publishing, 1967). Useful too were Wilfrid Sheed's *Muhammad Ali: A Portrait in Words and Photographs* (Crowell, 1975), Stephen Brunt's *Facing Ali: Fifteen Fighters / Fifteen Stories* (The Lyons Press, 2002), David Remnick's *King of the World* (Vintage Books, 1999), Mike Marqusee's *Redemption Song: Muhammad Ali and the Spirit of the Sixties* (Verso 1999), as well as two edited collections, Elliot Gorn's *Muhammad Ali: The People's Champ* (University of Illinois, 1995) and Gerald Lyn Early's *The Muhammad Ali Reader* (Rob Weisbach Books, 1998).

Several boxing biographies shed useful light on Muhammad Ali's place in boxing history, among them: Russell Sullivan, *Rocky Marciano: The Rock of his Times* (University of Illinois, 2002); Randy Roberts, *Papa Jack: Jack Johnson and the Era of White Hopes* (The Free Press, 1983), as well as Roberts's *Jack Dempsey: The Manassa Mauler* (LSU Press, 1984); Jeremy Schaap, *Cinderella Man: James J. Braddock, Max Baer, and the Greatest Upset in Boxing History* (Houghton Mifflin, 2005); Jack Newcombe, *Floyd Patterson: Heavyweight King* (Bartholomew House, 1961); and Nick Tosches, *The Devil and Sonny Liston* (Little, Brown and Company, 2000).

To tell the Mike Tyson story, I relied primarily on the following: Phil Berger, *Blood Season: Tyson and the World of Boxing* (Morrow, 1989); Mark Shaw, *Down for the Count: The Shocking Truth behind the Mike Tyson Rape Trial* (Sagamore Publishing, 1993); Richard Hoffer, *A Savage Business: The Comeback and Comedown of Mike Tyson* (Simon & Schuster, 1998); Daniel O'Connor, ed., *Iron Mike: A Mike Tyson Reader* (Thunder's Mouth Press, 2002); and Jack Newfield, *Only in America: The Life and Crimes of Don King* (William Morrow, 1995).

A few books on the larger subject of boxing proved enlightening. These included, most notably, Joyce Carol Oates's *On Boxing* (Ecco

ABOUT SOURCES

Edition, 2002), William Nack's *My Turf: Horses, Boxers, Blood Money, and the Sporting Life* (Da Capo, 2003), and Phil Berger's *Punch Lines: Berger on Boxing* (Four Walls Eight Windows, 1993).

As to the background of the era, I relied primarily on Todd Gitlin's comprehensive *The Sixties: Years of Hope, Days of Rage* (Bantam 1987) and Theodore Roszak's *The Making of a Counter Culture* (University of California Press, 1968) in addition to countless newspaper and journal articles as well as my own memory. Donna McCrohan's *Archie & Edith, Mike & Gloria: The Tumultuous History of All in the Family* (Workman Publishing, 1987) also helped.

On larger cultural issues, the timely release of Thomas Sowell's *Black Rednecks and White Liberals* (Encounter Books, 2005) proved a blessing. And, as often, I fall back on Shelby Steele's always timely *The Content of Our Character: A New Vision of Race in America* (St. Martin's Press, 1990).

As to video, essential viewing includes the following documentaries: William Clayton's *A.K.A. Cassius Clay* (1970), Leon Gast and Taylor Hackford's *When We Were Kings* (1997), and Phil Grabsky's *Muhammad Ali: Through the Eyes of the World* (2001). As to movies, there is *The Greatest*, a 1977 release directed by Tom Gries and starring Ali as himself, and the more credible 2001 epic *Ali*, directed by Michael Mann and starring Will Smith in the title role.

Kudos to the ESPN Classic channel for showing all of Ali's major fights and most of the minor ones and to the Newark Public Library for its help on New Jersey background information including that of my own family.

As the reader will see, I avoid footnotes as so much of the information is incontrovertible and can be found in multiple sources. Where the source does matter, I integrate that information into the text.

INDEX

INDEX

INDEX

INDEX